The MODERN World

TEN GREAT WRITERS

Malcolm Bradbury

The MODERN World

TEN GREAT WRITERS

Secker & Warburg
London

LLVN/TT
4
A CHANNEL
FOUR BOOK

First published in England 1988 by
Martin Secker & Warburg Limited
54 Poland Street, London W1V 3DF

Copyright © LWT 1988

British Library cataloguing in publication data

Bradbury, Malcolm, 1932–
    The modern world: ten great writers.
    1. English literature —— 20th century ——
    History and criticism
    I. Title
    820.9′00912   PR471

ISBN 0 436 06508 8

The illustrations of Dostoevsky, Ibsen, Conrad, Proust, Mann,
Joyce, Eliot and Woolf are courtesy of the BBC Hulton Picture
Library

Photoset in 11 on 14 pt Bembo and printed in Great Britain by
Richard Clay Ltd, Bungay, Suffolk

To Roberto and Gianna Celli

Then the time of exile began, the endless search
for justification, the aimless nostalgia, the
most painful, the most heartbreaking questions,
those of the heart which asks itself 'Where
can I feel at home?'

Albert Camus, *The Rebel*

CONTENTS

PREFACE

Melvyn Bragg

Laurence Olivier likes to tell the story of how William Wyler broke him into film acting. Olivier, like most British actors was convinced that the 'the-a-tre' was infinitely superior to the 'flicks'. Wyler was one of many who disagreed and thought that one root of the snobbish attitude might lie in the Standard British Actor's inability to act on celluloid. In *Wuthering Heights* the Old Vic met Hollywood head-on; Olivier emerged bruised but wiser.

Wyler directed him relentlessly – mocking his grand gestures, his dynamic voice, his actorliness. At one stage Olivier (even today he flushes with embarrassment to recall it) stepped forward and said to the tough all-American crew, 'Your anaemic little medium cannot support great acting.' It is thought that the laughter lingers around the rafters to this day.

When the film was completed, Wyler invited a reluctant Olivier to dinner and informed him that films were not an inferior medium; they could do anything. All you had to do was to find a way. Not Shakespeare, said Olivier. Even Shakespeare, said Wyler. Impossible, said Olivier – who went on to direct and star in *Henry V*, *Richard III* and *Hamlet*.

A similar snobbery has been directed at television. It is the newest medium, it is available to all, it is a carrier – on the same undifferentiating screen – of everything from pulp to grandeur. For all these crimes it has been judged inadequate. No matter that, in Britain at least, our finest dramatists have done some of their best work for television; no matter that anthropological films and documentaries on nature have established a refined new seam of vision . . . television is still suspected of being a poor relation.

Nowhere is this more apparent than in the area of arts broadcasting and, it has to be admitted, with some cause. Television arts programmes have often seemed too rushed, too thin or too flip. There has, though, been a steady tradition of arts programmes which have attempted to exploit the unique cluster of opportunities presented by British television: its comparative generosity with slots and budgets, its comprehension of minority programmes with their low ratings and usually difficult marketability, and its success in attracting groups or teams who can benefit from working alongside each other. *Monitor* under the late Sir Huw Wheldon was a prototype: I worked on *Monitor* in its later years and when LWT asked me to set up and edit what became *The South Bank Show*, I took over several of its ideas. One of the most important was to set up a team which would undertake arts programme in as committed and scrupulous a way as the best drama outfits, the best documentary units. Almost all the producers in the LWT Arts Department began as researchers: that continuity is essential, and not only in the best documentary units. It is only the consistent work of such a team, I believe, which by building on its own experience can secure a level of arts programming worthy of its subjects. In the end, it can not only be comparable with the best print journalism but, with luck, match the standard of the subject itself: i.e. a film as good in its way as the play or the film it treats.

There are several different areas of arts programmes – the discipline defines the approach – process films, profiles, performance-based, interview-based, mixtures of all four and variations on alternative methods . . . *The Modern World* draws on *The South Bank Show*'s films on writers: on William Golding, Harold Pinter, Arthur Miller, Marguerite Duras, Norman Mailer, Alberto Moravia, Françoise Sagan, Saul Bellow, Philip Larkin, John le Carré, Toni Morrison, Gore Vidal and dozens more.

About four years ago I put to Channel 4 the idea of making a series on some of the great writers around the turn of the century – Proust, Conrad, Joyce . . . Apart from wanting there to be such programmes as part of the currency of television, I thought that that the team we were assembling on the South Bank would enjoy turning their minds and talents from the contemporary to the past. We could employ some of the same techniques and attack we had cultivated on *The South Bank Show*: we could also put down a marker for ourselves and the viewers. Arts programmes, decently funded, made in a quantity which avoids their isolation as rather precious 'prestige' productions, need to extend their reach constantly. Television is still a new and in many ways an insecure medium: the job of those of us who make arts programmes is to ensure that they become a continuing seam.

The films we designed were ambitious. We chose to use drama to explore the fictionalized ideas of each writer and to concentrate on a single book, usually the principal work. We also gave ourselves the task of dramatizing, economically, the writer's life, personal experience, background and artistic philosophy – but we wanted the writing not the biography to be the focus. In short we devised a form which interweaves dramatic portrayal with documentary techniques and expert critical explanations.

It is inevitable that the plural be used of any television programme. Though the public might praise a Dennis Potter play, Leslie Woodhead's *Disappearing World*, David Attenborough's *Life on Earth* they would be the first to correct that. Television programmes are made by teams, only very occasionally is there a one-man/woman band. After getting the outline accepted by Channel 4 I asked two *South Bank Show* producers, David Thomas and Nigel Wattis (both former researchers on the programme) to take on the main shank of the shows. Gillian Greenwood, recently arrived from editing the *Literary Review*, was the chief researcher and Subniv Babuta took on that job for a couple of the programmes, just as Kim Evans and David Hinton – again, *South Bank Show* trained – were each to produce a programme. The core team in the first few months when we were setting out the strategy, the form and the budget was Thomas, Wattis, Greenwood, Michael Small (our Unit Manager) and myself.

Our first aim was to look at the range and intensity of the great explosion of Modernism in European writing at the turn of the century. One working title was Ezra Pound's *Make It New*. We thought that, in various ways, a number of authors then working were the first to imagine what it was like to live in the modern world. To some extent we still live in their shadow.

The thesis worked only so far. Individual authors refused to conform to a strict theme or a close pattern. Naturally we went with the authors while retaining the idea – commonplace for many years – that a radical and widely noted change of perception and consciousness occurred about a hundred years ago. Another strand was to look back from our turning century to that a century ago. Our critics – Steiner, Burgess, Kermode – translated the dead authors into the present.

The list of writers indicates that, rightly apprehensive of the rigidity of too central a hold, we let our hunches rove every now and then. The limitation of number – ten – meant that terrible cries rang out from our surgical meetings as Pound was amputated and Faulkner hacked away, as Musil was lopped off and Henry James expired on the insufficient but controlling grounds that we only had so much money and so many slots. In the end, almost arcane excuses of balance and commitment led us to our present list. Some omissions were for low-minded reasons and there is no point in concealing it. D. H. Lawrence, for instance, ought to be in this company but we had made a substantial film on Lawrence for *The South Bank Show* and for better and for worse, thought that limited air-time should not, finally, be spent on a repeat performance.

John Gross, that man of letters, was a valuable adviser in the first year but his work on the *New York Times* made it a little too difficult to keep up the regular contact we needed. Turning to Malcolm Bradbury was not only to exchange one man of letters for another but it was also a great benefit to have Professor Bradbury's accessibility and his deep intellectual grip of that time available. His book follows the series closely, choosing to concentrate on the books we ourselves selected and often using remarks made by those who appear in the programmes. It also, however, brings out in Bradbury some of the best and most incisive appraisals of great authors that he has done.

Thanks to him, then, and, back on the South Bank, to Production Assistants Jenny King, Xenia Ager, Ewa Radwanska, to Peter Pearson the Location Manager, Paul Bond the Lighting Cameraman and all their colleagues at LWT who enabled us to make a complex series with extraordinary efficiency and, by any standards, modest budgets. Half our budget was supplied by international globe-trotting producer and friend Reiner Moritz, to whom many thanks: the other half by Channel 4 – Michael Kustow, Arts Commissioning Editor has also been a friend to LWT Arts; and, also at 4, to Jeremy Isaacs, as the man who bit the literary bullet and waved us on. We are duly grateful and hope his successor will be as adventurous.

Finally, this programme attempts, as we do every season on *The South Bank Show*, to maintain the integrity and respect the complexity, the uniqueness of the artist who is our subject while taking into account two other factors – our own professionalism and that scattered audience which is television's great cultural opportunity. It is a tricky troika to master. If we have done so we will have illuminated those writers for many many people, kept faith with the authors and, perhaps, made what at best is one of the most exciting and underrated artefacts of our day – the intelligent and accessible arts-film.

Melvyn Bragg
24 September 1987

PRODUCTION
DETAILS

The television series was broadcast on Channel 4 in early 1988. The Series Editor was Melvyn Bragg, and the Series Producers David Thomas and Nigel Wattis. Malcolm Bradbury was the Series Consultant.

The casts and contributors to each film are listed below.

FYODOR DOSTOEVSKY

Commentator: John Jones
Cast   : Douglas Hodge, Charlie Drake, Patrick Malahide, Ian McDiarmid, Timothy Spall, Katy Behean, Sara Sugarman, Ann Way, Mair Coleman, Derek Deadman, Oh Tee
Produced and Directed by David Hinton
Researcher : Gillian Greenwood

HENRIK IBSEN

Commentators: Michael Meyer, D. M. Thomas, John Mortimer, Dr Anthony Storr
Produced and Directed by Nigel Wattis
Researcher   : Gillian Greenwood

JOSEPH CONRAD

Commentators: Sir V. S. Pritchett, Keith Carabine
Cast : Brian Glover, Francis Barber, Hywel Bennett, Jim Broadbent, Graham Crowden, Kenneth Colley, Peter Blythe, David Doyle
Produced and Directed by David Thomas
Researcher : Gillian Greenwood

THOMAS MANN

Commentator: Nigel Hamilton
Cast : John Shrapnel, John Grillo, Tim McInnerny, Paul Brooke, Iain Cuthbertson, Ben Daniels, Haydn Gwynne
Produced and Directed by David Thomas
Researcher : Gillian Greenwood

MARCEL PROUST

Commentators: Michel Butor, Terence Kilmartin
Cast : Roger Rees, Dominic Jephcott, Eleanor David, Zoë Mair, Julia Blalock, Paul Reynolds, Grace Wilkinson
Produced and Directed by Nigel Wattis
Researcher : Subniv Babuta

JAMES JOYCE

Commentators: Anthony Burgess, Dr Clive Hart
Cast : David Suchet, John Lynch, Sorcha Cusack, Tony Doyle, T. P. McKenna, Dermot Crowley, Patricia Quinn, Francesca Folan, Patricia Mort, Bryan Murray, James Aubrey, Dierdra Morris
Produced and Directed by Nigel Wattis
Researcher : Gillian Greenwood

T. S. ELIOT

Commentators: Sir Stephen Spender, Craig Raine, Peter Ackroyd, Professor Frank Kermode

Readers : Edward Fox, Eileen Atkins, Michael Gough (courtesy of Josephine Hart Productions)

Produced and Directed by David Thomas

Researcher : Gillian Greenwood

LUIGI PIRANDELLO

Commentators: Leonardo Sciascia, Julian Mitchell

Cast : John Woodvine, Jim Norton, Ian McNeice, Sylvestre le Touzel, Trisha Thorns, Douglas Hodge, Reginald Stewart

Produced and Directed by Nigel Wattis

Researcher : Gillian Greenwood

VIRGINIA WOOLF

Commentator: Hermione Lee

Cast : Eileen Atkins, Susan Tracy, John Castle, Robert Daws, Jenifer Landor, Eva Griffith, Gerard Logan, Oona Kirsch, Christina Greatrex

Produced and Directed by Kim Evans

Researcher : Gillian Greenwood

FRANZ KAFKA

Commentator: Professor George Steiner

Cast : Tim Roth, Michael Bryant, Bill Paterson, John Bennett, Oscar Quitak, Tattiana Colombo, David Barras, Mathew Marsh, Mark Williams

Produced and Directed by David Thomas

Researcher : Subniv Babuta

ACKNOWLEDGEMENTS

This book was written to keep company with a major television series of the same title, made by the South Bank Show at London Weekend Television, for transmission by Channel 4 in early 1988. Like everything to do with television it was a collaborative enterprise, devised by Melvyn Bragg and developed by David Thomas and Nigel Wattis. It was Melvyn Bragg who conceived a series that examined ten of the most important writers, from Dostoevsky to Kafka, Ibsen to Joyce, who were makers of the modern movement – the Cézannes, Matisses and Picassos of fiction, drama and poetry. The idea of a television series that would treat seriously the Modernist writers, visually and dramatically exploring their chief works, their lives, and their contemporary literary influence and critical importance, excited me from the start. I am pleased to have been literary consultant to the series, and delighted by the televised results.

And, of course, I am also deeply influenced by them, for this book has been inextricably bound up with the making of the series, the ideas behind it, the research done for it. The problems of recreating, rather than simply reporting, the great literary achievement of the seventy years from the 1860s and 1870s, when the new arts began to be made, and of constructing visual forms for the most complex modern works, were considerable. The ten scripts aimed to do justice to the often radical forms of the books, and to maintain the shock and surprise they provoked when they first appeared. All of this in turn

helped shape my way of writing this book. It too is a collaborative
enterprise, and I have drawn on the excellent work of the directors,
producers and researchers who made the programmes. There is also
another debt, to the many notable writers and critics who contributed
their thoughts and judgements to the series onscreen. I have drawn on
them too for the observations of the following pages. I am grateful to
them all, and especially to some who have been shaping my thoughts
on modern literature for many years – including Frank Kermode,
George Steiner, Stephen Spender, Michel Butor, V. S. Pritchett,
Hermione Lee, and Anthony Burgess.

So I have tried to follow the general spirit of the television programmes, to deal with the same authors (not always in the same
order), and consider similar arguments. At the same time I have tried
to write an independent book, and extend into wider issues and into
the general ideas of modernism. That brings me to another debt, to
my academic colleagues, especially those at the University of East
Anglia, a number of whom worked with me on an earlier book, the
Pelican Guide to European Literature volume *Modernism* (Har-
mondsworth, 1976). Much of my thinking on the subject was guided
by my co-editor on that volume, James McFarlane, as well as others
who contributed, or joined in its planning. I would particularly
mention John Fletcher, Brian Rowley, Franz Kuna, George Hyde,
Martin Esslin and Alan Bullock. Other colleagues – Chris Bigsby,
Lorna Sage, Helen McNeil, Ellman Crasnow and Guido Almansi –
have helped in different ways. In the wider world I have been especially indebted to Ihab Hassan, David Lodge, Robert Langbaum, Heide
Ziegler, Marc Chenetier and Gerhard Hoffmann. Then there is another
debt of a different kind; this book could not have been completed
without the time, quiet and academic comfort of the Villa Serbelloni
at Bellagio, on Lake Como in Italy. To the Rockefeller Foundation,
and to Roberto and Giana Celli, who create the wonderful atmosphere
of that splendid study-centre, I am lastingly grateful, as they will see
from the dedication.

In the project of the series, Melvyn Bragg, David Thomas and
Nigel Wattis have been superb to work with, both in their vision of
the programmes themselves and in their co-operation with this book.

I am also grateful to the rest of the team, especially Gillian Greenwood, Kim Evans and David Hinton. In the project of the book, everything has depended on the brilliant editing of John Blackwell at Secker & Warburg, and on the wonderful marital, organizational and literary assistance of Elizabeth Bradbury, my first true reader. It is thanks to both of them that this book happened in real rather than Proustian time – if reality, after all this, there still be. I have always doubted it.

Malcolm Bradbury
Norwich, 1987

INTRODUCTION: MAKE IT NEW

I

Sometime in the 1930s, the American poet Ezra Pound issued to his
literary contemporaries one of the most famous *Diktats* of modern
literature – *Make It New*, he declared. By this Pound meant a good
deal more than that his fellow authors should maintain the age-old
responsibility of the writer to be original and novel. Pound's phrase
was stirring – it still is – because he was asserting an idea that had
exercised extraordinary power over the greatest writers of the times:
an idea that in one way or another shaped all the writers of the modern
age who are explored in this book, and the Channel 4 television series
it accompanies. It is the idea that the modern arts have a special
obligation, an advanced or *avant-garde* duty, to go ahead of their own
age and transform it, and along with that the very nature of the arts
themselves. It is the idea of the 'tradition of the new' – the belief that
the time has come for the arts to break more or less entirely with the
past, and assert their connections to the present and above all the
future. 'We need new art forms,' cries Anton Chekhov's character
Trepilov in his play *The Seagull*. 'New forms are wanted and if they
aren't available, we might as well have nothing at all.' The task was
both creative and destructive, as Friedrich Nietzsche, the German
philosopher who exercised so much influence over the new ideas of
the twentieth century, suggested through his character of Zarathustra:
'Whoever wants to be creative in good and evil, he must first be an
annihilator and destroy values.'

The task of Making It New meant the need to go on ahead, finding
a new way through modern experience – a task of discovery and
dissent, a venture through the dangerous limits of the imagination, a
breaking free from the frozen structures of the past. Everything needed
to change – the philosophy underlying the arts, the basic vision they

expressed, the relationship between form and content, artist and audience, creative individual and society. As Nietzsche declared, this voyage into modern artistic knowledge had its own profound dangers. Dostoevsky's student Raskolnikov, in *Crime and Punishment*, intends to break free of the limits of thought, faith and morality: 'It seems to me what [people] are most afraid of is taking a new step or uttering a new word.' Rasknolnikov takes the step, utters the word, commits a modern crime, and finds a modern punishment. If it meant an act of courage, it could also be an act of Faustian self-destruction. In Thomas Mann's novella *Death in Venice*, the much-admired German writer Gustave von Aschenbach breaks from his literary mould and journeys to Venice, where he falls decadently in love with a handsome boy who comes to represent beauty as death and disease. Finally Aschenbach himself dies of the plague that empties the city. Just before his death, he remembers why Plato excluded the artist from his ideal state. He reflects on the artist's need for dangerous knowledge, the creative pressure in him to leave the ways of the wise and worthy citizen, and transgress. 'Our magisterial style is all folly and pretence, our honourable repute a farce, the crowd's belief in us merely laughable,' he thinks. 'Knowledge is all-knowing, understanding, forgiving . . . It has compassion with the abyss – it *is* the abyss.'

The dangers of the modern way were to become apparent even to Pound, whose own endeavour to Make It New was to reach a tragic outcome. An expatriate in Italy during the Second World War, Pound grew disappointed that President Roosevelt had not chosen to consult him on economic, cultural and political matters. He aligned himself with Benito Mussolini, who indeed had certain futurist views of his own on the arts. Pound ended the war in a cage in Pisa, held by the American army to await treason charges in the United States. This even had a certain logic, for Pound considered it the task of the artist to be the goad of the age, creating culture by revolting against the culture. By the end of his life, Pound was prepared at last to confess that his self-created ambition to transform the politics of culture had been a dangerous error, and one that questioned his artistic achievement and the very aim of Making It New. Like many of the modern artists, Pound went adrift in the political world that surrounded him.

One reason that the spirit of the modern arts began to die around the Second World War was that its paradoxical relation with the world of modern politics became all too clear.

Pound exemplified this. His desire to Make It New was a quarrel with modernity – the cultural bankruptcy of the modern state, the broken language of the modern age. Like many others, Pound revolted against modernity, but he believed in Modernism – the name we have come to give to that major transformation of the forms, the spirit, the nature of the arts which took place somewhere between the 1870s and the outbreak of the Second World War. It was a profound artistic revolution that stirred all of Europe and – thanks in part to Pound himself – the United States, and it radically changed the direction of all artistic expression. It was a crisis in the history of Western humanism, and a deep attempt to understand and apprehend the nature of modern existence. It had profound consequences, some intended and many that were not intended – especially in the realm of politics. It produced some of our greatest and most disturbing literature, and some of our most painful expressions of modern self-awareness and anxiety. It belonged to the transition of the Western world out of the Romantic movement and into a new age, out of the nineteenth century and into the twentieth. Its beginnings lie a century away from us, but it still shakes us and still manages to disturb. It has utterly reconstructed our artistic tradition, our sense of form and language, our contemporary values, our culture and our styles – the very look of our streets, houses, rooms and selves. It redirected the imagination of its age, and of our own succeeding age as well. It has given us some of our greatest literary art, and some of our most terrible imaginings.

In this movement, as it developed in Britain and the United States in the years before and after the Great War, Pound was one of the central figures. He was himself one of the great poets (there is dispute as to how great, but he is undeniably a major writer) of the first quarter of the twentieth century, when the entire verse-tradition in the English language was upturned, to a large extent under his influence. He was also one of the great entrepreneurs of change, an organizer, friend, guide and promoter for many of the radical new writers, painters and musicians who emerged in remarkable numbers in Britain, expatriate Paris and the United States over the years around the war. He was in London before it, Paris after it, at the time when many of the major events occurred. Everywhere he summoned up movements, printed manifestos, started or took over magazines, and grouped others around him, in the customary *avant-garde* way. Wyndham Lewis, his collaborator on the Vorticist movement that shook London in 1913–14, described him as an artistic Baden-Powell, always getting artists under canvas for the cause. He found patrons for the writers he most admired, knowing that they were far too novel to find an audience among any but the select few. The two major works that dominated the new arts in the English language largely owe their existence to Pound. He helped T. S. Eliot, a fellow American expatriate in London, working in a London bank and writing *The Waste Land*, which was dedicated to Pound. He also organized assistance for James Joyce, teaching in a language school in Trieste, and bringing to birth his great book *Ulysses*.

They were indeed works too advanced and outrageous for any but the select few, but Pound believed in the select few. 'Artists are the antennae of the race, though the bullet-headed many will never learn to trust their great artists,' he explained, declaring what was to become another major assumption of the modern movement, that the 'serious arts' were indeed *avant garde*, in advance of their times. The term *avant garde* suggests that the new arts were a military or political operation, and in many ways so they were. They were also a great historical gamble, an attempt to by-pass the bullet-headed many who preferred a more conventional and reassuring culture, in the faith that in the future the true audience will emerge to understand them. It was a gamble that had paid off, as in time readers did come to recognize the importance and centrality of those great works of modernity. The *avant-gardiste* is, in one sense, in revolt against his own age, dissenting from the modern and certainly from the conventional. He rejects the corrupted state of contemporary bourgeois culture, the smug values of a commercial, materialistic, imperial society, the middlebrow and reassuring tradition of its arts. At the same time he is the modern age in its full expression, the revealer of its deepest forms and principles, the distiller of its spirit and its contradictions.

In short the art of Making It New is also an art of crisis. The new fragmentary forms, the strange and often parodic structures, the pervasive sense of ambiguity and tragic irony that mark so many of its works, express this. Nietzsche said that modern men were 'the children of a fragmented, pluralistic, sick, weird period', and we can feel this in the spirit of the decadent writing of the later nineteenth century. Pound himself began as a poet in the atmosphere of the romantic decadence, but his writing took on a new rage and fracture around the time of the Great War, when the culture for which he had come to Europe collapsed into senseless mass destruction. The poets who had talked already of the Crisis of the Word now saw there was a Crisis of the World as well. Pound's own war poem, *Hugh Selwyn Mauberley*, published in 1919, used fractured forms to express his enraged reaction to the war, and explore the spectacle of a once-great artistic culture destroyed through commercialism and nationalism, producing a collapsed civilization, 'an old bitch gone in the teeth'. It was Pound's farewell to London, though it was also the precursor of another poem that saw London as the great example of modern sterility and the need for a spiritual renewal, Eliot's *The Waste Land*. Meanwhile Pound started another poem around the same time, the great life work that he called *The Cantos*, another fractured work, an epic – or rather perhaps an anti-epic – of the age of disunity and lost wholeness. Like many of the most ambitious works of Modernism, it was an endeavour to sift through the literary tradition, and find from its fragments the usable remnants. From this he hoped to construct the new modern *paideuma*, a fresh and complete state of culture in which the moral, commercial and linguistic currency was renewed. Pound indeed shared the double vision that ran through the modern arts – a distrust of the modern world and its direction, a commitment to modernity and Modernism.

It was this sense of the collapse of traditional culture that explained the need to construct a new art from the fragments and sensations of the present. As Rimbaud had declared, '*il faut être absolument moderne*' – it is necessary to be completely modern. So the old forms had to be dismantled, undermined, and perhaps reconstructed, the task that James Joyce performed on the Homeric epic in *Ulysses*. No thought

now lasts more than twenty years, says Ibsen's Dr Stockmann in the
play with the very modernist title of *An Enemy of the People*. The
tradition and the individual talent had divided, T. S. Eliot explained
in a famous essay, and the if the best of the past was to be recovered it
could only be by very great labour. A fundamental dissociation of
sensibility, a breakdown of cultural expression, had sent in. The word
was uprooted, the image had lost its coherence, thought and feeling
had separated, the symbol no longer had its transcendence, or the
poem its meaning. The pantheon of culture had to be reconstructed
on an unprecedented scale, and that remaking of the entire tradition
meant – as Pound insisted – that the modern writer had to learn not
only how to write again, but also how to read. Such views could be
thought particularly American, and Pound admitted (with considerable distaste) that they went back in part to Walt Whitman, the
inclusive, optimistic American poet who had tried to Make It New a
generation earlier. 'One main contrast of the ideas behind every page
of my verses, compared with establish'd poems, is their different relative attitude towards God, towards the objective universe, and still
more . . . the quite changed attitude of the ego, the one chanting or
talking towards himself and towards his fellow-humanity,' Whitman
had declared. But, he added, it was the spirit of American democracy
and the spread of his nation across the American continent that made
these 'new poetic messages, new forms and expressions' inevitable.

But for Pound and his main contemporaries, the 'new poetic
messages, new forms and expressions' did not come from a vast American or democratic optimism. They came from the breakdown of the
usable past, the collapse of certainty, the breakdown of the word and
the image. They did not spring from the soil of a single nation, but
from the great interfusions of forms, languages and new techniques
that were developing in the culture-capitals of Europe. Pound saw the
United States as a province of culture, a 'half-savage country, out of
date'. His new poet would be a world-scholar, read in Homer and
Catullus, Dante and the Provençal troubadours, knowing the importance of the Chinese ideogram and the centrality of the Japanese
short poem form, the *haiku*. He became, like so many of the Modernist
writers, an expatriate, a traveller not to the stable and traditional

culture of Europe, but to its spirit of modern experiment. 'The old conception of the fatherland no longer suffices for anyone intellectually mature,' wrote Henrik Ibsen; 'We can no longer rest content with the political community in which we live.' Pound would have agreed, and so would most of the Modernists.

2

It was in 1908 that Pound began the expatriation of a lifetime, when, a flamboyant bohemian figure, wearing one green earring, he travelled to Venice with a bundle of poems in his pocket that he wished to publish, and which already had the Italian title of *A Lume Spento*. He then travelled on to London, in search of his poetic hero, W. B. Yeats, a major figure of the 'Celtic Twilight' of the 1890s who had helped establish the modern tradition of the French symbolist poets in Britain. The 1890s had been a major period of change and innovation in the British arts, and had opened verse to continental influence. Thus Pound found London in a state of great artistic ferment – something, it must be admitted, that does not often happen. Indeed, his arrival coincided with a great transformation that had been sweeping through the ideas and arts of Europe as the new century started. The transition from one age to another, the massive burst of new invention and experiment in science and technology, philosophy and psychology, the great growth of cities, the spreading of factory processes, the coming of new means of communication like the motor-car and the telephone, the political gaps that were now opening in most of the Western societies, all of these things were creating an atmosphere of fracture. As Pound would have acknowledged, artistic change is not simply an aesthetic event. It arises from social and ideological change, the change of systems, beliefs, and ways of life. When Pound came, Europe was not some stable repository of traditional culture, but a changing map of frontiers, classes, values and ideas. The shifting world of modern society and technology was already making the world new.

And in London, Pound, like many other artists drawn to the central
cities in the years before the Great War, found the seedbed of Modernism, the foundations of his particular tradition of the new.

The new was not completely new. In fact throughout the last half
of the nineteenth century, in accelerating waves, a fresh spirit had
been moving through the arts and the ideas of Europe, as the founding
beliefs and expectations of the nineteenth century began to alter under
the great social, technical and political changes that had come from
the melting-pot of revolution and romanticism with which the
century had started. The world of the Rousseau-esque social contract,
of liberal-bourgeois optimism and possibility, had been transformed
by a century of growth. The Romantic view of a benign and divinely
invested nature had been upturned by the rise of great cities and the
gathering of life into masses, and the old Christian certainties had
been undermined by the spirit of new thought. In every area – in
social expectations, scientific awareness, religious and moral values –
fundamental upheaval had occurred. In the revolutionary year of 1848,
when most of Europe experienced the turmoil of new liberationist
movements, and the map of the continent changed, Marx and Engels
had produced their *Communist Manifesto* – an account of the emer-
gence of the new industrial proletariat challenging the now established
bourgeoisie, and even more importantly a statement of a revolutionary, secular, and materialist view of history and human expecta-
tion. In 1859 Charles Darwin, in *The Origin of Species*, had proposed a
theory of evolution in the natural world itself, and questioned the
Christian view of creation at its core.

These new sociological and scientific views, these secular accounts
of nature and history, challenged the old theocentric and romantic
vision. They brought about a new age of experiment, in which moral
and philosophical, medical and technological discovery gathered pace,
and a revolutionary sense of the task of the intellect grew. As the
best-known literary prophet of the new, the Norwegian playwright
Henrik Ibsen was reported as saying: 'The great task of our time is to
blow up all existing institutions – to destroy.' Throughout much of
Europe and in the United States the same new scientific and technological processes were producing an enormous sense of historical

acceleration, which intensified as the turn of the century approached, suggesting the likely destiny of the new century. In 1898 came the discovery of radium and the flight of the Zeppelin airship, in 1899 the first motorbus appeared on the London streets, and in 1900 quantum theory was announced. The age of electric light and telephones, motor vehicles and powered flight, was beginning to dominate. As Pound's fellow-American, the historian Henry Adams, put it, in entering the twentieth century men were entering not a universe but a multiverse, and learning to pray not to the Virgin, but to the Dynamo, the new mechanical energy.

The change in the world without was matched by a sense of a changed world within. As sociology and politics altered views of the social world, and science those of the physical world, so there were new notions of what constituted the nature of perception, intuition and consciousness. The great nineteenth-century narratives had been filled with crises of religious and moral conscience, as their heroes and heroines struggled between damnation and redemption. The arts and ideas of the later nineteenth century looked elsewhere, to new tumults of consciousness, the nature of impressions and perceptions, the world that lay below consciousness and came to be called the unconscious. Artists and thinkers emphasized the intricate inward existence of an immaterial world which was governed by fragile sensations and perceptions. Walter Pater, the spokesman for new and modern sensations, spoke of the 'quickened, multiplied consciousness' of modern times. In 1890 William James published his *Principles of Psychology*, emphasizing that 'reality' was not an objective given, but was subjectively perceived through consciousness — a view reflected in the later novels of his brother, Henry James. In talking of the mind hereafter, William James said, 'let us call it the stream of thought, of consciousness, or of the subjective life.' In 1900 Sigmund Freud published his *The Interpretation of Dreams*, one of the most profoundly influential books of the new century. In France the philosopher Henri Bergson emphasized the role of intuition rather than reason in human life, and stressed the fundamental role played by memory and inner time in our apprehension of reality. In Germany the decadent and aesthetic sense of stepping out of the prison of historical time fed the new fiction of Thomas Mann.

At a time when Freud was becoming known, Bergson influential, Strindberg a major playwright, the novels of Dostoevsky circulating widely in translation, the art of psychology and consciousness was itself taking on a new significance. It was fed by the sense of aesthetic independence and decadent freedom that had developed in the last half of the nineteenth century, as the literary and artistic imagination began increasingly to revolt against the scientific, the material, and the bourgeois social world. The artist was no longer to be a bourgeois moralist, but an independent instrument of discovery, a bearer of creative evolution. And the language of a plain and direct realism no longer expressed a sufficient sense of the shifting, moving, speeding, complex world. As the great new experiments in painting showed, art was not simply a matter of representing the social facts of an agreed world outside. It expressed itself, its own methods of composition, its own processes of perception and intuition. The arts had an independent existence, and interfused with and transformed each other – painting and architecture, drama and music, dance and design, fiction and poetry. Each fed the others, and just as poetry aspired to the condition of music, fiction aspired to the condition of painting, or drama to that of aesthetic reverie. Art became a symbol for its own existence, and the symbol grew more obscure, enigmatic and labyrinthine: as Yeats said, the poet's dreams 'shall have the capacity to defeat the actual at any point'. Artists too acquired their own independent country, which could perhaps be called Bohemia, as they tended toward the path of international exile. New literary and poetic messages were inevitable, and the idea of the new arts grew.

3

But what was modern, what was new? As Holbrook Jackson notes in his book *The Eighteen Nineties* (1913), by the last decade of the nineteenth century, even in Britain, the two terms had gained extensive

currency. The word 'new' was everywhere. 'The range of the
adjective gradually spread until it embraced the ideas of the whole
period,' he notes, 'and we find innumerable references to the "New
Spirit", the "New Humour", the "New Realism", the "New
Hedonism", the "New Drama", the "New Unionism", the "New
Party", and the "New Woman".' It was all part of a general international preoccupation with the idea of the Modern, which had been
growing for decades. The modern was the spirit of Henrik Ibsen, the
Scandinavian dramatist whose plays had upturned and transformed
the drama throughout Europe, and become the rage of the 1880s. It
was the philosophy of Nietzsche, the German philosopher who died
in madness as the new century was born, but who argued that the
world left behind by the Death of God demanded a new mental
architecture, a fresh act of energy and will. It was the influence of the
Russian novelists, above all Fyodor Dostoevsky, who was now being
widely translated. 'What's to be done? We have to break with what
must be broken with once and for all – that's what must be done; and
we have to take the suffering on ourselves,' declares Dostoevsky's
Raskolnikov in *Crime and Punishment*, which can fairly be called the
first of the modern novels, and a book that suggested the conflict and
crisis in the spirit of the age.

The ends of centuries, Jackson notes, are often marked by a revolutionary 'quickening' of thought. Now, as bourgeois life reigned
supreme, imperial and commercial competititon among the European
powers increased, and the *belle époque* flourished, the arts revealed the
drumming of a disturbing unease. Artists called themselves 'decadent',
and the term described not only a taste for bohemian life-style and a
dandyish flamboyance, but also a sense of transition and of world-
weary dismay at the age. Decadence was not new; it went back, like
the idea of bohemianism itself, to the Paris of the 1830s. Nor was the
campaign for 'art for art's sake' new; it had preoccupied the entire
Victorian era. 'Movements' in the arts had been around for a long
time. The idea of the 'modern' had been influential ever since Baudelaire. But the 'quickening' of the 1890s concentrated all of these
things. It was, said Jackson, a 'decade of a thousand movements'. It
was also in many ways the first modern decade – in part because it

saw itself *as* a decade, a time of transition, the last of the old, the first of the new. It was *fin de siècle*, aware of what was dying, and *aube de siècle*, awaiting the new birth. That is one reason why it insisted on the importance of immediate experience and sensation, the value of a flamboyant parade of new if momentary styles.

The 1890s in fact paid a high price for its decadence, in the ravaged careers, the sudden deaths of artists as they fell off their bar-stools or turned to suicide, the scandals like the Oscar Wilde trial, the public attacks on foulness that helped silence Naturalism and Ibsenism, and which stopped Thomas Hardy from writing more novels. The 1890s, Jackson suggests, began in decadence and ended in the great public celebration of Mafeking Night, and the generation seemed over, safely tucked away as the 'tragic generation'. Yet in fact it was all just beginning, and the new notions of the modern that spread across Europe were by no means stilled. Jackson published his own record in 1913, on the threshold of the Great War of 1914, which was to bring home the underlying instability in the social and political order, destroy much of what was left of traditional culture, and bring to birth the one great twentieth-century revolution, the Bolshevik Revolution in Russia, that bloody attempt to make the social world new. And modernism continued, some of its liveliest movements just preceding the Great War.

By now it was clear that it was a large international movement, which cast its radiation wide. It reached from Moscow in the East to Chicago in the West, the Scandinavia of Ibsen and Munch in the North to the Italy of D'Annunzio, Marinetti and Pirandello in the South. It had many centres, but the most obvious was Paris. Here came a succession of new movements, in poetry, drama, music, and above all painting. Especially there was Cubism, a new art of abstraction we usually date from the completion of Picasso's painting *Les Demoiselles d'Avignon* in 1907. Germany and Scandinavia were important, and the dramatic heritage of Ibsen and Strindberg became concentrated, around 1910, in the movement of Expressionism, which began in painting, drama and poetry, and made its way into film. In both Russia and Italy the dominant tendency was Futurism, though when Marinetti presented the first Futurist manifesto, glorying in modern speed and mechanical energy, in 1909, he did so in Paris. The movements kept multiplying, with names like Constructivism and Acmeism, Suprematism and Vorticism, *Die Brücke* and *Blaue Reiter*. Now they expressed less the spirit of decadence than the wonder of the new, the flickering strangeness of the modern metropolis, the joy of the machine, the new psychic and sexual relations of the age. Every form of literary art changed. The new theatre of Ibsen and Strindberg, Chekhov and Wedekind, Hauptmann and Maeterlinck, transformed not only the subjects the drama dealt with but the nature of theatre and production itself. The poetry of Mallarmé, Valéry and Rilke pointed to new verse forms which sought a fresh freedom of line and expression, a new image and symbol. The novel was transformed in many ways – by the vivid consciousness of Dostoevsky, the complex symbolism of the late Henry James, the irony of Thomas Mann, the time experiments of Marcel Proust.

The scale of recent change was brought home in Britain when, in 1910, Roger Fry organized an exhibition of Post-Impressionist paintings from France at London's Grafton Galleries which made Arnold Bennett acknowledge that, if he were a younger writer, he would have to start all over again. 'On or about December 1910 human character changed,' wrote Virginia Woolf, taking for her key date both the end of the Edwardian period and her friend Roger Fry's exhibition; 'All human relations shifted – those between masters and servants, husbands and wives, parents and children. And when human relations shift there is at the same time a change in religion, conduct, politics and literature.' In the years before 1914 the movements began to distil. Pound, in London, identified with the spirit of Making It New, and he invented Imagism; founded in a Kensington tea-shop, it was a movement in poetry that insisted on the end of Victorian discursiveness and a new hardness. Then he and Wyndham Lewis founded Vorticism, which insisted like Futurism on speed, energy and the vortex of abstract creation. Their magazine-manifesto was called *Blast*, and it was meant as an explosive blast against the Victorian past and bland commercial culture. Like much else in pre-war Modernism it has the air of a strange prediction, for, between the magazine's two issues, the Archduke Ferdinand was assassinated, and the blasts of the big guns started on the Western Front.

4

From the 1870s to the Great War there were many phases of Modernism – an artistic revolution that reached back certainly to the poetry of Baudelaire, the novel of Dostoevsky, the drama of Ibsen, and would reach forward to the outbreak of another World War in 1939. But there is no doubt that the Great War of 1914–18 stood at the centre, and was in its paradoxical way an expression or strange fulfilment both of the forebodings and uneasy expectations of Modernism, and of its preoccupation with the spirit of the new. It was a profound shock to the artists and the writers, as it was to the citizens of the Europe that was torn apart by its terrible events. In a famous letter of 1914, written shortly before his death, Henry James expressed the horror he felt at the 'plunge of civilization into this abyss of blood and darkness'. It, he wrote, 'so gives away the whole long age during which we have supposed the world to be, with whatever abatement, gradually bettering, that to have to take it all now for what the treacherous years were all the while really making for and *meaning* is too tragic for any words.' The years before had indeed been treacherous, but in retrospect the deep upheavals of the previous decades – in technology and science, politics and the arts – seemed to prefigure the crisis. Artists were the soldiers of the *avant garde*, and vortex, blast, energy, and the destruction of the dead museum of civilization had been important watchwords. And it was the old sentimental and romantic poetry of benign nature and patriotism that died on the battlefields, while the new arts of energy and ambiguity, of anxiety and extremity, suddenly acquired a greater and newer reality.

Above all the war gave a new meaning to the idea of the great fracture that went through the modern arts. 'On or about December 1910 human character changed,' Virginia Woolf had written. 'It was in 1915 the old world ended,' D. H. Lawrence wrote in *Kangaroo*, picking a date of far more historical moment, the point when an entire cultural tradition seemed to end in war. The modern was no longer a daring experiment in consciousness and new forms of expression, but a dark new condition that was to disorder life for the rest of the century. The anarchy that lay just below civilization, and could be glimpsed in the fiction of Dostoevsky, Conrad or Mann, the awareness that 'Things fall apart, the centre cannot hold' that was present in the poetry of Yeats or Rilke, now acquired a new meaning, and attached itself to a crisis evident in the world. The Futurists who had glorified war and violence ('Art and war are the great manifestations of sensuality; lust is their flower'), the Vorticists with their blasts and explosions (the Vortex would, said Pound, 'sweep out the past century as surely as Attila swept across Europe'), and the Expressionists with their revolt of energy against a rotten civilization, all seemed to express with a terrible directness the nature of the world that had come. To some the war was that purging of the past which the world so badly needed. In November 1914 Thomas Mann wrote that 'in Kant and Nietzsche we have the moralists of German militarism', and he suggested that the war might be 'purification, liberation, an enormous hope'.

It was a hope that died quickly. 'Where are we? Whither has the dream snatched us? Twilight, rain, filth,' Thomas Mann was later to write in *The Magic Mountain*, as he withdraws his hero, Hans Castorp, from our sight to fight on the wartime battlefields that replace the intellectual conflicts and crises of the earlier part of the book. *The Magic Mountain* was one of many major works that started in the hopeful experimentalism of the period before the Great War, and were completed after it. Another was E. M. Forster's *A Passage to India* (1924), with its dark glimpse of anarchy in the caves: 'Everything exists, nothing has value.' Marcel Proust's *Remembrance of Things Past* was begun around 1905, and its first volume, *Swann's Way*, appeared in 1913, but the further eight volumes came out during the 1920s and it became part of the postwar Modernist spirit. James Joyce's *Ulysses* was started by 1914, and Gertrude Stein's *The Making of Americans* very much earlier, though both books became part of the 1920s 'Revolution of the Word'. Franz Kafka's *The Trial*, with its terrible opening words – 'Someone must have been telling lies about Joseph K., for without having done anything wrong he was arrested one fine morning' – was begun in the August when the war started. Even Dostoevsky's *Crime and Punishment*, written in the 1860s, contains in its epilogue a curious prediction of a war fought in a new age when everyone was propounding his own theories, and no one could agree: 'Wholesale destruction stalked the earth.'

Most of the books that were written over the war also display the transformation of values that had taken place in it. They are, as it were, made out of different forces – the symbolist optimism that had grown in pre-war Modernism, out of the spirit of the 1890s, and the sense of post-war vacancy and fragility that the war expressed. When *Ulysses* appeared, T. S. Eliot greeted it in an essay as a modern anti-myth that revealed 'the immense panorama of futility and anarchy that is contemporary history.' If, as some have suggested, the phrase did not entirely fit the book, it certainly applied to Eliot's own poem of the same year, *The Waste Land*, with its vision of sterility and cultural collapse, of a universal fragmentation. When Virginia Woolf wrote *Mrs Dalloway*, she made one of its central characters, Septimus Smith, a shell-shocked ex-soldier whose visions of the battlefield feed the images of death that constantly recur during the novel, and whose death is, as it were, a substitute for Mrs Dalloway's own.

Thus the irony was that the Modernist spirit in the arts became relevant and true to postwar times, as it had not done in the prewar years. The novels of Dostoevsky, of Conrad, of Kafka – books that expressed a sense not just of outward political disorder, but of a terrible inner anguish and anxiety – took on a new relevance. The younger writers who attempted to capture the experience of their own age – writers like Hemingway, Faulkner, or Gide – thus took up the inheritance. The 'tragic generation' and the 'lost generation' found common cause in a linked inheritance of conscious decadence. 'Ours is a tragic age, but we refuse to take it tragically,' begins D. H. Lawrence's novel of sexual waste, *Lady Chatterley's Lover*. But many of the writers of the 1920s did take the times tragically, using modernist forms to express the fractured disorder of an era when abstract nouns seemed irrelevant, nature seemed an aggression against the self, and the self seemed to be able to discover only defacement, despair and defeat.

The sense of historical decline and human fragility may have grown in the years just after the war. But so did the achievements of the Modern movement, as the war dismantled for good the nineteenth-century tradition, and Making It New now seemed the best way forward. It was a time of major modernist publication, and in a short sequence of years during the 1920s the great books came. In 1922 there appeared *Ulysses* and *The Waste Land*, and W. B. Yeats's finest volume of poems, born out of the wartime Irish troubles, *Michael Robartes and the Dancer*. So did a new volume of Proust's great work, Rilke's *Sonnets to Orpheus*, Virginia Woolf's third novel *Jacob's Room*, two major plays, Pirandello's *Henry IV* and Eugene O'Neill's *Anna Christie* – and, quite crucially, Oswald Spengler's vast and despairing *The Decline of the West*. The next year, 1923, saw Rilke's *Duino Elegies*, Italo Svevo's *The Confessions of Zeno*, and Elmer Rice's Expressionist play *The Adding Machine*. In 1924 *The Magic Mountain* and *A Passage to India* appeared. So did Ernest Hemingway's first book *In Our Time*, Franz Kafka's *The Hunger Artist*, and from a Paris that was becoming a laboratory of new experimentalism came a declaration of the spirit of the post-war movements, André Breton's *Surrealist Manifesto*. In 1925 came Virginia Woolf's *Mrs Dalloway*, Kafka's *The Trial*, T. S. Eliot's *The Hollow Men*, John Dos Passos's *Manhattan Transfer*, Scott Fitzgerald's *The Great Gatsby*, Gertrude Stein's *The Making of Americans*, André Gide's *The Counterfeiters* – and a dark promise of what was to come, Adolf Hitler's Fascist bible, *Mein Kampf*.

Right on through the 1920s, the major publications continued. They made it very clear that a major new spirit in writing had become established, marked both by enormous literary ambitions and anxious modern despairs. These new arts had certain common characteristics. They were frequently hard, ironic, fragmentary. Their central characters were more often victims than actors, and the nature of existence was represented as weak and fragile. The literary form was often broken, and words seemed scarcely able to express experience. Yet the modern methods were also exciting and remarkable. Free verse in poetry, 'stream-of-consciousness' technique in the novel, expressionism in the theatre now seemed persistent conventions, indications of a new attitude to form and to life itself. But what had once seemed to be rarified and outrageous experiments now took on a different character; they now looked like necessary means for grasping the fevered and accelerated spirit of the postwar world.

When the 1920s died in the Great Crash of 1929, and the era of Depression and rising Fascism came, the spirit of Modernism was challenged. Hadn't it evaded politics in the interests of art, refused to face the process of history, and lost touch with moral responsibility? The Revolution of the Word came to seem less important than the revolution in the world, and when the 1930s ended in a second World War, the modern movement appeared to come to its end. At the same time the scale of its own revolution was being increasingly acknowledged. In a book of 1931, *Axel's Castle*, the American critic Edmund Wilson looked back over the entire enterprise since the 1870s, and argued that 'writers such as W. B. Yeats, James Joyce, T. S. Eliot, Gertrude Stein, Marcel Proust and Paul Valéry represent the culmination of a self-conscious and very important literary movement.' Other critics considered that the revolution that had taken place was of even more massive proportions. Herbert Read in *Art Now* (1935) saw an unprecedented transformation: 'it is not so much a revolution, which implies a turning over, even a turning back, but rather a break-up, a devolution, some would say a dissolution . . . Its character is catastrophic.'

But whatever had happened to the modern arts, the movement that had seemed to go on for more than sixty years reached a new break in 1939. In that year, James Joyce finished and published the 'history of the world' that for the previous seventeen years had been his work-in-progress. He intended *Finnegans Wake* to be the culmination of the modern experiment, and so in a way it was. It was a great encyclopaedia of experiment, written in a mega-language that related it to the vast narrative and mythic traditons of the world. But the war that had been impending broke out in September of that year, and Joyce moved to Switzerland. He died shortly thereafter, and other literary deaths – of Yeats, Freud, Virginia Woolf – marked the end of an era. The new generation of writers who came along after the war felt that the times had changed profoundly, and that their tasks were different. The movement that meant to be modern for ever now seemed over, the *avant garde* no longer seemed *avant*, and a

new term, 'Postmodern', became current to describe a new artistic
and social condition.

5

This book – like the television series of the same title, the making of
which brought it into existence and shaped many of its themes, images
and ideas – is a consideration of some of the very greatest writers of
that modern movement, a view of their work, their achievement,
their interconnections, their influence, and their perception of the
modern world. Like the modern world itself, they have not gone
from us, and their significance and influence is far from over. The
important fact about that movement, which was really many
movements, is that it was not simply a new spirit and attitude, a way
of responding to the age, as I have emphasized so far, but an extraordinary and dense creative achievement, one that is in many respects
incomparable. Few ages have summoned from themselves an art so
extraordinary and so complex. It was a great gathering of talent and
discovery, as movement followed movement in an unprecedented
fertility of artistic change. And if, as I have said, it was an *avant-garde*
gamble with the future, it has indeed changed our sense of art and our
view of life for good. In coming to recognize it, we have also come
to recognize the centrality and urgency of its vision of crisis, the
justice of its tragic irony, the need for its anxiety, and the basis of its
quarrel with the age.

The modern movement was an extended and ever-changing
achievement, spanning more than sixty years. It was the art of an era
of intellectual and cultural internationalism, and of great social
upheaval, and it passed its ideas from culture to culture. It was therefore an art of great cosmopolitanism, some of it willingly sought
through the age-old process of literary travel and expatriation (as was
the case with Pound, Eliot, Joyce and his successor Samuel Beckett)
and some of it enforced by the historical disorder that drove many

modern writers into exile (as was the case with Dostoevsky, to some extent Ibsen, and then Mann, Brecht, and Nabokov). There are, as George Steiner has said, very good historical reasons why much of our modern art has been produced by writers 'unhoused', detached from their national culture, their tradition, or their own native language, and why the word 'modern' has much to do with rootlessness and disorientation. And there are equally good reasons why the sensations of exile – the irony, the alienation, the rootlessness, the loss of domestic and familiar qualities – should be the dominant qualities of a good part of its achievement, and why it is an art that disturbs us as profoundly as it wins our admiration.

Because the modern movement was an international affair, which came to flower at around the same time in a great variety of countries, it needs to be seen under the international gaze. It drew its writers into the modern cities of art, where its ideas flowed, its spirit flourished, its tensions grew. These were often the great cosmopolitan cities like Paris, Munich, Vienna, Rome, Paris and more lately New York, which became clearing-houses where many tendencies met. The changeable and fleeting excitements, the enormous flickering contrasts, of the great modern cities had a good deal to do with the modern spirit. *Crime and Punishment* is a great work of modern extremity, the story of a young man for whom existence had never been enough, and always wanted more – but it is also a novel of Saint Petersburg and its dark tenements, its squalor, its disoriented and anguished intellectuals and its displaced underground men. Conrad built his *The Secret Agent* on 'the vision of an enormous town' vaster than some continents, the imperial city of London. Joyce's *Ulysses* is written in one city, Zurich, about another, the paralysed city of Dublin in 1904. Virginia Woolf's *Mrs Dalloway* evokes the war-shocked but still very imperial London of 1923, and Eliot's *The Waste Land* summons up all the unreal and falling cities of the world into one, a very different London from Mrs Woolf's, where the crowds sightlessly cross London Bridge and a modern sterility reigns. But the cosmopolitan cities did more than provide modern writing with one of its most essential subjects and sensations. They provided the meeting-places, the cafés, *avant-garde* magazines and publishers, the patrons, the specialized audiences, and the experimental environments and arguments out of which the new arts came. They dismayed, stimulated, and created, and most of Modernism can fairly be called a city art.

The modern movement was made up of many stages of development, many nationalities, many different provinces and literary capitals. And so there is no one figure who totally dominates it, no Shakespeare or Goethe, though there are many major talents, above all those dealt with here. Similarly no one movement or tendency clearly sums up its entire direction, and many of its greatest writers stood apart from the movements to pursue their own sense of art. 'Every new work has had as its purpose for me that of serving as a process of spiritual emancipation and purification,' Ibsen wrote, and for each of the writers in this book that emancipation and purification was the essential quest. Fractures, breaks and turning-points were always part of the argument behind Modernism – but no one moment will ever quite clarify for us why the deep change in the spirit in the arts occurred, or why we or its artists felt the modern age to be so different from the times that went before it. Various literary critics have attempted to give a theory or an inclusive explanation and as time goes on these explanations have tended to grow ever more daring (thus the French Structuralist critic Roland Barthes has argued that 'Around 1850 . . . classical writing therefore disintegrated, and the whole of literature, from Flaubert to the present day, became the problematics of language'). But no single overall view will fully envelop a modern spirit that constantly multiplied in direction and endlessly disagreed with itself. Similar disputes surround the meaning of what it all stood for. It has been said that it marked the end of Western humanism – and yet humanism, and the desire to preserve art, culture and reason, was one of the essential impulses. It has been seen as politically of the right, and yet many of its figures kept company with the left. It is said to mark the Death of the Book, and yet its books are many, and fortunately we continue to read them.

We continue to read them, I believe, because the great works of the modern movement – some of them thought wicked or obscene, obscure or eccentric in their day – are major monuments of art and understanding. They were attempts not just to capture their time but to bring art to a new spirit of discovery, a fresh self-consciousness. That is one reason why its best work is often so technically complex and so narcissistically self-aware, one reason why one of its most obvious subjects is the making of that particular work of art itself. That idea of being beyond the tradition, of creating each work separately and anew, is one of the many inheritances the Modern movements has passed on to the writers who came after. Indeed it would be difficult for any writer today not to acknowledge the power and influence of the tradition of the new. Many — like Philip Larkin in poetry, or the postwar British novelists who looked back in hunger to the Victorian realists — have questioned the influence, but it is there. The great writers of our time — Samuel Beckett, Jorge Luis Borges, Vladimir Nabokov, Italo Calvino, Saul Bellow, William Golding, John Fowles — have in various ways acknowledged this, and though many of the justifications for the *avant-garde* revolt have gone in a new age of universal bohemianism, the Modernist spirit continues.

If Modernism remains important for our writers, and has become the great tradition that lies closest to us, so it is for modern readers. We still live in the anxious, international, politically disordered age of modernity. We too live close to the turning of a century, though this time it is also the turn of an entire Christian millenium. We continue to live, then, on the change and turn of things. That 'quickening' of thought and art that Holbrook Jackson finds in the arts of the modern, that sense of living in an age where creation and negation go hand in hand, in a period that is fragmented, pluralistic, sick and weird, is still with us. So is that hunger for new forms of expression and new visions of experience which always marked the modernist spirit. The great writers here still remain our contemporaries — sometimes to a far greater degree than many of the writers of our own time. They offer us, still, some of the finest art, some of the deepest moral and historical exploration, that we can find from literature. They did, indeed, Make It New, and we live both in the new age they saw and among the new images of reality they constructed.

FYODOR DOSTOEVSKY

'I am a sick man. . . . I am a spiteful man. I am an unattractive man. I believe my liver is diseased.' The person addressing us is an 'underground man', the unnamed figure – we cannot call him the hero, for he refuses to be one – who pours out his bitter story in Fyodor Dostoevsky's short novel *Notes from Underground*. He is one of those clerkly, poverty-stricken, orphaned characters who abound in mid-nineteenth century fiction, in the novels of Balzac and Stendhal, Dickens and Melville, working unnoticed and angry behind their desks, a cross between a romantic dreamer and a bureaucratic slave. He is forty, a former government official in the imperial capital of Saint Petersburg who has had a small legacy and withdrawn into his seedy 'corner', a poor apartment in the suburbs. He addresses us from, he says, 'beneath the floorboards'. It is a metaphorical place, the place where the dissident intellectuals and revolutionaries common in Dostoevsky's writings hid their subversive printing presses, and also a hidden position from which he can spy 'through the chinks' on the life and intellectual condition of his age.

Dostoevsky meant his underground man as a representative figure of the times. 'It is clear that such persons as the writer of these notes not only may, but positively must, exist in our society, when we consider the circumstances in the midst of which our society is formed,' he wrote in a note he added to the *Notes*. 'He is one of the representatives of a generation still living.' He is modern man, in his fragile, irritable state: 'I'm very touchy, sensitive and quick to take offence.' He has withdrawn from real life and people into his own consciousness, but despises it: 'I am firmly persuaded that a great deal of consciousness, every sort of consciousness, in fact, is a disease.' His tone is ironic, his sensibility sick, and he knows the distorted quality

of his own nature, but blames it on the distortions of the times. He
takes pleasure in degrading himself, and others. He cannot feel, and
though he suffers he does not believe in his suffering. He is cruel,
jealous, and enraged – 'and all out of boredom, gentlemen, all out of
boredom; I'm crushed by tedium.' He cannot succeed in becoming
anything, 'neither spiteful nor kind, neither a rascal nor an honest man,
neither a hero nor an insect.' He is the superfluous man, exiled from
himself, a type Dostoevsky saw as the man of the modern age. As
Walter Pater put it in *The Renaissance*: 'To regard all things and principles of things as inconsistent modes or fashions has become more
and more the tendency of modern thought.'

Notes from Underground came out in 1864, when its author was in
his forties, in mid-life, mid-career, and in the midst of great personal,
intellectual and financial crisis. The fiery and temperamental Dostoevsky was penniless, bankrupt, in every kind of debt. He had to sell
his work before it was written, and everywhere his creditors, family
and dependents were hounding him for money. He was observed by
the police, and had recently spent ten years in a Siberian prison camp
for the liberal ideals of his youth. He was one of a vast new underclass
that had grown up in Russia, the intelligentsia, the educated sons of
the gentry who had been entranced by the new romantic and revolutionary ideas that had swept through modernizing Western
Europe. Such people existed all over Europe; they were the new avant-
garde, the bohemians. 'Bohemia possesses nothing, yet contrives to
exist on that nothing,' wrote Dostoevsky's literary hero, the French
novelist Balzac; 'Its religion is hope; its code, faith in itself; its income,
insofar as it appears to have one, charity. All these young people rise
superior to their misfortunes; poverty they must endure, but their
destiny they can shape for themselves.'

But Tsarist Russia was still a feudal, autocratic society, a nation of
great nobles and landowners and of brutally used serfs. The new
intelligentsia of Russia who discussed ideas, wrote novels to express
those ideas, and dreamed of moving the nation from feudalism to
modernity in one great leap, were even more impotent than those of
Western Europe, kept in check by a strict censorship, police spies, and
a lack of employment and influence. They could be neither men of

power nor men of the people, and their ideas, deprived of an outlet, turned to impatience and extremity. They gathered penniless and discontented in the two great capitals, Saint Petersburg and Moscow, living, like Dostoevsky, in a damp, diseased environment of sordid tenements, noise and dirt, violence and beggary, family hangers-on, pawnshops and promissory notes, turning to ideas, writing, and the solitary confinement of thought. And they had nowhere to go except into a corner, like the underground man, or into an extreme action that expressed their wild desire for moral freedom and a self-shaped destiny, as was to be the case with Dostoevsky's next literary hero, Raskolnikov.

Notes from Underground, as its title suggests, is about this underbelly of the world. It is intended as a subversive book, as its title also suggests; 'underground' is still where a significant part of Russian literature comes from. Its subversion, though, was aimed less at the regime (which nonetheless censored one chapter) than at the liberal and radical ideas he had once shared. His term in the prison camp had changed him deeply. He had become more committed to his Slavic inheritance, more concerned with common humanity, more aware of the deep contradictions that lay in human nature. He distrusted the spirit of utilitarianism and the ideas of enlightened self-interest which led many intellectuals to hope for a revolutionary socialist state based on human virtue, the good and the beautiful. Like the underground man, he sensed a doubleness in human behaviour, and found in mankind a deep instinct for chaos, negation and nihilism.

The underground man is a doubled man himself – not good and not bad, just divided. Virtue and vice war inside him: 'I felt them positively swarming in me, these opposite elements.' In him romantic self-consciousness has turned to irony and self-contempt. He lacks a character, for, as he says, 'a man in the nineteenth century must and morally ought to be a characterless creature; a man of character, an active man, is pre-eminently a limited creature.' If he despises himself, he despises even more those around him. An intellectual, he rejects other intellectuals, who believe in the good and the beautiful but ensure they have a good state pension. He sees an absurd division between thought and action, the intellectual's disease. Indeed his notes

from underground can never be fully completed, for he does not
believe in them himself, Always there are gaps – between literature,
which can console us, and 'living life', which does not, and which
therefore we avoid. For in these times no one knows what, or where,
real life is: 'We even feel it difficult to be human beings, with real
flesh and blood *of our own*; we're ashamed of it and always striving to
be some kind of unprecedented sort of generalized human being.'

Thus he makes the very confession he writes into an ironic object –
not literature, he says, just 'corrective punishment'. The task is absurd,
and he might as well stop:

> Why, to tell long stories, showing how I have spoiled my life
> through morally rotting in my corner through lack of fitting
> environment, through divorce from real life, and rankling spite
> in my underground world, would certainly not be interesting; a
> novel needs a hero, and all the traits of an anti-hero are *expressly*
> gathered here, and what matters most, it all presents an un-
> pleasant impression, for we are all divorced from life, we are all
> cripples, every one of us, more or less. We are so divorced from
> it that we feel at once a sort of loathing for real life . . . it is
> better in books . . . Why are we so perverse and seek for some-
> thing else?

The underground man is thus the modern anti-hero. But supposing,
under such conditions, a modern man seeks to act, and not foolishly,
to escape from the solitary confinement of thought and affect the
nature of the times? Might he then be a form of the modern hero?
What kind of action would he perform? These were the questions
Dostoevsky now went on to consider, and out of them he created his
next, and most famous, fictional hero, the young student Raskolnikov,
the central figure of *Crime and Punishment*.

The underground man is the precursor of Raskolnikov, and both
are men for their times. But both became precursors of something
more – nothing less than the spirit of modern literature and modern
ideas. From his concealed corner, the underground man was to cast a
vast shadow over the literature of modernism. In his characterless

character a new modern figure was born, and his bitter ironic confessional voice, self-conscious and distrusting his own authenticity, was
to sound throughout the pages of modern fiction. If he was the anti-
hero there was the new hero, the heir of Raskolnikov, an arrogant
superman, convinced he is exceptional and so entitled to commit any
'free' act in the name of self-liberation or history. In the outcast and
the criminal, the anti-hero and the superhero. Dostoevsky wanted to
display the contradictions and extremities of his own day. But the age
that followed was persistently to recognize them, in their conflicts,
dilemmas and irritable rages, and make them into a fundamental part
of modernity in literature.

To say this is to suggest that 'modernity' – the spirit of the age as it
is recognized and explored by its great writers, the bearers of the
literary conscience – is itself divided, anxious, self-doubting and
dismayed. But so it has been; modern literature, like modern life,
moves always closer to the abyss, in the world of action or the world
of inward consciousness. More than virtually any other nineteenth-
century writer, the author of *Notes from Underground* and the great
sequence of books it started – *Crime and Punishment* and *The Gambler*
in 1866, *The Idiot* in 1869, *The Possessed* in 1872, and finally *The
Brothers Karamazov* in 1880, the year before he died – would dominate
the imagination and anxieties of the generations and ages that
followed, as that modernity that Dostoevsky always attended to
became more deeply apprehended. It has rightly been said that it took
the twentieth century, and its experience of history, to understand
Dostoevsky. He was, like Kafka, his natural successor amid the greater
uncertainties of the new age, a writer of enormous and terrible prediction. He was an intellectual novelist who raged against the domination of the intellect, an intensely modern writer who revolted
against much in modernity. When the old feudal Russia reached, in
1917, the moment of revolutionary terror that so much of his work
seems to predict or try to forestall, the essential choices had already
been foretold in *The Possessed*. In the characters of that extraordinary
book we can find those urgent, intellectual, revolutionary desires that
were to shape so much in the twentieth century – the hunger for
ideology, the need to dominate by the will, the justification for terror

and totalitarianism, the vision of an order of society where 'only the necessary is necessary'.

Dostoevsky seemed to catch at modernity's very flavour in politics, in philosophy, in psychology, and in the form of art. When Friedrich Nietzsche, the German philosopher whose ideas of modernity were so to influence the world of the early twentieth century, spoke of the need to step 'beyond good and evil', that step had already been taken by Raskolnikov. And when Nietzsche picked up *Notes from Underground*, he acknowledged the book at once. 'The instinct of kinship . . . spoke up immediately; my joy was extraordinary,' he said. Freud acknowledged his complex insight into psychology, and in turn attempted to psychologize him. Kafka was one of his most avid readers, and when Kafka's friend Max Brod complained that there were too many mad people in his fictional world, he answered: 'Completely wrong. They aren't ill. The illness is merely a way to characterize them, and moreover a very delicate and fruitful one.' Kafka's characters are the children of Dostoevsky in a changed age, and they hand him on to the present. If the underground man cannot, as he says, quite 'become an insect', those children can. In Kafka's story 'The Metamorphosis', the central character does indeed become an insect, and is swept away with the rubbish. The men without qualities, the figures who are not Prince Hamlet nor were meant to be, the vacant spaces in so much modern fiction where the hero should stand, all show their trace of Dostoevsky.

Dostoevsky both helped to construct and also to trouble the modern imagination. Virtually no major writer of the twentieth century has been able to avoid his massive presence, and his implications for the attitudes and methods of modern fiction. Russian culture divided between its two great nineteenth-century giants, Tolstoy and Dostoevsky – Tolstoy the social and historical novelist, the writer of reason and panoramic breadth, Dostoevsky the great inward novelist, the psychological visionary who wrote of modern suffering, anguish and, in the later books, the need for faith and mysticism. His fame spread through Europe in the early twentieth century, especially around the years of the Great War, and the writers of Germany, France and Britain responded to his power. Conrad declared there was something too Russian in Dostoevsky for him, but *The Secret Agent* and *Under Western Eyes* both show his obvious influence. Proust expressed his admiration for his art of construction, but also observed that his preoccupation with murder 'is something extraordinary which makes him very alien to me.' Virginia Woolf was one of his greatest English admirers, but acknowledged that there was something in him that stood apart from the British temperament, and which she defined as the Russian 'soul'. D. H. Lawrence typically admired his extremity and despised his characters, 'suffering their way to Jesus'.

Of all the nineteenth-century novelists Dostoevsky exerted most influence over modern writing, though he also represented something extreme in the modern spirit. He himself considered there was something distinctive in the Russian imagination that separated it from that of Western Europe, and said that the spirit of European Romanticism grew more extreme as it swept into Russia. His fiction both expressed and revolted against that extremity – one reason why he seems modern. That conflict came partly from the struggling world of the spirit within, as it fought the battles of will and consciousness, intellect and feeling, revolutionary optimism and mystical faith that belonged to the age. But it also came from the divided, ghostly Russian world outside, split between the old and apparently unchangeable order of things and those raging intimations of the new that demanded their right of expression.

The extremity and the modernity were inseparable. As D. H. Lawrence acknowledged, 'Two bodies of modern literature seem to me to have come to the real verge: the Russian and the American.' Both, he said, reached during the nineteenth century 'a pitch of extreme consciousness' that even the highest frenzies of modernist experiments never reached. Standing apart from the social and moral realism of the European mainstream, they reached into the places of spiritual exile and anguish in ways fundamental to the modern imagination. If Dostoevsky was, as he is, a genius presiding over the spirit of modern literature, this was one reason why. There was also another. He took not just the experience but the form of the nineteenth-century novel into new places, into the underground of art itself.

2

That sense of extremity in Dostoevsky's writing came both from his place inside, and often outside, Russian culture, and from his own morose and fiery temperament. Fyodor Dostoevsky was born in 1821 in Moscow, the son of a doctor who was himself given over to great moroseness and violent rages. When he was 16, his mother died, and one year after he went to college his father, who had become a drunkard, was murdered by the serfs on the country estate he had acquired. This undoubtedly had a profound effect on the son (Freud, in his writings on him, saw it as the basis of his personality) and contributed to his mixture of proud independence and his hunger for identity with the peasant soul. But by then Fyodor was already at the Military Engineering Academy in the other capital, Saint Petersburg, training for a military career, though his main interest now lay in the literature of Romanticism. He evidently possessed his father's impetuous temperament, and friends recorded him as solitary, highly strung, morbidly sensitive, spendthrift and deeply ambitious. There was, evidently, a good deal of the Raskolnikov in him.

It was not long before he found his military career 'dull as potatoes', and in 1844 he resigned from it to try to make his living from literature – a depressed career which inevitably returned him to poverty and uncertainty. In fact the experience of poverty became the theme of his first novel, *Poor Folk*, which appeared in 1846. For it he was hailed as a genius, and treated as a young literary celebrity. But a second novel, *The Double*, which in fact began to explore the psychological interests of his later books – it deals with paranoid psychology – was not well received. Nonetheless Dostoevsky became an important figure in Saint Petersburg literary circles, and like most intellectuals of his time he became excited by the German and French romantic movements and by the liberal ideas coming out of Europe. In 1848 came the revolutionary flowering of those ideas, in the various waves of nationalistic and libertarian revolution that passed through Europe, and were to dominate intellectual life thereafter. And it was one year later, in 1849, that there came the most terrible event of Dostoevsky's life, the event that shaped all his work from that moment.

This was the Petrashevsky affair. Dostoevsky had joined an intellectual circle around Mikhail Petrashevsky, a young foreign-office official, who was a follower of various European radical thinkers, especially the French communitarian, Charles Fourier. There was talk of setting up intellectual communities and even discussion of liberal revolution. The group had been penetrated by a secret agent, for autocracy and surveillance prevailed in Russia, sometimes in an oddly tolerant way. But tolerance was not in evidence under the severe regime of Tsar Nicholas I, especially in the wake of 1848. Dostoevsky, along with others, was arrested, at four in the morning, and kept in the Peter-Paul Fortress (its commander was General Nabokov, an ancestor of a much later modernist writer). He refused to answer questions, and in a written statement he defended the principles of liberalism. It was in effect a self-condemnation, and a military court passed death sentences on the defendants. The Tsar did not intend this to be carried out, but allowed the men to be led to the place of execution and put in white shirts before a firing squad. Only at the last minute was a reprieve read out, and Dostoevsky was instead condemned to four years in a Siberian labour camp.

The moment of exposure to death, the degradation and violence suffered by a young intellectual in the terrible camp over the next years, these things were always imprinted on Dostoevsky's mind, and came to dominate his writing. The experience of the Siberian camp became the subject of *The House of the Dead*, and the mock execution is in *The Idiot*. Raskolnikov's experience in prison at the end of *Crime and Punishment* resembles Dostoevsky's – he too was separated from the other convicts by his social background and his solitary temperament, and found himself despised, distrusted and assaulted. He began to consider the nature of the criminal, and the temperament of the murderer, who often murders from will rather than instinct. At the same time he came to respect and honour the acceptance of suffering, the religious humility and simple faith, of his fellow convicts, and that too is part of the theme of *Crime and Punishment*, and of his later identification with the simple peasant soul.

The four-year experience completely changed Dostoevsky, physically and intellectually. He began to suffer from the epilepsy that
plagued him thereafter, and to adopt a more complex and bitter view
of the world, which moved him away from his earlier liberalism. Nor
was his punishment over. He had to serve five further years as a
common soldier near the Mongolian frontier, forbidden to return to
Saint Petersburg or to publish his writings. By the time he returned
to the city in 1859, a new Tsar ruled, and the intellectual climate had
changed and, for a brief time, grown more open. There was a new
nihilism in the intellectual breeze, as well as a new Slavic nationalism.
He returned to poverty and new difficulties. The wife he had married
while on military service grew ill, and he started a magazine with his
brother Mikhail which began to accumulate great debts. The harsh,
poor and overwhelming life of Saint Petersburg now engulfed him,
and became the dominant subject of his writing. Indeed the Dostoevsky who was drawn to the soul of the Russian peasant was to become
one of the great novelists of modern, crowded, pressing and oppressive
city life, like Balzac or Dickens.

And in that city life his difficulties grew to become almost insup-
portable. The magazine he edited with his brother was silenced by
the censor in 1863, leaving debts; censors and creditors were always to
plague him. He increased his problems himself by a wild compulsion
for gambling, which he exercised on travels in Europe in which casinos
figured prominently. There was a troubled, disappointing love affair.
His marriage had not been happy, but now his wife died, and so did
his brother and literary collaborator Mikhail. Fyodor assumed his
debts and responsibility for the family, and of his wife's troublesome
son by a previous marriage, and found himself bankrupt. Writing was
his only solution, for predatory editors who required manuscripts at
speed. Yet it was in this atmosphere, and largely in an attempt to
clear his debts and make the ground for a sudden new marriage, that
he began to write his greatest fiction.

The books reveal the burden of these years. *Notes from Underground*
is a story of withdrawal from the intellectual romanticism of the time,
and the beginning of a new kind of ironic confessional literature. It
shows his own bitterness and pain, and his division between an ironic

sense of himself and a feeling of responsibility for the agonizing crowds of humanity that fill the great city and tear at the conscience. He explored his gambling mania in *The Gambler*, a book hastily written back-to-back with *Crime and Punishment*. According to story, that novel, his most famous, came from the roulette table too, when a bout of gambling in Wiesbaden in Germany left him penniless and totally alone there, dependent on pawnbrokers. Now he conceived his great-est book, which was based on all his recent experiences – destitution, the claims of dependent relatives, intellectual crisis, the relation be-tween the 'exceptional' man and the human mass, modern boredom and anxiety, the nature of the criminal and the murderer, crime and guilt, punishment and imprisonment.

The seeds of the idea already lay in *Notes from the Underground* – the book in which Dostoevsky's imagination itself seems to go under-ground, into the underside of life and psychology. They also lay in his ideas for a novel called *The Drunkards*, never written, but intended to deal with the pressing city problems of the day – drunkenness, and all that surrounded it, including poverty, crime, prostitution and neglect of children. All this went into *Crime and Punishment*, chiefly into the story of the Marmeladov family, the tale of a genteel family corrupted by the father's drinking, but also into the book's general vision of the insulted and injured, of suffering and degraded common humanity. This is the world from which Raskolnikov considers himself separated by his exceptional qualities, but into which he is always drawn, and whose wrongs he would like to redress. His isolation and his com-passion mingle to create his belief that he has the exceptional right to act in defiance of conventional law, by constructing through violence a new economy of justice and utility. Thus the essential idea of the book became the study of such a crime, and its inward punishment.

3

Dostoevsky first sketched the idea for his most famous and successful book in a letter he sent from Wiesbaden to a magazine editor he wanted to interest in it. 'This will be the psychological study of a crime,' he wrote; 'It is a novel of contemporary life and the action takes place this year. A young man, a former student of Petersburg University who is very hard up, becomes obsessed with the "half-baked" ideas that are in the air now because of his general mental instability. He decides to do something that would save him immediately from his desperate position. He makes up his mind to kill an old woman moneylender. The old woman is stupid, greedy, deaf, and ill . . . absolutely worthless, there seems to be no justification for her existence, etc. All these considerations completely unhinge the mind of the young man.' Though many more ideas would come later, this is a vivid description of the book we know. Dostoevsky also says the crime will not be detected: 'He is never under suspicion, nor indeed can there be any suspicion against him. But it is here the whole psychological process of the crime unfolds itself. The murderer is suddenly confronted by insoluble problems, and hitherto undreamt-of feelings begin to torment him.' And, he adds, 'The murderer himself decides to accept his punishment in order to expiate his crime.' The idea, Dostoevsky said, was 'difficult to explain', but he pointed to several examples of recent crimes committed by intelligent young men: 'Our papers are full of stories which show the general feeling of instability which leads young men to commit terrible crimes.'

Dostoevsky has often been called an instinctive and even an inartistic writer. He certainly believed that books, like our view of life itself, should come from deep feeling rather than abstract conceptions. He wrote his books, he said, in travail and pain of soul, and wanted them to be full of life's immediacy and authenticity. But the notebooks he kept for the novel show how carefully the book was planned, and its design is complete and solid. At first, they show, he wanted it to take a form close to that of *Notes from Underground*, and be a first-person narrative by Raskolnikov – a diary, a court confession, or a reminiscence after his sentence. The early manuscripts show how similar he is to the underground man; 'Why, why am I here? Why do I feel an alien?' he cries in one draft that survives, and the notebooks stress he should be presented as someone not in his right mind. But then came a fundamental change of plan that was to transform the book and give it a far greater universality. 'Narration from the point of view of the author, a sort of invisible but omniscient being, who doesn't leave the hero for a moment.' The intense method of psychological rendering that makes the book so remarkable had now been born.

At the same time Dostoevsky believed that the author must experience and discover the book along with his major characters. And it is clear that, like a great many novels, *Crime and Punishment* is a book where many of the discoveries took place in the writing, including the very motives of the hero. 'The murder is done almost unexpectedly (I myself did not expect it),' he noted at one point. This is what gives the book its enormous immediacy, and our feeling of sharing every emotion and instinct felt by its hero. Dostoevsky scarcely departs from his side and sensations for a moment, except for a few scenes (the death of Svidrigaylov, for example) where Raskolnikov is absent. So the book observes from his viewpoint, reacts to his every response and state of mind, and yet sees him from outside. It experiences life as we see, feel, sense and hear it, at the moment of sensation, but it also observes the morbidity of his sensations, and the confusion of his temperament. That vivid psychological consciousness is one of the things that makes the book feel modern.

Another is the vivid, even fantastic treatment of the city of Saint Petersburg, which Dostoevsky once called 'the most fantastic city in the world'. Like many of the great nineteenth-century writers of fiction, Dostoevsky is essentially an urban writer. At the same time his approach is novel, comparable to Baudelaire's treatment of the modern city in his poetry as an unreal place of strange sensations and random dreams. Dostoevsky observed what he called the 'Petersburg nightmare', where strange dreams prosper, and the walls fall away into terrible visions. 'Here,' he once wrote, 'one cannot take a step without seeing, hearing and feeling the contemporary moment and the idea of the present moment.' Svidrigaylov speaks of Saint Petersburg as a city of half-crazy people, filled with gloomy, harsh and strange influences. Raskolnikov constantly walks the city, reflecting that even its magnificence is 'the embodiment of some blank and dead spirit',

while the life of its streets is what overwhelms him and maintains his
sense of psychological extremity.

Dostoevsky's Petersburg is indeed the unreal city of modern life,
but that life is both strange and profoundly vivid, unceasing and ever-
present, and never for a moment is Raskolnikov out of the noise, the
shouting violence, the universal pain of it. All his characters wander,
as Dostoevsky did himself, its dark streets, its public spaces, its bars, its
random and packed traffic routes, its tenements, with their squalid
rooms, paper-thin walls, unlit stoves, and stairwells covered with slops
and eggshells. It is a place of diseases and fevers, suicides and sudden
deaths, street accidents and violent fights, a nightmare without that
matches nightmare within. Everything seems like an unplanned col-
lision, and yet everything connects. It is a place of extreme contrasts,
with its wealthy noblemen, its government officials and clerks, its
secret policemen and investigating magistrates, its poor students, and,
everywhere, its insulted and injured. It is also a place of hectic ideas,
expressed in endless discussions and in the magazines and newspapers
that are read alike by the intellectuals and the police. A surreal city,
like an hallucination, it becomes as much a part of Raskolnikov's inner
life as the abstract thoughts of his mind. In fact one of Dostoevsky's
best critics, the Russian critic Mikhail Bakhtin, observed that Dostoevsky created from it a new form, the 'polyphonic' novel, exactly opposite to *Notes from Underground* in that the narrative is told not as a
monologue but as a great polyphony of many voices endlessly compet-
ing for dominance.

And if the city of the novel is the modern city, Raskolnikov is very
clearly a modern intellectual, one of the displaced and alienated figures of
what the underground man has called 'the most abstract and intentional
city in the world', adding that there are intentional and unintentional,
intellectual and unintellectual, cities. The word '*raskolnik*' means
'schismatic' or 'dissenter', and Raskolnikov is taken by the newest
ideas of the times. Like his dark double, Svidrigaylov, he is a man
born of contemporary anger and boredom, an atheist and nihilist who
believes in the libertarian right to create his own morality and transcend religious and moral law in the interests of a self-created higher
good. He explores the dreadful freedom of a world where lives are

rootless, injustice is endemic, society is a place of universal suffering, God appears absent, and public law is irrelevant. He believes in the 'Napoleonic' idea of the world-historical individual, the man entitled by his exceptional powers to commit any act in order to deliver the future. He is, as the corpulent and chubby investigating magistrate, Porfiry, says, a modern man, and the crime that has taken place is a modern crime: 'We're dealing with quite a fantastic affair here, a modern one, a case characteristic of our time, when men's hearts have grown rank and foul ... We're dealing with bookish dreams here, with a heart exacerbated by theories.'

For all this Dostoevsky found a modern method of writing, the method he called 'fantastic realism': 'I have my own idea of art, and it is this: what most people regard as fantastic and lacking in universality, *I* hold to be the inmost essence of truth. Arid observation of everyday trivialities I have long since ceased to regard as realism – it is quite the reverse. In any newspaper one takes up, one comes across reports of wholly authentic facts, which nevertheless strike one as extraordinary.' 'Do you read any newspapers?' he asked one correspondent, explaining how a writer must get at the heart of his own epoch, by reading them and sensing the underlying wholeness, 'in order that the visible connection of all matters, public and private, may become consistently stronger and clearer.' What Dostoevsky makes fantastic, through the visible connection of all matters, is the contemporary world, the world that seeks to seize on the present and turn it into the future. The book is made both from an intense sense of the inner emotional and psychological life of the hero, and a deeply dramatic, vivid, and public method of invention. That combination makes it one of the most powerful and coherent of nineteenth-century novels, and yet also a book that prefigures the modern sense of human nature.

Crime and Punishment has been seen as many things. It has been seen as the most profound of detective stories, one of the greatest of the genre, in which the detection of the crime involves the remorseless pursuit of its motives, and where the essential detective is the criminal himself. It has been read as a metaphysical thriller, in which the very nature of sin is analysed. It has been regarded as a tale of tragic pride, in which the hero is unremittingly haunted to the heart of his soul by the deed of blood he has done – and one critic has said that it reads like the fifth acts of all the tragedies. It has been seen as a profound work of modern nihilism and egotism, in which the modern superman attempts to step beyond the rule of good and evil. It has also been regarded, by the great Spanish critic Ortega y Gasset, as the novel that escapes 'the general shipwreck of nineteenth-century novels' because its strange realism arises not from random events and the facts of life but from the wholeness of its formal vision, as in the major twentieth-century novels. But perhaps these are all ways of saying a similar thing: that in some compelling fashion this is indeed the first of the modern novels.

4

The structure of *Crime and Punishment* is very clear. The book consists of six parts and an epilogue, and by the end of the first part, within the first hundred pages, the crime is done. The following five parts, the bulk of the book, deal with the punishment, which is essentially a process of psychological crisis and complex self-excoriation, ending at last with his confession, first in the public street, and then in the police station. In the epilogue we see Raskolnikov suffering his official punishment, like his own creator, in a penal colony in Siberia, though his punishment is still not complete. Earlier in the novel he has mockingly asked the prostitute Sonia, who seeks to return him to humanity through suffering and repentance, to read the passage from the Bible about the raising of Lazarus from the dead. But we leave Raskolnikov at the end of the story still in the house of the dead, his redemption still not complete. The meaning of the book is centred on an observation in his notebooks that Dostoevsky emphasized: 'Man is not born for happiness. Man earns his happiness, and always by suffering. There is no injustice here, for knowledge and consciousness of life . . . is acquired by experience pro and contra, which one must get through on one's own.'

As Dostoevsky said, the book is the psychological study of a crime, in which the psychology of it largely unfolds after it is committed. From the very first page it is clear that the crime is intended, in thought if not in deed. Like the underground man, we find Raskolnikov, as the story begins, confined in his coffin-like room under the stairs which is more like a cupboard than a room. He has, we learn, grown used to lying in bed and thinking 'all sorts of absurd things'. He is so completely absorbed in himself that he does not want to meet others, and when he passes the kitchen of his landlady, to whom he is heavily in debt, and whose daughter, we learn later, he has wooed to solve some of his problems, he 'experiences a sickening sensation of terror'. Yet he despises those who are 'afraid of taking a new step or uttering a new word'. Even so the action he wants to perform – we do not know yet what it is – is something he does not fully understand, and he wonders why he is going out and doing *that*. 'It isn't serious at all,' he tells himself. 'Just amusing myself by indulging in fantastic dreams.'

Raskolnikov is an intellectual, but it is clear from the start that his ideas are at the service of his passions and random emotions. In fact the book never allows him to develop his ideas in the abstract. His solitude is always intruded on, by the endless threatening noise and violence of a city in which there is virtually no privacy, and by the method of the novelist, who describes his every small and involuntary movement of sensation and feeling. Though he tries to keep himself apart from or above the world, he is at every instant a part of it, as the world mirrors each sensation, and the random events outside him could equally well be elements of his morbid and hallucinatory state. In fact everything seems a portent to him, tugging at or revealing his own vacillating spirit.

Thus his walk through the streets at the start of the book is made up of a complex welter of feelings and sensations. He feels disgust, terror, anxiety and self-confidence. He feels shame about his tattered clothes. This turns to fear, as the clothes may mean he has overlooked some detail of his plan, for his actions are a theatrical rehearsal that he must be able to perform, a mock version of a later action. He visits an old woman moneylender, makes a transaction, asks questions, and leaves. In a public house he goes into afterwards, he feels cheerful, but 'could not help feeling rather vaguely that this tendency of his to take a cheerful view of things was itself morbid.' Like the underground man he is an expert in the contradictions of his own sensations, a man who is always watching himself. Each event becomes vivid both because of the massive intensity of social and urban detail that Dostoevsky creates as the background to the story – he describes topography and measures distances exactly – and because everything Raskolnikov does is studied by him as if a walk in life is something on which he will later be examined.

In this scene he meets Marmeladov, a former member of the civil service, now destitute through his drinking. We are told his eyes glitter with a mixture of intelligence and madness, and he begins to speak of modern British theories of utilitarianism, where even pity has been outlawed by science, which is why he needs to still his soul with drink. The tale he tells is a tragic one, of genteel decline through drunkenness which has led to his daughter, Sonia, becoming a prostitute. He is now drinking her earnings, and he asks to be crucified, not pitied, and God alone will be the judge. Raskolnikov takes him back to his apartment and meets Sonia, leaving a few of his own much-needed coins on the window sill. Afterwards, he regrets his compassion, and regards what he has seen as a lesson in the way men become used, like beasts, to anything and everything. And if man is not a beast, 'there is nothing to stop you from doing anything you like, and that's as it should be!'

Crime and Punishment begins as it continues, in a great accumulation of human misery, which surrounds and beats at Raskolnikov's spirit, but from which he tries to remain separate to retain his own individuality. But the misery enfolds him on every side. His sister is being pursued by a vicious employer, Svidrigaylov, who will play an important part in Raskolnikov's fate. She, like Sonia, intends to sacrifice her life for her loved ones, by making a loveless marriage; his mother asks him to intervene. Everything that happens seems to call him out of thought and passivity, bringing into his mind 'the form of a fearful, wild and fantastic question . . . clamouring for an immediate solution.' Dostoevsky concentrates this in a terrible dream, of peasants flogging a horse to death, which seems to purge Raskolnikov's mind of the murderous plan he has been forming. Yet each new event, each accumulation of chance, seems a fresh signal, always pointing in one direction. A chance street conversation he overhears tells him that the old moneylender's simple sister, Lisaveta, will be out the following evening. He recalls overhearing another chance conversation between a student and an army officer, a discussion of the balance of human misery, in which the question is asked: 'What does the life of a sickly, wicked old hag amount to when weighed in the scales of the general good of mankind?'

So, like a series of signs and pointers to a superstitious man, everything seems to confirm an intention that has already been there. Raskolnikov is a thinker, but what we see are not his theories but the chance pressures and feelings that forge a strange connection between his mind and the random world outside: 'Always afterwards he was inclined to see in all this something strange and mysterious – the presence, as it were, of some influences and coincidences.' His state is one of morbid intensity, while the world outside, however dense and detailed, is strange and hallucinatory. The method Dostoevsky had detailed in his notebook, of recording everything through an invisible but omniscient author who doesn't leave the hero for a moment, works to construct a surreal immediacy, a fantastic realism. And in fact the author is not always invisible to us. Just before the crime itself he speaks clearly: 'Let us, incidentally, observe a peculiarity in connexion with all these final decisions he had taken in the matter. They all possessed one strange characteristic: the more final they became, the more absurd and more horrible they at once appeared in his eyes.'

That separation of the novelist from the character is his literary preparation for the central and terrible scenes of the crime itself – perhaps the most terrible and remarkable scenes in all modern literature, which has not been short of such things. Now the absurd relation between thought and action increases, the novelist steps back, to allow actions to be freed from any explanations, and there is a strange coming and going of consciousness. We do not really see why Raskolnikov sets out for the moneylender's apartment, and his thoughts are now random and disordered. He thinks, for example, about improving the amenities in a park he passes. Nothing he does quite follows the intellectual plan. He feels as though 'someone had taken him by the hand and drawn him after himself, blindly, irresistibly, with supernatural force, and without any objection on his part.' He has developed the theory that what makes criminals betray themselves is that their reason and willpower break down during the crime, like a disease. He imagines this will not happen to him, since 'what he intended to do was "not a crime."' Yet he himself falls into a state of oblivion, and nothing he does goes quite to plan.

Most terrible of all is the fact that after he has murdered the woman moneylender with a hatchet, her sister Lisaveta returns unexpectedly. Part of his 'justification' for the death of the old woman is that she has misused her sister, but now he must kill her too. The most vivid scene in the book is that where Lisaveta backs away from him, somehow unable to cry out:

> He rushed at her with the hatchet. Her lips were twisted painfully, like those of little children who are beginning to be afraid of something and, without taking their eyes off the object of their fright, are about to scream. And so simple, crushed, and cowed was this unhappy Lisaveta that she did not even lift her hands to protect her face, though that was the most natural and inevitable gesture at that moment, for the hatchet was raised straight above her face. All she did was to lift her free left hand a little, at some distance from her face, and extend it slowly toward the hatchet as though pushing it away. The blow fell straight across her skull . . .

What makes this most terrible is not simply the vividness of the detail, nor even the touching, innocent and simple gestures of the victim. It is also that, thanks to Dostoevsky's literary method, we see what happens as if it has a victim but no perpetrator. Raskolnikov's actions are not shown as his, and the struggle seems to be between Lisaveta and the hatchet itself.

No scene better displays the strange, hallucinatory nature of the writing, or the way it becomes a method exactly appropriate to the novel's theme. This terrible detachment of the doer from the deed is like the separation of thought from action which has brought Raskolnikov this far. For his actions are a part of his self-alienation, an approach to life which has allowed this act to take place. They are in effect acts of the unconscious, which will later have to be made conscious. This is a novel about the unimaginable becoming real, about disconnections becoming connections, random events needing to be seen as human responsibilities, thoughts becoming deeds, and deeds requiring doers. The terror the scene strikes arises from the fact that abstract thoughts and strange sensations have become a dreadful actuality. 'When the hour struck, everything happened not at all as he anticipated, but somehow by sheer accident, almost unexpectedly,' Dostoevsky writes. He also observed in his notebook that the murder was unexpected even to him, and we can see how his own method made this so, and turned his scene into one of the most terrible of literary truths.

5

Dostoevsky's intention for his novel was very plain. He would start quickly with the crime, and then devote the rest to its psychological consequences, which would dominate the book. It is this that gives the book the impression, it has been said, that it is written backwards. 'All as swiftly as possible,' he said in his notebook, about the opening. 'The event and then begins the corruption of his own psychology. Because only now he regained consciousness.' As he said, after the act, the psychological process of the crime unfolds, and this psychological unfolding is the true heart of the novel. It was to take several forms. One is the movement of the act from the level of the unconscious, in which it has been so brilliantly presented, to the level of consciousness, where it can be confronted by moral analysis. 'From the crime itself begins his moral development, the possibility of such questions as earlier were impossible,' Dostoevsky observed in his notebook, and

'Out of despair there comes a new perspective.' That new awareness, as Dostoevsky makes clear, can itself be corrupting as well as improving; Dostoevsky is always a writer of the double face of human nature.

Along with the bringing of the crime to consciousness comes the question of its motivation. Dostoevsky had resolved to keep Raskolnikov's motives indeterminate at the start of the novel, and indeed had chosen not fully to understand them himself. The process of discovery would occur in the writing, and be not just his hero's but his own. The brilliant Russian critic Shklovsky – who argued that the mark of modernity in fiction is *defamiliarization*, making strange, the removal of conventional sensations and expectations – said of Dostoevsky's novels that in them a double or even triple motive is given for every action. First it is told to us, but then, as the interaction of the characters grows, it is deepened or replaced. This is what happens in *Crime and Punishment*. After the crime, Raskolnikov becomes a bundle of contradictions, of fevers and irascible sensations, dreams and hallucinations, sometimes believing himself an heroic and exceptional man, sometimes a louse. Dostoevsky's sense of the vastness and even the indeterminacy of human motive is remarkable, but he seeks to define the specific motive, which is made up both of an external justification – the general good of humanity – and an existential hunger, to be an exceptional man.

The reason *Crime and Punishment* reads like a detective novel is that it is the story of an investigation. This investigation is largely conducted by the criminal himself, but it is also conducted by an investigating magistrate, the extraordinary Porfiry, one of several great creations in the book. We learn at the end of the novel that he has suspected Raskolnikov even before he commits his crime, after reading an article by him in a magazine about the exceptional man who is entitled to commit great crimes in the interests of humanity and history. He asks Raskolnikov, in one of their several interviews, some of the most gripping scenes in the book, how such individuals are to be distinguished – 'a special uniform . . . or be branded in some way?' Thus he undermines Raskolnikov's arrogant sense of himself as a Napoleonic world-historical individual. He is a formidable intellectual adversary, the modern policeman who matches the modern criminal. Soon it becomes hard for us to decide who is hunter and who is prey, as Raskolnikov circles not only around his interrogator but around himself, hunting himself down. In effect Porfiry has his solution already, but requires the criminal to discover it. 'I waited for you impatiently,' he says, noting that the crime was psychological, but 'all this blasted psychology is a double-edged weapon.' And, as he leaves Raskolnikov to discover his own crime, so he leaves him to discover his own punishment, waiting for him to come at last and make his confession.

For the other major question of the novel is the purging of the crime, the problem of redemption and punishment. This, too, is a process Raskolnikov must undertake for himself. Punishment is almost Raskolnikov's first thought, after the crime is done, when he dreams that night that his landlady is being beaten, and wakes to think this the first stage of punishment. He is then called to the police station, to find it is because his landlady has reported him for his debts. Nonetheless, hearing talk of crime, he faints, sowing the first seeds of public suspicion. Then he starts haunting the scene of the crime, and debates it with others. With great confidence he even mocks the police for the errors of their investigation. At the same time he feels he is losing all contact with others, cut off from them as by scissors. His rage and contempt intensify, and he can find little compassion for humanity. He enters a world of strange relations, of adversaries and doubles, accusers and accused, street deaths and accidents, in which the universal sense of stain multiplies but comes ever closer to himself. The paths divide, between arrogant independence and humble repentance.

The two characters who represent his choice are the bored voluptuary, Svidrigaylov, and the meek and Christian prostitute, Sonia, the daughter of Marmeladov. In his notebook Dostoevsky made the nature of the choice very clear. 'Svidrigaylov is despair, the most cynical,' he noted, 'Sonia is hope, the most unrealizable. Raskolnikov himself must say that. He is attached passionately to both of them . . .' Svidrigaylov makes his first visit to Raskolnikov as he wakes from a terrible dream in which the old moneylender is alive and laughs at him as he keeps trying helplessly to kill her. His entrance appears as a continuation of the dream, a remarkable touch in the book's hallucinatory technique. He proves to be Raskolnikov's double, a murderer himself, having killed his wife, and a pursuer of corrupt sensations, who regards good as equal to evil. He overhears Raskolnikov confessing his crime to Sonia, and uses the knowledge to attempt to seduce Raskolnikov's sister. His end is the one that in one plan for the story Dostoevsky intended for Raskolnikov. Bored and indifferent, he finally settles his affairs, gives money to Sonia, explains he is going 'to America', and, in a brilliantly constructed scene, shoots himself in front of a Jewish soldier in a watchtower, the final witness to his crucifixion.

Sonia is one of Dostoevsky's fundamental characters, the 'meek' witness to the need for confession and redemption. Raskolnikov is at first enraged by her simple faith, and her willingness to sacrifice herself for others. He tries to convince her towards his own path of independence and domination, though it is to her that he has to confess that, in killing the moneylender, he has killed himself. Slowly she points him along the path of confession, crucifixion and redemption. It is she who tells him that he must make his confession in the public street, and kiss the ground in humility, before the crowds from whom he has cut himself off, in the interests of serving some vaster idea of humanity. It is she who waits outside the police station as he enters and makes his declaration; 'It was I who killed the old woman moneylender and her sister Lisaveta with a hatchet and robbed them.' And it is she who follows him to Siberia and tends him and the other prisoners as he serves his sentence in the penal colony.

The epilogue to the book retains the inexorable quality that marks everything in this extraordinary novel of psychological crime and psychological crisis. Raskolnikov still does not fully acknowledge his crime; 'My conscience is clear,' he says. He remains separated from the other prisoners, dreaming an ambiguous dream of a future in which a great plague comes which causes men to believe that truth resides only in them. He also knows now that he cannot solve his problems through reason and consciousness; he can only feel. 'Life had taken the place of dialectics, and something quite different had worked itself out in his mind.' But that working out is not completed in the novel, and Raskolnikov still holds on to some of his intellectual pride. He will need, the book declares, to find his regeneration somewhere else – not in the place of official punishment, but through an act of heroism and passage into 'a new and hitherto unknown reality. That might be the subject of a new story – our present story is ended.'

6

Crime and Punishment was successful, Dostoevsky made a happy marriage, and his life improved. But he continued to be plagued by debt and his compulsive gambling, and up to the 1870s he was regularly forced to live outside Russia to escape his creditors. Over this time he wrote a group of major novels which are as important in ideas as *Crime and Punishment*, though they lack the extraordinary metaphysical vitality given to that book by its detective-story form and its psychological suspense. Fame arrived, but he continued to battle with the authorities, and in 1874 he was again arrested for violating the censorship. He developed a deeper mysticism and a fuller idea of what he implies in Raskolnikov's story, the Christian idea of self-sacrifice and suffering. He died in 1881, regarded as a great Russian writer, though a deeply dangerous one. In 1905 Maxim Gorky attacked him as Russia's 'evil genius', and soon after the dream of men turned to warfare by the madness of their individual and nihilistic feelings came about. The war that brought the upturning of Europe also bred the Russian revolution of 1917, which turned into a triumph of that revolutionary nihilism and world-historical transgression about which he had written. Though Lenin had wished to raise statues to both Tolstoy and Dostoevsky, his message seemed dangerous, and under Stalin he suffered from the censors again. As late as 1953, the national curriculum for university study of Dostoevsky required that he be taught as 'an expression of reactionary bourgeois-individualistic ideology', though in recent years he has come to a greater recognition.

Dostoevsky has always troubled his readers, and will continue to do so. His books remind us of much that is terrible in the modern imagination, and it is the underground man's self-irony, Raskolnikov's great intellectual pride, that remain in our mind. But what troubles our literature is also what is in it, just as it is in the fiction of Dostoevsky, who addressed what most challenged him from inside, and even gave to it a certain secret sympathy. The traces of his diverse, extraordinary and intensely psychological and existential imagination are everywhere in modern writing. The whole method of the psychological novel, the novel of consciousness and the under-consciousness, owes almost everything to him, as Proust and Viginia Woolf acknowledged. Conrad's dark irony lies in his shade. So does the irony, the sense of modern disease, and the desire for a great new dialectic, that fills the fiction of Thomas Mann. The modernist fiction of ironic self-confession – Italo Svevo's *The Confessions of Zeno*, for example – comes in his wake. So do the tales of a psychic and political oppression that lies both outside and inside the self in the work of Franz Kafka. The novel of the great and inclusive city, like Joyce's *Ulysses*, belongs in his tradition of a sceptical and fantastic realism; so does the modern metaphysical thriller, from André Gide to Graham Greene. Existential fiction, the fiction of the absurd, the writing of Jean-Paul Sartre and Albert Camus, shows his mark. It is an extraordinary bequest, all the more remarkable for a writer who – in theory at least – set himself *against* the self-alienating modern imagination, and tried to find the way of redemption.

HENRIK IBSEN

I

One way to capture the spirit of Henrik Ibsen – the dramatist who dominated the early modern movement as no other writer did – is to turn to a drawing by a fellow-Norwegian, the painter Edvard Munch. A morbid and introverted artist, Munch was a painter of darkness and light, of painful self-analysis and of the *élan vital*. His famous painting 'The Shout' was a grim cry of pain that kept on resounding through twentieth-century art. For Munch became a leading influence in the Expressionist movement, which dominated German painting in its art-centres of Dresden and Munich in the years before the Great War, much as Cubism dominated Paris. He was a major figure of the early twentieth-century generation who lived on into his eighties, and into the Second World War. The subject of his drawing, Ibsen, was an even vaster figure, the man who one generation earlier had created much of the revolution from which Munch's work came, and changed the artistic tradition not just of Scandinavia but of the entire Western world.

'It may be questioned whether any man has held so firm an empire over the thinking world in modern times,' wrote a youthful admirer called James Joyce in 1900, as the century whose closing decades Ibsen had dominated came to its end. Another admirer, the influential Danish critic Georg Brandes, linked him with Nietzsche as a transformer of the modern spirit, and joined him with Renan and John Stuart Mill as 'men of the modern breakthrough', the men who had opened the chasm between today and yesterday. He was the greatest playwright of the day, the great individualist and over-reacher who was also an entire movement in himself. His work covered the second half of the nineteenth century very exactly. His first play, a rather wooden historical drama called *Cataline*, was published on a shoestring in 1850. He wrote his last work, the remarkable symbolist play *When We Dead Awaken*, which James Joyce said 'may rank with the greatest of the author's work – if, indeed, it be not the greatest', in 1899. The next year, as the century turned, he suffered a stroke, and he died in 1906. Like Nietzsche, he closed his page at the end of the century he dominated.

But over those fifty years he wrote twenty-five plays, starting at a time when there was no native drama in Norway and when the dramatic tradition of Europe was moribund, the only serious drama being Romantic drama written not for performance but for reading. His fame came slowly, but from the 1870s up to his death, and beyond it, he dominated and transformed the whole idea of modern theatre, as well as conducting a revolt of modern ideas. By the time he died theatre was a major art form, comparable to poetry and the novel. No other figure of the modern movement had changed not just the spirit of the arts but an entire genre. And Ibsen did not simply change the idea of what a play might be, or what sort of future drama should take. His way of writing changed the look and shape of the theatre itself, the design of the stage, the practice of acting, the entire relation of drama and dramatist to audience.

By the 1890s Ibsen's work was known almost everywhere, and as Joyce, writing in 1900, said, 'the great genius of the man is day by day coming out as a hero comes out amid the earthly trials.' Against massive hostility, Ibsen had begun to triumph. Something called Ibsenism was alive throughout Europe, and Bernard Shaw sought to distil it in his book *The Quintessence of Ibsenism* (1891). Ibsen's plays, said Shaw, are more important to us than Shakespeare's: 'He gives us not only ourselves, but ourselves in our own situation.' Indeed during the 1890s it was, as a German poem had it, 'Ibsen, Ibsen everywhere!' 'Over the whole globe Ibsen fever rages,' it went on, 'The whole world is Ibsen-mad, even though unwillingly . . .' Even Britain, which had managed to stave off the fever for a decade, had succumbed, and the translations poured out – from William Archer, Edmund Gosse, and Eleanor Marx Aveling, Karl Marx's daughter. The conservative newspapers condemned his work as an open drain and an unbandaged wound, but the new minds saw that nothing in theatre – and for that matter in modern thought – would ever be the same again.

For Ibsen did not only transform an entire literary genre. He used the genre to transform modern ideas. 'How the ideas tumble about us now,' says the idealistic John Rosmer in the late play *Rosmersholm*. 'All that we've been living on until now is but scraps from the table of last century's revolution. Liberty, equality and fraternity are no longer the same as they were in the days of the guillotine . . .' Ibsen was a self-educated man, for whom ideas were not words in books but principles for living life, though his own was withdrawn, reticent and conservative. But, like Rosmer, he wanted to produce a 're-volution of the spirit', and saw it as his task to carry the burden of the nineteenth-century revolution, towards reform, emancipation, indi-vidual self-realization. His work was compared with Nietzsche's in its desire to declare the task of the modern, the nature of the new, a task which was not simply social or political. It meant a revolution within, a transformation of the psyche, a revolt against all that dulled the life instinct: against convention, smugness, hypocrisy, religiosity, the dead hand of the past. It could be called bourgeois, individualistic, based on a naive nineteenth-century optimism, though anyone who reads Ibsen's work as a whole (that was, he said, how he wanted it to be read) will see that its aspiration and emancipation often leads to tragedy.

Certainly Ibsen was a very nineteenth-century writer, a man of his age. In this he differs from Dostoevsky, that more terrible precursor of modern darkness and alienation. But both started to write in the spirit of Romanticism, and both were stirred by the revolutionary events of 1848, the 'momentous era', Ibsen called it. Ibsen too began his work in the era of Romantic nationalism, and his early plays were mostly Romantic historical verse-dramas. But when the idealism of 1848 began to die, and a new spirit, that of Realism, swept through Europe, emphasizing the social problems, the conflicts and great en-vironmental changes of the times, Ibsen's work expressed this. As Realism moved towards Naturalism, the secular, scientific and material-ist approach to life and art, which saw individual lives constrained by powerful environmental and genetic forces and vitalistic energies, Ibsen responded; if Emile Zola in France became the great novelist of Naturalism, Ibsen became its great dramatist. Yet while his plays grew familiar and vernacular, they retained the sweep of the great classical tragedies. And when Naturalism began to dissolve into Impressionism, Expressionism and Symbolism, a less realistic, more psychological and intuitive form of writing, Ibsen again was in the forefront, leading the way into the less literal and more complex arts of the twentieth century.

As the young James Joyce was to say in amazement, one thing that was remarkable about Ibsen's work was its sheer regularity, the 'clockwork routine, seldom found in the case of genius'. Yet each new play was an advance on the last, a new step in artistry, a new option for drama. Ibsen took pride in constant advance, and in moving ahead of his audiences once they had begun to catch up with him. Thus he could be seen in many different guises. For Shaw, he was (like GBS himself) the great reforming dramatist and the master of stage argument; he had turned theatre itself from being a children's doll's house into an adult theatre that put the new ideas onto the stage and into public discussion. For Joyce, he was the artist of 'soul-drama' who helped Joyce's own struggle to break free of nationality, religion, and convention. For other thinkers of his day and since, he was the creator of the art of modern tragedy, a new form of theatre which brought the inexorable and fatal sense of tragic awareness out of the world of kings and princes and into the bourgeois drawing-room. For others he was simply offensive and obscene, the playwright who had brought a new priggishness *and* a new filth to the stage, a 'muck-ferreting dog', said one British critic.

It was not surprising that in the 1890s, when he returned to Norway towards the end of his days and at the height of his fame, the admirers gathered round him as he sat in the café of the Grand Hotel in Christiania (as Oslo was then called) and the painters came to paint him. Munch was one such admirer – he regarded the late play *John Gabriel Borkman* as 'the most powerful winter landscape in Scandinavian art' – and he began a series of lithographs that attempted to capture the great figure. The task was considered very difficult, partly because of Ibsen's strange eyes ('One eye, half-closed, seemed to reflect and ponder, while the other observed,' said one actor who worked with him) which seemed to express his doubleness of vision, one eye turned inward to the soul and the psyche, the other on the social world. Munch was agreed to have caught him as no other artist did.

In a lithograph of 1902 Munch captures the famous head – with its great brain-pan, which Ibsen boasted had been judged by a physician as the largest he had seen, the double vision of the eyes, the famous, carefully cultivated great mane of white hair, the divided points of his beard – as if it is disembodied, so that it appears like a white comet surrounded by an intense blackness. It resembles the head of a pastor or preacher, like some of Ibsen's protagonists. Though sombre and severe, the look is also visionary and prophetic, in the manner of William Blake. The surrounding blackness comes partly from Ibsen's dark clothes; he was famously conservative in his dress, just as he was punctilious and obsessively tidy in his personal life. He wore white cuffs when no one else wore them, and invariably the heavy black coat which darkens the drawing. So too does a heavy curtain hanging behind him – like a theatrical curtain opening onto a stage set. We seem to be in one of the rooms of Ibsen's plays, those dark, heavy, nineteenth-century rooms hung with the portraits of the past and the ghosts of old feelings, but which open up through the window to a larger life outside, waiting to be lived. And to one side of the drawing we see life beyond the window, the passing parade of the street in the rain, filled with the stick-like but Naturalistic figures typical of Munch's paintings.

In fact the drawing is a cross between Naturalism and Expressionism, Realism and Symbolism, like Ibsen's own late work. And it captures not only Ibsen but the actual relation between the two artists – Ibsen the man of the nineteenth century, the contemporary of Marx and Darwin, Kierkegaard and Nietzsche, and Munch the man of the next age, the contemporary of Freud and Einstein, Strindberg and Maeterlinck. It builds the bridge between the generations, and also between the two key figures of the Nordic temperament which played so powerful a role in the making of the modern arts. It is hard to say why Scandinavia became one of the great provinces of Modernism, but so it did. The temperament was quite different from the mystical temperament of Dostoevsky's Russian imagination, very different from the symbolist and impressionist spirit of the French. It was Northern, morbid, introverted, protestant, given to cycles of gloom and

light, Naturalistic pessimism and Expressionist vitality. Yet it produced
the first existentialist philosopher, Kierkegaard, the major music of
Grieg and Sibelius, the novels of Knut Hamsun and Per Lagerkvist,
the drama of Bjørnson and Strindberg, the painting of Munch and
Nolde. Above all it produced Ibsen, who in every sense put that
imagination firmly onto the world stage.

2

Ibsen was a rebellious spirit and his relation to his Norwegian background was always a quarrel, like much else in his life. As he told a
friend:

> Anyone who wishes to understand me fully must know Norway.
> The spectacular but severe landscape which people have around
> them in the north, and the lonely shut-off life – the houses often
> lie miles from each other – force them not to bother with other
> people, but only their concerns, so that they become reflective
> and serious, they brood and doubt and often despair. In Norway
> every second man is a philosopher. And those dark winters, with
> the thick mists outside – ah, how they long for the sun!

That brooding, doubting, despairing temper, the lonely and shut-off
life, these were all in Ibsen's nature, and part of the spirit of his writing.
Throughout his work runs the story of the man who has known mists
and darkness and longs for the sun. The Ibsen who comes to us from
Michael Meyer's brilliant modern biography is not in all ways an attractive man. He was ruthless in his sincerity, imperious, ill-tempered,
quick to take offence, braver in thought than deed. For a man who
came to see himself as an outcast and exile, and who rejected the
nationalist state, he was oddly keen to obtain state honours and re-
wards. As he said himself, the heroes of his plays – the rigid pastor
Brand, the sinful, self-seeking Peer Gynt, the over-reaching master

builder Solness, the sculptor Rubek, trapped in a loveless life — were versions of himself, expressions of the contradictoriness and hunger of his nature.

Ibsen's was a Norwegian temper, but it led by an inevitable logic into that exile which was the lot of so many modern writers. The Norway in which he grew up was the province of a province, formerly part of the Danish Empire, now part of the Swedish. It had its own proud tradition of independence and democracy (Henry James, another admirer of Ibsen, called it 'the little Northern democracy') yet it was cut off from many of the thought-movements of the time. Its harsh terrain not only divided and isolated its people but even divided the language, and each fjord spoke a different dialect. The official language was a form of Danish, but a desire persisted for a vernacular language based on popular speech. Ibsen may have broken loose in rebellion to become a world playwright, but, never good at other languages, he wrote in an already divided language that was known to very few outside. His work was filled with Norwegian elements: the Norse gods and trolls, the sagas and eddas, as well as the landscapes and seascapes of the country. But in becoming an exile he internationalized these things, and at home he was never quite accepted as a Norwegian writer.

And nearly all his major work was created, and his happiest years spent, elsewhere — in Rome, Dresden and Munich, three centres of art and exile always attractive to Northern and Scandinavian writers. Here his work took on the great movements of thought that were sweeping through central Europe, and here he found his most sympathetic audiences. At home his plays were as often reviled as honoured, and the outrage he so often provoked seemed strongest there. Honours came his way, but it was in Denmark, Sweden or Germany he seemed better understood. In a poem addressed to his country, he thanked it for its 'gifts that help and harden', its 'purifying pain'. 'Norway is a difficult country to have as a fatherland,' he wrote; Norway might have answered that it is difficult to have a great writer as a son. Toward the end of his life, after twenty-seven years of exile, he did return, a world-famous figure. He wrote to his good friend, Georg Brandes, who had hailed him as a 'man of the modern breakthrough':

'Oh, my dear Brandes, one does not live twenty-seven years out in the great, free, liberating world of culture for nothing. Here among the fjords is my native land. But – but – but – where shall I find my home?'

Not until the age of 36, when he left Norway, was Ibsen anything more than a failure. Not until he was over 50 did he become a world dramatist. He was born in 1828 at the small town of Skien, on the eastern coast of Norway south of the capital Christiania. His father, a respected figure in the town, who ran the general store, suffered sudden financial ruin which embittered him. It also dismayed his son, and there were added rumours of illegitimacy, a strong theme in Ibsen's work. As a child he was considered withdrawn and naturally rebellious, and when he had to leave school at 15 to become an apothecary's assistant in another southern Norwegian town he soon became known as a radical, a freethinker, an atheist and a revolutionary. The 'momentous era' of 1848, when he was twenty, stirred his literary instincts. He wrote poems to the revolutionaries, and his first play, a blank-verse historical drama on a revolutionary theme, *Cataline*. He submitted it unsuccessfully to the theatre in Christiania, but did succeed, in 1850, in publishing it privately. He was largely self-educated, studying at night to go to the university in Christiania to read medicine, but when he entered the preparatory course most of his time was devoted to writing: verse drama, poetry, essays, political journalism. Another play, *The Burial Mound*, was staged in 1850, and he contributed essays to a radical journal until it was suppressed and its editors imprisoned.

His career in theatre now began, and the 'clockwork routine' of his playwriting. He left without a degree to join the small theatre in Bergen as a writer and dogsbody, encountering here contemporary European drama, most importantly the French social dramatist Scribe. He also met and later married Suzannah Thoreson, that strong-minded woman of literary and artistic interests who was to be his firm, and sometimes unyielding, support throughout his life. In 1857 he moved to the Norwegian Theatre in Christiania, and wrote, designed and directed. But national drama in Norway was moribund, his productions were unpopular, and his own plays mostly failed. He began to drink heavily, dismayed by lack of success and recognition, and more than once was seen insensible in the gutter. The great opportunity came in 1864, when, after many unsuccessful applications, he was awarded a travel grant that enabled him to go and write in Rome. Outraged by the failure of the Norwegians to support the Danes in their war with the Prussians, Ibsen saw it as political exile, though his own lack of recognition and the provinciality that surrounded him were motives just as important.

Italy was the natural choice, the land of sun, art and classical serenity, the great destination for the writers of Northern Europe seeking artistic and emotional release. As the American writer Nathaniel Hawthorne, another refugee from Puritanism, wrote in his novel *The Marble Faun* in 1860, Rome was 'the central clime, whither the eyes and heart of every artist turn'. In Thomas Mann's story *Death in Venice*, written just after Ibsen's death, the central character, the famous and rigorous North European writer Gustave von Aschenbach, leaves 'the daily theatre of a rigid, cold, and passionate service' to seek 'freedom, release, forgetfulness' in Italy – if with rather more disastrous results. For Ibsen it was a great imaginative release, as he declared later, recalling the experience of crossing the Alps. 'Over the high mountains the clouds hung like great, dark curtains, and beneath these we drove through the tunnel and, suddenly ... that marvellously bright light which is the beauty of the south revealed itself to me, gleaming like white marble. It was to affect all my later work, even if the content thereof was not always beautiful.' It was, he said, 'a feeling of being released from the darkness into light, of emerging from mists through a tunnel into the sunshine.'

Ibsen had found the sun, the great image of artistic and emotional release that runs through his later work. The transformation came almost immediately. The two plays he wrote next, the two verse-dramas *Brand* and *Peer Gynt*, are the first of the great Ibsen plays. *Brand* (which won Ibsen the state pension he craved) is the story of a preacher rigid and uncompromising in his devotion to truth and duty, whose message is 'I require All or Nothing.' *Peer Gynt*, filled with trolls and the stuff of Nordic legend, and later set to music by Grieg, is the story of a more limited man who gives himself in all directions,

seeking to follow the injunction of 'To thine own self be true,' only
to find that this leads to the self-indulgence of 'To thine own self be
enough.' These works, intended for reading rather than performance,
still belong to the era of Romantic tragedy, but on a new and more
ambitious scale. Both represented sides of Ibsen's own temperament,
and explored the Nietzsche-like struggle between the Apollonian, rational powers and the forces of Dionysus that raged within him – and,
according to Nietzsche, all tragic writing. They are also plays of
modern individualism, tragedies of the single lonely individual seeking
the path of 'To thine own self be true,' a path that Ibsen was always
to see both as life-giving and death-bringing, leading to stark isolation
or to excess, yet requiring courage of the spirit – themes that would
develop through the very different plays that were to follow.

3

Ibsen's work can be conveniently divided into four periods, though
the qualities overlap from phase to phase. There were the early historical and classical dramas; the two great Romantic pieces of the Rome
period, *Brand* and *Peer Gynt*; then the plays of the 'modern' Ibsen,
which divide between the great sociological and problem plays of the
1870s and 1880s, and the remarkable, bewildering tragedies at the end
of his work. Each phase seems to lead naturally into what follows,
and the Romantic poet still survives in the problem drama, just as the
problem plays predict the psychological intensity of the last works.
Each stage was more or less marked by a change of country, the problem plays being largely written in Germany, the reflective late tragedies of individualism mostly coming after the return to Norway.
Every stage shows Ibsen profoundly alert to the ideas of the day. He
may not have kept many books in his home, and he was no man for
literary groups and movements, but he was an avid observer, a close
reader of newspapers, an attentive analyst of behaviour, and a man
closely in touch with the conflicts within himself. As he once said:

'Everything that I have written is most minutely connected with what I have lived through. Every new work has had for me the object of serving as a process of spiritual liberation, for every man shares the responsibility and the guilt of the society to which he belongs.'

In 1868 Ibsen left Italy for Southern Germany, and would spend most of the next twenty years first in Dresden and then in the Bavarian capital of Munich. As it happened, the Dresden he now moved to was also home to Dostoevsky, who was writing *The Possessed* in his usual flight from the authorities and his creditors. The two writers never met, but were often to be compared as creators of the modern tragic masterpieces of an age of upheaval. Ibsen's move meant a new and fruitful relation to the Germanic culture that, as a Norwegian nationalist, he had once despised. Though his plays were regularly published in Norway, it was German theatre that would establish the basis of his international recognition. And it was now – 'influenced no doubt by the heavy German air,' he said, but also by the strong winds of new international ideas that were blowing through it – that his work began to move toward the spirit we call Naturalism.

Like many movements, Naturalism was made up of conflicting strands. But essentially it developed in France, and the leading figure was Emile Zola, who said of his novels that 'I have done on living bodies the work of analysis which surgeons perform on corpses.' The novel was an experimental form, he said, but experimental in the sense that a scientific or medical study is an experiment. 'Heredity has its laws, like weight,' he wrote. Ibsen acknowledged many of the positivist, materialist and determinist ideas that went with the tendency. But when we speak of him as a Naturalist we usually mean the extraordinary and immediate effect of his plays; they come off the stage as if they were life itself. We also mean their awareness of the social problems of the time, and his sense that all life is an evolutionary struggle. Naturalist ideas flourished in Germany, and were an important reason for the ready reception Ibsen was to receive in its theatres, and the strength of his influence over other playwrights. To some critics, like Bernard Shaw, Ibsenism and Naturalism were always to remain much the same, but that was not quite how it appeared to Ibsen himself.

Yet he was taken by many of the ideas of a new, scientific and radical realism that flourished in the early 1870s in Germany and Scandinavia. Thus Georg Brandes took up the movement, and argued in a famous lecture series at Copenhagen University in 1871 that 'A literature in our day shows it is alive by taking up problems for discussion.' When he sent copies of the lectures, Ibsen responded excitedly, saying that no more dangerous book could fall into the hands of a pregnant writer: 'It is one of those books that set a yawning gulf between today and yesterday.' They met in Dresden and had long talks which Brandes recorded. Ibsen described Scandinavia as outside the cultural mainstream: 'We will never get anywhere until the rest of Europe has moved on.' He spoke for individualism and emancipation, against the compromises of liberalism and its limited idea of freedom: 'The true freedom was social freedom, spiritual freedom, freedom of thought, freedom of conscience.' (This greatly contrasts with Zola's determinism: 'I chose characters completely dominated by their nerves and their blood, deprived of free-will . . .') He considered the major advance of the age was that literature was becoming more 'psychological'. Not surprisingly, Brandes thereafter acclaimed Ibsen as one of the great 'men of the modern breakthrough', transforming and emancipating the ideas of the age.

Ibsen's new drama was indeed new. It has rightly been said that Ibsen's decision to turn from poetry to prose was one of the most important events both for his career and for the future of modern drama. With that choice went the acknowledgement that the themes he now wished to explore were themes of contemporary relevance, essential issues of the age – above all, the conflict between the conventional and traditional world of society and morality and the emancipation summoned by the future. As Brandes urged, modernity itself was the proper subject of literature. Naturalism was thus more than the problem play or novel, more than the airing of social issues. It was an identification with the transforming powers of the age itself, and the conflicts of spirit and soul they generated. It required a new dramatic method and a new psychology, the task Ibsen set himself to pursue over the 1870s. In 1869 he wrote *The League of Youth*, a contemporary political comedy, fairly straightforwardly written. In 1873 came the play he always thought his masterpiece, *Emperor and Galilean*, a 'world-historical drama' dealing with the eternal conflict between Christianity and paganism, which seemed like a return to Romantic historical drama. But Ibsen wrote it in prose, and he intended its theme as an essential myth for the age.

But the key moment of Ibsen's evolution into a major playwright came in 1877, with *The Pillars of Society*, the play that really started the Ibsen revolution. It is set in a Norway that is more than Norway, a country of the mind. It becomes a repository of the Victorian spirit, where the ghosts of past faiths and attitudes endlessly quarrel with the new conscience of the present. It is a place of confinement, of narrow-mindedness, mercantilism and hypocrisy. This is typified onstage by the bourgeois room in which the action is essentially set, though what happens there is shaped by great events outside. In this tight and airless room, the most striking dramatic gesture occurs at the end of the first act. Lona, a 'modern' woman, returns from America, and she pulls aside the curtains to let in the light and bring, as she says, some fresh air to society. The gesture was the spirit of Ibsen's new drama itself, just as the person who performs it, the 'new woman', was so often to be the spokesperson of change. At the (rather weak) end of the play, the reformed central character announces that women are the true pillars of society. But Lona doubtless speaks for the playwright when she corrects him and gives a slightly different meaning to the events: 'No, my friend; the spirit of truth and the spirit of freedom – they are the pillars of society.'

The Pillars of Society came like a declaration. It reminded those who were pillars of society of their duties, and dealt with problems of the age, and the processes that were changing it: the need for a Plimsoll line on ships, and the momentous coming of the railways. It showed that the stuff of contemporary drama was the conflict between fundamental issues and ideas: between smug and self-serving hypocrisy and an enlightened new morality, men and women, old and young, past and future. The very fact that the play was deeply resented in Scandinavia emphasized Ibsen's literary and moral freedom and independence, and it began his international reputation among those who considered themselves enlightened. In Berlin alone there were five

productions of the play in 1878, and it reached other major centres as
an expression of the spirit of the age. Even though Britain was more
or less to suppress Ibsen for another decade, there was a version of it
in London done by Ibsen's young British admirer William Archer,
who hailed its author as 'one of the great negative voices of a negative
age.'

Thus began Ibsen's role as a major controversial playwright. But
this was little compared with the controversies to follow. For now
came a whole group of major plays (*A Doll's House* in 1879, *Ghosts* in
1881, and *An Enemy of the People* in 1882) of ever-increasing subtlety.
They represent the central, the most familiar, Ibsen. They are Naturalist, in the sense that each puts at centre-stage a major subject for
discussion – smug hypocrisy and bourgeois self-confidence, the nature
of modern marriage, the problem of venereal disease, or the attempt
of civic worthies to suppress news of the pollution of a town spa.
They give a clear representation of the familiar and felt life of the
times, and a remorseless attention to the issues that trouble that life
and will be immediately recognizable to the audience. They are 'well-
made' plays, tightly and at times mechanically constructed, so that
they develop coherently and inevitably through a great process. The
forces in conflict are the essential historical processes at work in the
age, above all the struggle between old morality and inevitable forms
of evolution. At the same time they are part of larger, more ambiguous, and more transcendental conflicts: the conflicts *within* individualism, the tragedies that limit self-realization, and the endless war
between life and idealism.

The art of realistic Naturalism is thus the kind of theatre that shows
us all this on familiar ground, in the lives of ordinary citizens, in the
politics of marriage, the relation of parents and children. The problems
of the problem play are revealed at meetings of charitable Societies
for Fallen Women, in the planning of an orphanage, in the visit of the
local pastor, or a meeting of the town elders. People shop and trade in
the background, and beyond the window we can see the garden, the
street or the sea. In this world lovelessness and moral blindness generally prevail, and the human spirit needs to act radically to break
free. It can seem an art of surfaces, but Ibsen had learned his methods

in a wider, more classical idea of theatre. His methods went deeper, letting Ibsen find a profundity he had not previously achieved, even in more epic and poetic dramatic forms. But as the plays went on it was clear that for Ibsen the Naturalistic method opened out into a complex symbolism, and a new and modern form of tragedy.

A Doll's House was the play that seemed at first to pose the largest challenge, raising the 'woman question' and the 'marriage problem' right across Europe. It caused massive debate, upset and dismay in many a household, and there were public demonstrations for and against it. It has been called the most influential play ever written, and the famous ending of the last act – when Nora, the 'child-wife', walks out on her husband and slams the door offstage in a final gesture of departure – the best-remembered ending in modern drama. That door-slam was to resound through modern social attitudes and modern sexual relationships, and Nora's final declaration to her husband who attempts to keep her and who reminds her of her duties ('I have to educate myself first, and you can't do that for me . . . I have another duty, equally sacred, my duty to myself . . .') has been a clarion call of the women's movement ever since, and a general promise of the self-realization that is afforded to those who choose to break free of what confines them and declare their own individuality and need for self-fulfilment.

Yet it is important to recall that Ibsen conceived the play as a tragedy, and headed his plans for the play 'Notes for a Tragedy of Modern Times'. 'There are two kinds of moral law, two kinds of conscience, one in man and a completely different one in women,' he noted; 'They do not understand each other; but in matters of practical living the woman is judged by the man's law, as if she was not a woman but a man.' This produces a tragic consequence: 'Mental conflict . . . Everything must be borne alone . . . Despair, resistance, defeat.' Nora, the 'child-wife' who leaves her 'doll's house' at the end, is not a repository of moral virtue, as is the case with many of those who embody life-energy in Ibsen's drama. Indeed her ambiguous energy is displayed in the famous dance she performs, the tarantella, the spider dance. Her desire at last to grow up and discover her own laws of life is what makes her an Ibsen heroine, but we are not to know

what becomes of it, other than the troubled hint that Ibsen has left us
in his notes: 'Everything must be borne alone . . . Despair, resistance,
defeat.'

It has often been said that each Ibsen play comes out of the one
before. And his next work, *Ghosts*, the greatest work of this period of
his writing, certainly came out of *A Doll's House*. 'I couldn't remain
standing at *A Doll's House*; after Nora, Mrs Alving of necessity had to
come,' he wrote. *Ghosts* was the play that caused the greatest outcry
of all, and everywhere it was performed it was surrounded by
outraged controversy. In Germany the modern critic Otto Brahm
acknowledged: 'All is now permissible, all the writer need do is to set
to work.' When the major new independent theatre in Berlin, Freie
Bühne, started in 1889 it made its first play a production of *Ghosts*.
Ibsen himself declared that it was time 'to move some boundary posts',
and so he did. The play not only displayed the ghosts that haunt the
apparent respectability of the society of his time. It dealt with Zola's
theme of the fundamental power of heredity, and presented it in the
most horrifying form, the form of inherited syphilis. It returned to
the theme of marriage, but in its most agonized aspects. But *Ghosts*
was not simply a radical, scandalous play. It was also a modern tragedy, the form that Ibsen can be said to have invented for us.

4

The curtain rises in *Ghosts* to reveal a kind of set familiar from Ibsen's
two previous plays, though here it will prove to be a prison from
which no major character escapes. There is a garden room with an
attached conservatory, 'shut in by glass walls', and beyond a view of a
gloomy fjord, veiled by heavy rain. It is the essential set of Ibsen's
drama – a closed space, a hard landscape with a brooding sense of
nature, a hint of possible escape beyond the glass walls. On a centre
table are some books and magazines, which, like the gun in Chekhov's
famous definition of drama, are likely to go off later on. The action

starts on a commonplace note, as the servant girl Regina talks to her father, the dissolute carpenter Engstrand. This sets the scene but also starts the sense that a past drama is being replayed, as we find that he may not be her true father after all. Meanwhile the mistress of the house, Mrs Alving, is upstairs taking chocolate to her son Oswald, tired after his return from Paris, where he has been for two years, becoming an artist. The boat has docked, bringing a minister, Pastor Manders, who inspects the books on the table and is displeased. When Mrs Alving comes downstairs, we learn he has come to settle the arrangements for the dedication of an orphanage built in memory of her husband, Captain Alving, who is ten years dead. But his presence comes back when Oswald appears, smoking a pipe like his father's. With these commonplace details Ibsen has already filled the stage with his 'ghosts'.

Ibsen's writing notes display that he is no conventional Naturalist in his construction of the play. For his notes are not social facts or data, and the story he begins with is not quite that we now see. What he does is to identify the central symbols that form the spine of the play, and give it its depth and meaning; his Naturalism is a disguise for symbolism. The notes contain the idea that a 'monument' is erected to a 'model man', a pillar of society (it will become the orphanage). A terrible nemesis will be vested on a son who tries to escape (it will become hereditary syphilis). The central character will be a woman who desires to live but finds 'everything is ghosts' (this will become Mrs Alving, whose play it is). He even drew an interesting parallel between the structure of the play and his own creative processes: 'First comes what is inorganic, and afterwards what is organic. First dead matter, then living. The same holds for art. From promising material I will always first make a sketch, but it turns out as a drama.' The characters are in the same position as the creative artist, though he said later: 'My intention was to try to give the reader an impression of experiencing a piece of reality . . . In none of my plays is the author so extrinsic, so completely absent.'

Another note explores the position of Mrs Alving: 'These women of the modern age, mistreated as daughters, as sisters, as wives . . .' debarred from following their mission, deprived of their inheritance,

embittered in mind – these are the ones who supply the mothers for
the new generation. What will be the result?' The result becomes
steadily clearer by the end of the first act, as we realize that Mrs
Alving and the Pastor are in a terrible competition for the soul of
Oswald. Manders tells Oswald he has inherited the mantle of a good
and worthy man, and that his responsibility lies not in bohemian Paris
but in the home of his fathers. Mrs Alving justifies the path Oswald
has taken – it will prove later she has encouraged him to it exactly in
order to avoid inheriting the mantle of his father. When Oswald talks
of the 'great, free, glorious life' he has seen in Paris, among the modern
ménages of the bohemian artists, Manders is outraged, but Mrs Alving
supports Oswald. The books on her table express the same modern
ideas. 'All your efforts have been toward emancipation and law-
lessness. You have never known how to endure any bond,' Manders
rebukes her, and recalls the time when Mrs Alving fled to him from
her marriage and home, and he, the guiding hand of providence, had
sent her back.

Mrs Alving questions his decision. For Alving had continued with
the life of dissolution she was fleeing, and had seduced the servant
girl, Regina's mother, in the house in Mrs Alving's own hearing. She
has attempted to maintain her husband's reputation by endowing the
orphanage, but there is another reason – to prevent the money going
to Oswald, because she does not want him to inherit anything from
his father. She has not, however, told Oswald about his father's nature,
a concealment that is to have dramatic consequences. Indeed at the
very end of the first act they are beginning to take shape, as the past
begins to repeat itself in the present. The two now overhear Oswald
making a similar approach to the servant girl (who will prove to be
his own half-sister). On this terrible irony, as the past comes back into
the present and the son seems the child of the father, the act closes as
Mrs Alving speaks the title of the play: 'Ghosts!'

For the rest of the play the 'ghosts' are everywhere, and they are
not just memories but repetitions. Like many of Ibsen's late plays, this
one seems to start remarkably late in its own story, in the aftermath
of great events that have taken place at other times and in other
places, but are now concentrated into the small domestic set. As James

Joyce said: 'His analytic method is thus made use of to the fullest extent, and into the comparatively short space of two days the life in life of all his characters is compressed.' The ghosts are not just memories of the past, nor previous actions repeated. They are the consequences of moral choices once made, and they construct a new drama from the old, producing not just re-enactments but terrible new crises. They acquire their extraordinary depth, their symbolic resonance, from the fact that they are both present actions *and* re-creations of things gone before that have been concealed and suppressed. Each person is in a psychological as well as a social prison – when Ibsen called his naturalistic drama 'psychological', he was speaking truly. The history of repression and past conflict is essential to the present story. The 'inorganic matter', the 'dead nature', from the past is recreated as a new and terrible drama of life.

Then what are these 'ghosts'? Ibsen multiplies their meaning. They are the traces of past events now returning, but also the ghosts of traditional duties and conventions, which once stopped Mrs Alving deserting her husband and now prevent her revealing the truth to Oswald. They are the ghosts of heredity (suggested by the pipe that Oswald smokes and by his attempted seduction of the servant girl) which will grow more terrible as the play develops, but also the ghosts of defunct ideas that can still somehow dominate behaviour. As Mrs Alving puts it, in the play's most famous speech:

> When I saw Oswald and Regina in there just now, it was as if I saw ghosts. I almost think that we're all ghosts, all of us, Pastor Manders. It isn't just what we've inherited from our father and mother that walks in us. It's all sorts of dead ideas, and all sorts of old and obsolete beliefs. They're not alive in us; but they're lodged in us and we can never free ourselves from them. . . . There must be ghosts the whole country over, as thick as the sands of the sea. And then we are, one and all, so pitifully afraid of the light.

The ghosts are thus far more than the deterministic forces found in most Naturalist writing – the social conditions that shape us, the

genes that form us, the kind of facts that Darwin, Marx or the contemporary sociologists might emphasize. Ibsen is already exploring
many ideas that Freud would examine, about the way past guilts and
repressions form our present behaviour and nature, and our hunger to
be released from those repressions and find 'joy'.

But the ghosts within cannot be laid, nor the power of conscience and
guilt represented by Pastor Manders escaped. At the play's end, in-
exorably, Oswald's brain is softening from his Alving inheritance of
syphilis, and he waits to die, staring dully up at the rising sun, the futile
emblem of joy and freedom. Mrs Alving ends the play ministering to
him, and waiting to become the agent of his death when the agony
grows too great. This may be Naturalism; but it is Naturalism in the
form of tragedy. For tragedy is the vision of an implacable and inevitable
world that will not be reformed by a simple revolution of the spirit.
Ghosts has rightly been compared with Greek drama for its ominous
inevitability, and the prison Ibsen weaves round Mrs Alving is complete.
Despite the symbol that outraged everyone – congenital syphilis – Ibsen
was writing not a problem play but a great modern tragedy.

Ghosts prefigures the final plays, but the outrage provoked by the
play itself did stir Ibsen to one last Naturalist drama. What better title
could it have than *An Enemy of the People*? 'The majority is never
right,' says the hero, Dr Stockmann, who risks everything to tell the
truth about the polluted waters of a spa, '*I* am right – I and one or
two other individuals like me.' Ibsen wishes to show that pollution
exists already, and it is those who point it out who suffer. These are
his true heroes, the individualists, not the men of politics and civic
duty. Ibsen now stood aloof from politics himself, dismaying some of
his supporters. As his Dr Stockmann says, 'The life of a normally constituted idea is generally about seventeen or eighteen years, at most
twenty.' It was not ideas but aspirations that mattered, and the price
in life that was paid for them. This was the theme of what was to
follow, the late dramas of human aspiration, from which the cloak of
Naturalism is dropped. As he put it: 'I have been more of a poet and
less of a social philosopher than people generally tend to suppose. My
task has been the portrayal of human beings.' Here was the theme of
the late plays.

5

In 1891, as the century came toward its close, a French Naturalist writer, Paul Alexis, sent one of the most famous of all literary telegrams. 'NATURALISM NOT DEAD,' he cabled a Paris journalist investigating the future tendencies of art, 'LETTER FOLLOWS.' In that letter Alexis claimed that Naturalism would become the great twentieth-century art, bringing the world to reform and happiness. As we know, Alexis's prophecy was not borne out. The world does not reform easily, happiness and the twentieth century have been uncomfortable bed-fellows, and the scientific and sociological view of life that Alexis emphasized has been persistently challenged from the standpoint of subjectivity and modern relativism. The arts of intuition and impression that emerged during the 1890s were a challenge to Naturalism. As Edmund Wilson suggested in *Axel's Castle*, the modern method in the arts arose when Naturalism, with its often naive and simplified view of reality, was challenged by and interfused with the major new spirit of modern Symbolism.

1891 was the year Ibsen returned to his homeland, Norway, and to the fjords, mountains and snows that would be backdrop to much of his final work. He was in his sixties, the white-maned prophet of Munch's drawing, and his fame was universal. Ibsen fever had raged through Germany in the 1880s, reaching a Britain suddenly opening out to new continental ideas in the early 1890s. Throughout Europe, when people said the new word, 'modern', they thought of Ibsen. They thought probably of the problem dramas, but already they were seeing the spirit of a later Ibsen, which showed that for him Naturalism was indeed virtually dead. Symbolism was becoming his method, and the tragedy of human aspiration his theme. Behind it was the concern with the new psychology that fascinated the thinking people of the day, and was to culminate in the appearance in 1900 of Freud's *The Interpretation of Dreams*. Famous and of great influence, Ibsen could write what he wished, and so came the plays of his late maturity, the final phase. With *The Wild Duck* of 1884 he wrote his first clearly Symbolist play about the fragile and wounded nature of the idealists of modern existence, focused round the symbolic bird of its title, the wild duck which, when wounded, dives to the bottom of the lake.

This developed into the deeper psychology of his next play, *Rosmersholm*, which was to be given the homage of a psychological interpretation by Freud himself. The two central characters are the typical Ibsen heroine and hero – Rebecca West, the 'new woman', with her unremitting energy for life, a woman in search of herself, and John Rosmer, the idealist who is seeking a revolution of the spirit. But both are driven by unconscious forces, by ghosts they cannot quite comprehend. Rebecca comes into Rosmer's home, desires him, and drives his wife to suicide. Once she has done this, her desire begins to die. Freud was particularly interested in the scene where Rebecca attempts to describe her motives as she drove Mrs Rosmer to her death: 'Every step I took, every move forward, something screamed inside me, "Stop, no further, stop!" But I could not let it be. I had to push a little bit more, and then one more and always one more. That is how such things happen.' This play, like most of those that follow, ends in death and a version of tragedy. A death-tryst between Rebecca and Rosmer becomes the only way they have of consummating their love. As August Strindberg, Ibsen's successor in the development of Expressionist theatre, said in an essay aptly called 'Soul-Murder', the play was 'unintelligible to the theatre public, mystical to the semi-educated, but crystal-clear to anyone with a knowledge of modern psychology.'

In 1888 came a personal event which evidently caused Ibsen to reassess his own life. He was 60, world-famous, admired by the young, the man who spoke for liberation and self-realization, the endless quest for fulfilment and joy. He had aspired high, and achieved the art he wanted. In Austria that year he met an eighteen-year-old girl, Emilie Bardach, who fell in love with him, and Ibsen declared his attachment. She was the vital muse who drew him higher, but whether through caution or inner conflict Ibsen's interest palled. A similar relationship with another girl followed in Munich. Ibsen did not, as a more flamboyant and less personally conventional artist might, follow the path offered to the artist of fame. But that image of an older man, a great artist or achiever, caught in the dead relationships of the past and seeking to waken to the future, dominates the later plays, which declare both the need for and the tragedy of high aspiration. As he wrote: 'So to conduct one's life as to realize one's self – this seems to me the highest attainment possible in a human being. It is the task of one and all of us, but most of us bungle it.'

These preoccupations shape the plays of the 1890s – *Hedda Gabler* in 1890, *The Master Builder* in 1892, *Little Eyolf* in 1894, *John Gabriel Borkman* in 1896, and finally *When We Dead Awaken* in 1899. These are not 'well-made plays' or works of naturalism, and they seek to step away from the closed rooms of Ibsen's earlier drama, into a greater and freer air which increasingly becomes the fjords and mountains of his own native Norway. They are fables of those who, like himself, have sought the heights but still feel trapped in the limited relationships of the world below. *Hedda Gabler* is the story of a destructive woman who seeks a Dionysian release in 'free and fearless action', but is herself afraid of life. She is finally driven to terrible destructiveness by fear of scandal. The destructive side of human aspirations conflicts with its worth and value in all the later plays. This is very clear in *The Master Builder*, which is often read as a parable of Ibsen's own life and achievement. In it the architect Solness, who has always aspired to build a kingdom of his own, resembling God's, on earth, is reminded of his high aspiration in late life by a young girl who admires him. She encourages Solness to climb the spire he is building on his house, and he falls to his death. Images of high and dangerous aspiration dominate these last plays. John Gabriel Borkman climbs a mountain in search of freedom of the will, and dies in the mountain snows. So does the sculptor Rubek in *When We Dead Awaken*, who tries to break free from death in life ('When we dead awaken, we will see that we have never lived') and climbs another mountain with his former model Irene, where both of them disappear in an avalanche of purifying snow.

Ibsen called *When We Dead Awaken* the 'epilogue' to his late phase, and in fact it was his last play. It expressed its final theme in all its ambiguity, for Rubek's death is both his punishment and his artistic recovery. It was Ibsen's last great image of himself as someone who always aimed at the heights of art, even at the sacrifice of his own life and emotions, and at the price of the lives of others. The play disappears into the strange whiteness which is both art and death, creativity and destructiveness, and it would be revisited often in the twentieth century, not least in Thomas Mann's *The Magic Mountain*. To the end, Ibsen led his theatre into unexpected places, from reform to a tragic vision of the nature of art itself. He had forced the theatre to look across the Alps, and into a harsher sunlight. Each stage of Ibsen's work would have some influence and impact on the drama that followed, the drama of Strindberg and Wedekind, Maeterlinck and O'Neill, Brecht and Pirandello. Modern theatre could never be the same again. Like Ibsen's final heroes, it now needed, at whatever cost, to go on.

JOSEPH CONRAD

I

In the years before the Great War, London was the world's largest and greatest city. 'The richest town in the world, the biggest port, the greatest manufacturing town, the Imperial city – the centre of civilization, the heart of the world!' wrote H. G. Wells in his novel *Tono-Bungay* (1909). Its streets hummed with modern traffic, its Royal Exchange dominated international banking and finance, its great docklands handled the trade and serviced the merchant fleet of a great and far-flung empire, and the Royal Observatory on the hill at Greenwich measured the mean of time for the entire globe. It was a place of enormous tentacular growth, teeming variety, strange contrasts. The public buildings and great private houses of its West End displayed the grandeur of imperial power and social privilege. The sprawling tenements and enormous poverty of its East End formed what George Gissing called a 'nether world'. Others described it as an abyss, an unexplored and dangerous jungle, a place of darkness. When General William Booth, who marched at the head of the Salvation Army, wrote about the East End, he compared the task of exploring it with the work of the African traveller H. M. Stanley, and gave his book on the subject the title *In Darkest London and The Way Out*.

At the centre of the web of the world's largest empire, London was at its most cosmopolitan. It was, said the American Herbert Hoover, the best place in the world to live if you had money. It was a bourgeois capital in a mercantile and imperial age, but it also had both social and artistic attraction, and it became a centre for major artistic activity – one reason why for a time London was indeed one of the capital cities of the Modern movement. Artists and writers from its Empire and Commonwealth, from Ireland and the United States and many

other countries came to paint, write, and participate in and stimulate
the atmosphere of artistic ferment. Explaining why, as a writer, he
had chosen London rather than Paris or Rome, Henry James, who
settled in London in 1876, said simply that it was the place where
there was most to observe. 'It is the biggest aggregation of human
life – the most complete compendium of the world,' he wrote to a
friend.

And there were other *émigrés* too – political refugees from more
turbulent and less tolerant European nations, who had fled from
imprisonment or persecution, usually for their revolutionary principles. After the revolutions that swept through Europe in 1848 the
numbers increased. Karl Marx wrote *Das Kapital* in the haven of the
British Museum, and the spokesmen of Socialism, Communism and
Anarchism constantly met or found safety in Britain. With its traditional democratic institutions and respect for law, Britain seemed safe
from some of the more violent and starkly ideological events that
troubled Europe, but it had its share of turbulence and outrage, and
even James at times suspected the coming of revolution. After the
French commune of 1879 and the growth in the numbers of those in
flight from Tsarist oppression in Russia, the turbulence increased. The
London of the 1880s saw several dynamite explosions; with rising
Irish troubles, there came the Phoenix Park murders in Dublin. Some
of the disorder was the work of Fenians, but some bore the marks of
the growing movement of international anarchism, dedicated to
'creative violence' and the destruction of all public institutions in the
hope of bringing a new world to birth. In 1881 a meeting of international revolutionaries was held in London, and the anarchist Prince
Kropotkin attended. It declared the aim of revolution through ter-
rorism, and a wave of attacks on European heads of state, and assas-
sinations of leading political figures in Europe, Britain and the United
States, soon followed.

London was a challenge to its writers. They tried to capture in
poetry and fiction its strange impressions, its variety, its contrasts, and
increasingly its political turbulence. This was what gave Henry James
the theme of his most political and strangest novel, *The Princess
Casamassima* (1886), a book about the 'great grey Babylon' of London,

and the revolutionary and anarchist impulses that were growing amid its 'horrible numerosity'. For anarchism was acquiring considerable intellectual appeal, and figures like William Morris and Bernard Shaw expressed support for its cleansing aims. Up to the turn of the century violence continued, the anarchist press grew, especially after the break between Marx and Bakunin, and both the British police and European governments took an interest in the revolutionaries who found asylum in Britain. The British police grew adept at penetrating these re-volutionary groups, and planted informers. European governments employed *agents provocateurs* with the aim of creating outrages designed to provoke the British government into withdrawing rights of asylum from radicals and revolutionaries who threatened their governments at home. In 1894 a particularly bizarre terrorist event – it became known as the Greenwich Bomb Outrage – took place. An anarchist called Martial Bourdin was blown to pieces by a bomb he was carrying toward the Greenwich Observatory. The affair was mysterious, and apparently senseless. But it was accepted in anarchist circles, and by many British observers, that his brother-in-law, working as an *agent provocateur*, had played a large part in the whole explosive event.

This was natural material for fiction, and it came to attract the eye of another novelist. He was almost as unlikely an *émigré* as the charac-ters who populate his deeply ironic tale about the complex plots and counterplots of anarchist and revolutionary London – figures like his seedy central character, Mr Verloc, who had 'arrived in London (like the influenza) from the continent'. The book, published in 1907, was called *The Secret Agent: A Simple Tale*. Its author was born Josef Teodor Konrad Korzeniowski, but we know him as Joseph Conrad. And, though London is its setting and major subject, *The Secret Agent* is a very European novel. For Conrad's own life and upbringing had given him plentiful experience of the world of revolutionary idealists, repressive regimes, strange conspiracies, and the power of the 'de-structive element' in the world. It was the book that brought to Eng-lish fiction something of the spirit of Dostoevsky – even though Conrad professed to dislike his work. *The Brothers Karamazov* was, he said, 'terrifically bad and impressive and exasperating. I don't know what Dostoevsky stands for or reveals, but I do know he is too Russian for me.'

Conrad's quarrel with the Russian metaphysical temperament could not, however, conceal a deep emotional link with it. He had been born in 1857, the son of a highly educated and literary Polish patriot, in the lost Polish empire of the Ukraine, now under Tsarist Russia. His father was arrested for conspiracy after the Rising of 1863, and was exiled to the Urals, along with the five-year-old Josef. When his father died in Crakow when Josef was 12, he took part in the patriotic street parade. Josef grew up with a Polish sense of adventure, which made him want to go to the West – where, in the wake of the dismemberment of their country, many Poles had emigrated – and become a sailor. He joined relatives in Marseilles, sailed on French ships, became involved in love and money worries, attempted suicide, possibly fought a duel. He had become a romantic wanderer without a country, though he found one in time. For, to escape his problems and avoid the risk of conscription into the Russian army, he joined the British merchant navy, a world of mercantile discipline coupled with imperial adventure.

Here he acquired a feeling for the orderly life of ships, a new language, English, and in 1886, after he became a sea-captain, a new country. He took British nationality, though at that time he had still yet to see much of Britain, and he certainly had still to become a writer. Britain offered him a sense of historical stability, and he attached his strange sense of fidelity to it. As he wrote to a fellow-Pole who had made the same choice of country:

> I agree with you that in a free and hospitable land even the most persecuted of our race may find relative peace and a certain amount of happiness, materially at least; consequently I understood and readily accepted your reference to 'Home'. When speaking, writing or thinking in English, the word 'home' always means for me the hospitable shores of Great Britain.

Britain brought out his sense of romantic conservatism, though (like Henry James) he saw England too was at risk from the prospect of international revolution. For the moment, it was the 'only barrier to the pressure of infernal doctrines born in continental back-slums'. But, he added, 'the destiny of this nation and of all nations is to be accomplished in darkness amid much weeping and gnashing of teeth, to pass through robbery, equality, anarchy and misery under the iron rule of military despotism.'

In 1890 Conrad made a voyage to the Congo that damaged his health badly, and afterwards he settled onshore and, following his father's tradition, set out to become a writer. His first novels – *Almayer's Folly* in 1895, *An Outcast of the Islands* in 1896, *The Nigger of the 'Narcissus'* in 1898, and the best of them, *Lord Jim*, in 1900 – were, essentially, sea-stories, exotic romances, mostly set in testing circumstances on board ship or else in the countries of the Far East. They were imperial novels for imperial times, dealing with the British Empire, its trade and its duties, the crises at its outposts. They were not directly political, and not directly about Europe. By chance – and chance, Conrad always insisted, was the essential force in human lives – he had become an English author, but the world he knew was the unhoused, international, multilingual world of the sea. And one of the essential themes with which he dealt was the personally disturbing question of fidelity and betrayal – of one's country, one's cause, one's self.

Indeed this was one of a group of themes that, from the start, made his work tragic, impressive, and imbued with metaphysical feeling. There was the essential contrast between the small hierarchical society of men on shipboard and the vagaries of the sea, between the isolated trader outpost and the savagery that lay beyond. There was the contrast between fidelity – that simple idea on which the world rests, Conrad said – and betrayal, between the habits of order and chaos and anarchy, between what in *Lord Jim* is called 'the sovereign power enthroned in a fixed standard of conduct' and what he called 'the destructive element.' There was the contrast between the solidarity of shipboard life and the profound underlying loneliness of existence – that 'loneliness impenetrable and transparent, elusive and everlasting . . . that surrounds, envelops, clothes every human soul from the cradle to the grave, and perhaps beyond.'

It is not hard to see why Conrad came to seem a novelist of modern anxiety – a writer who brought a dark and troubled vision that, though he half-denied it, owed a good deal more to Dostoevsky than it did to the more secure and social British tradition of fiction. One critic has described him as 'the first important modern novelist in English', because 'the world of significance he creates is at the furthest remove from the world of public significance created by the great Victorian and eighteenth-century novelists,' and, if we leave aside Dickens, that is true. And the books that followed the turn of the century – *Heart of Darkness* in 1902, *Nostromo* in 1904, *The Secret Agent* in 1907, *Under Western Eyes* in 1911, *The Secret Sharer* in 1912, and *The Shadow Line* in 1917 – increasingly revealed him as the great, ironic, ambiguous modern writer that we recognize today, though not all readers saw it at the time. They all kept their character as adventure stories, but increasingly they dealt, at metaphysical depth, with the encounter between the human need for order and meaning and a cosmos that lacks all ethical and moral substance. 'In the destructive element immerse,' Conrad had written in *Lord Jim*, and a sense of anarchy fills these books. On another occasion he saw that the theme had much to do with his own origins: 'Under a destructive pressure of which Western Europe can have no notion, applied by forces that were not only crushing but corrupting, we [the Poles] kept our sanity.'

There was another important idea very significant for Conrad's creation of *The Secret Agent*: the idea of secrecy itself. The word 'secret' is in the title of two of Conrad's later books, and secrets are everywhere in them. As in Dostoevsky, his characters often come face to face with some double, a secret sharer, who resembles them, reminds them of the ambiguity of the world and the psychological incompleteness of the self, and initiates them into an awareness of chaos and duplicity. Likewise modern imperial civilization had its own secret hidden within it, in the form of an inner darkness. The double face of things is a recurrent Modernist theme; everything is touched by its ironic opposite. Fidelity and civilization themselves depend on maintaining a precarious fiction – a fiction or gamble that Conrad defends while being unable to assert it with any form of absolute certainty.

This is a central theme of *Heart of Darkness* – the short book that is one of the great works of the modern movement, to which T. S. Eliot paid homage when he used a key phrase from it as the epigraph to his poem *The Hollow Men*. It begins in the heart of London, on a ship on the river near Gravesend; in the background a mournful gloom hangs over 'the biggest, and the greatest, city on earth.' It then takes its narrator, Marlow, on what has been called a 'night journey' up the Congo and, through the circles of hell, into the dark heart of Africa, 'the earliest beginnings of the world'. Here amid the undignified scramble to exploit and colonize the continent the white man Kurtz is dying, and his final words express the moral anarchy he has found there: 'The horror! The horror!' Marlow returns to the apparent light of London, and goes to see Kurtz's fiancée, 'The Intended'. When she demands to know Kurtz's last words, Marlow tells the precarious lie that lets civilization survive: 'The last word he spoke was – your name.' Order and idealism are allowed to triumph, but the shadow of horror remains. As Marlow says, London too has been one of the dark places of the earth.

So when, a little later, Conrad turned to the idea of *The Secret Agent*, he was concerned with far more than the story of a strange anarchist plot that had gone wrong ten years before. The basic themes of his writing – fidelity and betrayal, moral heroism and moral cowardice, order and 'the destructive element', stability and anarchy – were to be part of the story. And so was the matter of his own ambiguous attitude toward the radical and revolutionary assault on the contemporary social order. Thomas Mann, who greatly admired the book and wrote an introduction to the German translation in 1926, just after Conrad's death, recognized it as a work in which 'Polish Russophobia is expressing itself in British.' Conrad had become, in effect, an English gentleman, but with a Polish accent and sensibility. To the end of his life he continued to describe himself as a writer who 'can't claim English literature as my inheritance.' When *The Secret Agent* was not the popular success he had hoped for, he had his explanation: 'Foreignness, I suppose.'

There was another explanation. *The Secret Agent* dealt with basic themes he had explored in his sea adventures. But it also marked a great change in his writing, and a new pessimism and despair in his vision. The heart of darkness had settled in his work. He himself saw it as a work in a new genre, that of the political thriller. And it was also his first metropolitan novel, a book where he explored the world of the British Empire not through its outposts, but at the very centre. It was a novel of the great modern city, the place of complex contrasts, light and darkness – the kind of ambiguous, fleeting city that lies behind many of the works of Modernism. In fact this notion was part of what Henry James would call the essential 'germ' of the story, which came out of the imagining of strange forms, 'sharp in outline but imperfectly apprehended.' But then, he says in the 1920 preface to the book, 'the vision of an enormous town presented itself, of a monstrous town more populous than some continents and in its man-made might as if indifferent to heaven's frowns and smiles: a cruel devourer of the world's light. There was room enough there to place any story, depth enough for any passion, variety enough there for any setting, darkness enough to bury five millions of lives.' The great city became the background for his further meditations, until from its obscurity two stories emerged – the story of Winnie Verloc, with her conviction that 'life doesn't stand much looking into,' and the strange explosion in Greenwich Park.

2

So, despite its ironic sub-title, *The Secret Agent* is very far from being a simple tale, as in fact almost every reader of it has declared. From the moment Mr Verloc steps out from the darkness of his seedy shop in Soho, selling cheap pornography, rubberware, and revolutionary sentiments, and passes through the lighted, orderly, and respectable parts of London towards Knightsbridge – a London of opulence and luxury watched over by a bloodshot sun with an air 'of punctual and benign vigilance' – little is as it seems. As the seedy stout Mr Verloc goes westwards 'through a town without shadows in an atmosphere of powdered old gold,' he sees his own task not as being to challenge but to preserve this respectability, his mission being 'the protection of the social mechanism, not its perfectionment or even its criticism'. He is in fact a man of consummate idleness – but when he arrives at the Embassy that employs him, he proves to be an *agent provocateur*, though he has obviously provoked very little. He is also a shopkeeper and a solidly married man: 'And you a professed anarchist too!' cries Mr Vladimir of the Embassy. Everything has a touch of contradiction about it, and even the language halts and turns on itself. Mr Verloc is a 'rock', but this is amended; he is a 'soft kind of rock'. Even at the level of words, nothing is as it seems.

Mr Verloc's visit to the Embassy is also the start of a complex plot which will have extraordinary and unexpected results. The respectable Mr Vladimir demands that Verloc organize a terrorist outrage – not to advance the cause of revolution, but to upset it. The aim is to provoke the British public into suppressing the revolutionaries who reside in the country. It therefore should not be an assassination, or the usual forms of terror. It cannot even be an outrage against religion, or art; none of this would upset the British middle classes at all. The attack must be against science, time, the idea of order itself, and hence the Greenwich Observatory. 'Go for the first meridian. You don't know the middle classes as well as I do. Their sensibilities are jaded,' says Mr Vladimir. And the respectable Mr Verloc goes off to his seedy end of London with an impossible task to perform.

So the comic, ironic oppositions of the novel begin; and soon they multiply. We meet Verloc's band of revolutionaries, gathered in his dim little shop: Michaelis, the ticket-of-leave revolutionary, who speaks of the power of the historical process, which therefore requires very little action from him; toothless old Karl Yundt, the terrorist, who waveringly asks men to be strong enough to become destroyers; Comrade Ossipon, the scientific revolutionary who shares the conviction of Lombroso that criminals and degenerates can be identified by the lobes of their ears, and himself preys on young women. The revolutionaries talk in endless, brilliant circles of the various ideas of radical reform, human suffering, social cannibalism. But the only person who is actually stirred by this to any real feeling of compassion is Verloc's brother-in-law Stevie, an idiot and, for Ossipon, an example of degeneracy. Sitting at the kitchen table, drawing his own endless circles, he listens to the radical talk and grows more and more upset.

Irony, as Conrad was to explain in his preface, was the essential method of the novel: the artistic task to be done was that of 'applying an ironic method to a subject of this kind.' But irony in fiction can mean many things. Here it meant a method of distance, as Conrad displayed his characters as blind examples of paradox and contradiction. But it meant more, for irony is the principle behind the entire story. Nothing works out as it should, and everything has a double face. The blindness of the characters to their own fates and to the ironies inherent in the human condition is part of it all. Nor is the irony solely directed against the anarchists, and in favour of the *status quo*. After all, the anarchists themselves are already pawns in the hands of the conspiratorial embassy authorities. 'If I had the necessary talent I would like to go for the true anarchist, which is the millionaire,' Conrad was to remark. What he does actually go for is the social order as a whole – in effect, for the whole 'monstrous city' through whose duplicities and paradoxes Mr Verloc has walked. For the anarchists are imperfectly aware of the contradiction in all things; and that is Conrad's fundamental theme.

Thus, as another character we soon meet, the Professor – he is described as 'the perfect anarchist' – observes, terror and law are simply two sides of the same coin: 'Like to like. The terrorist and the policeman both come from the same basket. Revolution, legality – countermoves in the same game; forms of idleness at bottom identical.' What the Professor means by 'idleness' – and this is an important theme in the book – is the willingness to accept one's vision as it is, to idealize the world rather than looking at it directly. The Professor believes he looks at it directly, and his faith is in total destruction, death as perfection. He is a man of disappointed ambitions and great hatred, both of the system and the popular masses, who has turned his rage into the determination to annihilate completely, like Kurtz with his desire to 'exterminate the brutes'. His own contradictions turn him into a figure of profound danger. He is small and unnoticed as he passes through the obscure jungles of London: but he considers himself the Superman, assuring his freedom of all legal restraint and social convention by means of the flask of explosives he carries in his pocket, ready for detonation. He seeks for the 'perfect detonator', but there is irony here too. For the perfect detonator he provides to Verloc is imperfect, and it causes the horrifying death of the man who, in fulfilment of Vladimir's mission against the Greenwich Observatory, does blow himself to nothingness.

The image of total physical destruction of the flesh, rendered as meat, dominates the book. But the obscure event produces the mystery at the heart of the story, and begins the investigative theme. Just as Dostoevsky had shown that crime and punishment, self-made morality and social need, are intricately interwoven, so Conrad shows that terror and law are indeed closely interlocked. But he does so not with Dostoevsky's romantic identification with the characters and their moral dilemmas, though rather with the same cosmic irony. For even those who speak for and defend society share the same 'pangs of moral discontent' as those they pursue, and live in the same urban fog of indirection and uncertainty. Society, it seems, is a complex and arbitrary creation in which, whether we serve it or oppose it, we are all secret agents, administering the bureaucracy of existence in a world where, like Mrs Verloc, we are never quite able 'to look into things'. And the issue of the book becomes not anarchism but a universal anarchy, which can only be confronted with an ironic anxiety.

In the main investigator, Chief Inspector Heat, Conrad constructs a brilliant invention, a man on a moral tightrope, undermined from within by the society and institutions he seeks to protect. Heat is used to dealing with thieves, whom he finds as natural to the good order of things as property itself: 'Thieving is not sheer absurdity. It was a form of social industry, perverse indeed, but still an industry exercised in an industrious world . . .'. The thief accepts the social rules as they are, and wins or loses by them. But anarchism, as Heat finds, cannot be dealt with by rule, and secret agents are frequently double agents. Heat has every reason to protect Verloc, who is also as it happens a police informer, and every reason not to arrest the Professor, who has the protection of the detonator in his pocket. He does have every reason to arrest Michaelis, who is an obvious suspect, even though he is not the guilty party. But in any case he is distrusted by his own superior, the Assistant Commissioner, who decides to conduct his own independent investigation.

The Assistant Commissioner is in turn chained to his own ironic fate, and he has his own pangs of moral discontent. His wife is a friend of Michaelis's rich patroness, who regards the 'ticket-of-leave apostle's' aim of destroying the economic base of society as entirely humanitarian, and is in favour of universal ruin if it would leave the social values untouched ('. . . she did not really see where was the moral harm of it. It would do away with all the multitude of parvenus, whom she disliked and distrusted . . . The disappearance of the last place of money would not affect people of position. She could not conceive of how it would affect her position, for instance'). He mistrusts Heat; indeed a 'mistrust of established reputations was strictly in character with the Assistant Commissioner's ability as detector.' He sees dangerous reservations in all fidelities, and, as he tells the Great Personage, Sir Ethelred, the Secretary of State, another protector of secrets, his aim is to vindicate innocence. But he is also bent on 'finding out', and, like Heat, makes his descent into the streets of the monstrous city. Here he must lose his moral identity and take on a 'sense of loneliness and evil freedom' that is 'rather pleasant'. Allowing his public persona to fade – 'he himself had become displaced' – he imbibes the anarchy that comes from the city itself.

Confusion, disorder, ambiguity and indirection are thus everywhere in *The Secret Agent* – and not least in Conrad's method of narrating the sequence of events. Frank Kermode once called the book a story 'with an enormous hole in the plot', and that is true in several ways. Conrad, for instance, avoids the conventional methods of chronological narration, folding the story in on itself. The explosion at Greenwich Park has already happened by the beginning of Chapter 4, and Comrade Ossipon reads the news from the press to the Professor, who then acknowledges he has supplied the bomb to Verloc, who is thus assumed to be the victim. Soon afterwards the Professor encounters Chief Inspector Heat, who, we learn, has already inspected the terrible hole and seen the mangled, cannibalized remains of the body. Then the story folds back on itself, and we see again Verloc, Winnie, and her brother Stevie, who takes a cab-ride with a cruel driver which becomes his experience of anarchy, as he learns that the world is a bad one for poor people, and that the police protect the rich from the poor. Only late in the story, and never by a direct method of telling, do we learn that the victim blown up by the bomb he was carrying was Stevie.

The 'enormous hole in the plot' is evident in other ways. *The Secret Agent* is a novel without a hero. Most fiction works by soliciting our sympathy for one or several of the characters, who then help us find our position in the novel, and give us a secure centre of values. But here the irony eliminates those centres of value as they appear, and there are no secure points of identification in the novel. There are, indeed, characters who invite our sympathetic attention. Stevie is one of them, but he is a victim and an idiot. But, though he owes something to Prince Myshkin, the saintly figure of Dostoevsky's *The Idiot*, he is never a source of true insight or wisdom. His view of the world is simple rather than innocent, and he is seen very largely through the eyes of other characters. The one who admires and protects him is his sister Winnie, Verloc's wife, but she has spent her life trying to ensure that Verloc will be his protector. He is simply the victim, both of the imperfect views of the world that are fed to him, and of the indifference of Verloc, who, lost in his own difficulties and meditations, and his enormous self-satisfaction, uses him as a convenient and expendable item in a plot that was not intended to go wrong.

The other central character is Winnie Verloc herself. She, as Conrad acknowledged, became his main point of interest in the story. It is her slow discovery of the details of the outrage, most of them overheard by chance, that brings her to the point of violence, when she takes the knife from the meat and uses it to stab her husband. His death is an extreme example of self-satisfied delusion, for in his sublime marital confidence he has assumed that her real interest will not be in her brother but in his own considerable dilemma, as he faces a future of imprisonment or exile. In any case, what Winnie needs is a good cry, and things could have been much worse: 'What would it have been if you had lost me?' The scene of the murder has been rightly praised as the brilliant centre of a brilliant book, with its marvellous management of the mutual incomprehension between the couple, as each of the Verlocs follows a different 'insane logic'. As Verloc attempts to placate his wife with visions of the future, Winnie in turn has her own visions of 'meretricious splendour'. She has taken care of Stevie, and sacrificed a better marriage in order to find a protector for him, only to find the protector is his killer. Besides, with the boy's death she no longer needs to stay with Verloc, and can have her 'freedom'. The complex moment comes to its peak when Verloc calls her name in what she recognizes as 'the note of wooing'. In an extraordinary slow-motion scene, Verloc realizes that the moment that is coming to him is not sexual gratification but murder.

Winnie Verloc may be a central character, and the heart of the story. She takes on tragic but not heroic proportions, and her fate does not dissipate the universal irony. She has 'become a free woman with a perfection of freedom which left her nothing to desire and absolutely nothing to do, since Stevie's urgent claim on her devotion no longer existed. Mrs Verloc, who thought in images, was not troubled now by visions, because she did not think at all. She was a woman enjoying her complete irresponsibility and endless leisure, almost in the manner of a corpse.' It is in the final scenes of the book – where she breaks away from the bourgeois, marital and maternal values that have enfolded her so far, and finds herself in a world of desperate freedom – that we become aware of the deep anarchy of life. Betrayed by Ossipon, who sees her as a moral degenerate like her brother and takes her purse, and divided between 'vigour of vitality' and the awareness of terror and despair, she takes her own life on the cross-channel ferry by which she had hoped to make her escape.

But the book itself stands with a renewed vision of the monstrous town bigger than some continents. Ossipon walks through 'distant parts of the enormous town slumbering monstrously on a carpet of mud under a veil of raw mist', and soon reads of the impenetrable mystery that is destined to hang for ever over Winnie's act of madness or despair. The Professor makes a final appeal to just such a madness or despair, which might dispel mediocrity and move the fate of the world. Then he too walks through the monstrous city, with his perverse and outrageous message,

> averting his eyes from the odious multitude of mankind. He had no future. He disdained it. He was a force. His thoughts caressed the images of ruin and destruction. He walked frail, insignificant, shabby, miserable – and terrible in the simplicity of his idea calling madness and despair to the regeneration of the world. Nobody looked at him. He passed on unsuspected and deadly, like a pest in the street full of men.

It is not on Winnie but on a new irony that the book comes to rest, as her impassioned act becomes a deadly philosophy. This is a novel in which everything seems to have been prepared for, and all the elements are paid off – every key phrase, every key image. The book is made of story, but also of a complex, ironic web of words and phrases – ruin and destruction, impenetrable mystery, madness and despair, 'not worth looking into', the monstrous city. And it is on this linguistic web, and the finer subtler web of discourse that has held together the strange duplicity of the novel, that this most remarkable of books ends, and on a vision of extremity so dark that it may explain why, along with Winnie, so many people see life as not worth the looking into.

3

The Secret Agent is a very remarkable book indeed, and to my mind it is one of the greatest works of modern irony, a form of very justified address to the modern world. Conrad had hoped that the serious melodrama, the thriller that constituted a full vision of modern life, would make him into a popular writer, something he craved. It did not happen with the book, and Conrad finally pronounced it 'an honorable failure. It brought me neither love nor the promise of

literary success. I own that I am cast down.' In the preface he wrote
to the edition of 1920, when on the strength of other, later books he
had indeed become a popular writer, he felt compelled to explain it,
and was still defending himself against the charge of having written a
work of moral squalor. He writes of his 'inspiring indignation and
underlying pity and contempt' in his treatment of the tale, and the
deliberate choice of the ironic method, which would 'enable me to
say all I felt I would have to say in scorn as well as in pity.' He then
adds: 'I confess that it makes a grisly skeleton. But I still will submit
that telling Winnie Verloc's story to its anarchistic end of utter de-
solation, madness, and despair, and telling it as I have told it here, I
have not intended to commit a gratuitous outrage on the feelings of
mankind.'

The Secret Agent is a paramount work of modern scepticism, which
regards not just the instincts of anarchism but the aim of penetrating
the meaning of life itself as a process leading either to absurdity or
madness and despair. It has, in short, a very modern vision, philosophically comparable to existentialism. But there seems no doubt
that in considering his own work in retrospect, Conrad was made
uneasy, and this sometimes led him to suggest that it had no great
aims. 'The whole thing is superficial and but a tale. I had no idea to
consider Anarchism politically or to treat it in its philosophical aspect;
as a manifestation of human nature in its discontent and imbecility,' he
wrote in a rather typically ambiguous letter to his friend John
Galsworthy. It is true that he does not mean in the book to deal with
anarchism as a serious political philosophy, but the work is clearly not
superficial, and far more than a conventional tale. He was similarly
obscure about his knowledge of the Greenwich Outrage, telling his
correspondents, quite incorrectly, that he was out of Britain at the
time, and had small knowledge of it. We know that in fact he knew a
good deal about it, researched it, and gathered information from various friends like Ford Madox Hueffer, who had anarchist connections,
and many of the details of his story, which he sets in the 1880s, closely
parallel the actual events of 1894.

But clearly Conrad was not interested in giving an accurate record
of the event, or for that matter in doing justice to anarchism for its

own philosophical sake. What he saw was a 'blood-stained inanity' which was somehow related to ideas of perfect freedom and the revolutionary transformation of the world. In fact Conrad began a group of stories on related political themes in 1906, just after the failed Russian revolution and at a time of personal depression. There were two pieces called 'The Informer' and 'An Anarchist', which were collected in *A Set of Six* (1908). The third story he started was called 'Mr Verloc', and it was this which extended, through several versions, into *The Secret Agent*. But the true companion-piece to *The Secret Agent* was to be his novel of 1911, *Under Western Eyes*, which deals with Russian revolutionaries as they make their existence in St Petersburg and then in Geneva, under Western eyes. This brilliant novel is a fuller and far more realistic treatment of the issues that Conrad saw moving the age, showing, once more, his preoccupation with growing disorder and the way in which moral nihilism pointed to social nihilism. Thus all these works deal in different ways with the rise of revolutionary affairs and violent ideologies, and it is clear that the revolutionary impulses that had fed the failed revolution of 1905, and would in time feed the Bolshevik Revolution of 1917, were in his mind. So were those ideas of the Nietzschean transformation of modern man into a new freedom which are in various ways expressed by Ossipon and the Professor, who want to bring idealism and reality into concord, and which have so much to do with the early twentieth-century mood.

The Secret Agent and *Under Western Eyes* have thus been taken as important examples of the modern political novel, and so they are. At the same time they have been criticized, not surprisingly, by those who want to call novelists to their political duties, and expect them to intervene positively and progressively in the great advancement of history. Politics, of course, are supposed to matter in their own right, especially in a secular age that must set its Utopias within history. In fact, in the pure, ideological sense, they have had more to do with totalitarianism, state-owned reality, zealotry and self-interested delusion than they have with freedom, and they have not resolved but multiplied our haunting sense of living in a modern absurdity. Today, after the rise of Stalinism, Fascism, and the new fundamentalisms of a zealotic age in the Middle East, we might grant rather more to the view that the political passions have probably added much more to the agonies and atrocities than they have to the betterment of the world. The visionaries and leaders have, like the Professor, persistently exploited the folly and frenzy of the crowd, and the emotions of madness and despair. Conrad's interest is not simply in revolutionary anarchism for itself, but in the underlying dreams and contradictions of emotion which create it. It also goes deeper, into the whole modern notion that there is somehow an absolute and imperious freedom of selfhood which is visionary and may be possessed.

Politics, we are often told, deserves something better than irony. Thus the American critic Irving Howe has complained that this is a work surrounded 'by a thick fog of irony which steadily eats away at the features, the energies, and the very vitals of its major characters'. This is true, though in this it compares with much that has been done in the name of modern politics. The book is a work of extreme vision, a profound penetration through irony into the duplicity of human experience. It was Thomas Mann – who once indicated that there is a kinship between Conrad's book and what he had done later in *The Magic Mountain* – who gave the novel what is in many ways a better, and certainly a far less defensive, preface than Conrad's own. Writing his introduction to the German translation of the novel in the political circumstances of Germany in 1926, he saw it was a work written in the space that art could open up between the contradictory ideologies of the age, those of bourgeois capitalism and revolutionary socialism. It was a book written not in the old forms of tragedy or comedy, but in a new, post-bourgeois form. That form was tragi-comedy, the form of the modern grotesque. Thus the book was a cry for the independent and elusive freedom of literary vision, managed through the spirit of irony.

That is one of the important things to say about *The Secret Agent*, a work enormously important for its literary method. When Conrad talked of his method, he preferred to use the modernist term he shared with Henry James, Ford Madox Hueffer, and Stephen Crane, and called it 'impressionism'. By this, he meant that the novel's task was to make vivid through its appeal to the senses, to offer a 'light of magical suggestiveness . . . brought to play for an evanescent instant over the commonplace surface of words.' 'My task which I am trying to achieve is, by the power of the written word to make you hear, to make you feel – it is, before all, to make you *see*.' However, this suggests that Conrad's method is scenic, and that to a point is true. It is also, however, deliberately oblique and suggestive. As Conrad said himself, the novel works by indirection, its tone, imagery, narrative line and spirit being guided by something complete, a figure in the carpet, that makes it a view of life. Thus, as Mann suggested, *The Secret Agent* is a work of *total* vision – the vision of ironic grotesquerie. Its view of life is, as I have been arguing, one of profound moral irony. For annihilation is, as the Professor sees, the true anarchism, and the absurd, impenetrable mystery of existence is the true secret agent.

It has taken time to recognize the importance of the book, though by the time of Conrad's preface in the 1920s the significance of the darker side of Conrad's writing was already growing more evident. The events of following years would make the book's vision far more central, as political disaster and extremity increased, the security of liberalism declined, the dangerous anarchies of new forms of revolutionary socialism and fascism rose, and the political spy and the secret agent took a bigger part in history. Conrad was to have the singular distinction of being acknowledged as an important predecessor by writers like Virginia Woolf on the one hand, and Graham Greene and Jean-Paul Sartre on the other. The work of pervasive modern irony has become more and more our kind of book, for very good reason. So has the serious melodrama, as a world that once seemed to belong to the exotic fringes of society seems much closer to its very centre. Tales of divided loyalties, corrupted missions and secret agents have become vital forms of modern fiction, in writers from Arthur Koestler to John le Carré. And just as important have been Conrad's oblique, ironic methods of viewing the world of nihilistic forces and destructive history – methods that were, he suggested, ways of confronting the moral ambiguity of a world which indeed needs a very great deal of looking into.

THOMAS
MANN

I

In a train from Hamburg to Davos in Switzerland sits an ordinary
and unassuming young man, Hans Castorp. He is wearing his summer
overcoat, his winter overcoat hangs on the train peg, and beside him
is a book called *Ocean Steamships*. These are the years of German
expansion, not too long before the coming of the Great War of 1914.
The orphan son of a good Hamburg family, Hans's destiny seems
clear enough. He has just passed his engineering examinations, and is
about to take up employment with the firm of Tunder and Wilms,
shipbuilders. He comes of a good and sturdy burgher background,
and though his parents have died the family has supported him. In
fact, if he maintains his devotion to work, his future seems pleasantly
assured: 'Some day he would sit in the Assembly, or on the Board of
Directors, he would help make the laws . . .' The three-week break he
is taking from the normal and predictable pattern of his patterned life
is simply a short trip he is making to visit his cousin Joachim. Joachim
is a healthy-seeming young man who intends to join the army, but
his life has been interrupted in a bigger way. He is suffering from
tuberculosis, and he is recuperating at the Sanatorium Berghof, on the
mountain above Davos, where Hans's train-journey is taking him
now.

This is the opening of Thomas Mann's great novel *The Magic
Mountain* – the book he wrote after completing his novella *Death in
Venice*, the extraordinary story of a distinguished and famous German
writer, Gustave von Aschenbach, who suddenly breaks out of 'the
daily theatre of a rigid, cold, and passionate service' and the bourgeois
German world. A writer notable for his classical control, Aschenbach
travels on a romantic whim to the beautiful, grotesque, artistic, decadent city of Venice. Here he is lured by erotic feeling into a profound

inward conflict of morality and emotion, focused around a beautiful young boy he sees on the beach. As bubonic plague begins to rage through the city, Aschenbach comes to accept it as his romantic fate, and the story ends with his death. The theme of the book – Mann described it as 'the fascination of death, the triumph of disorder in a life founded on order' – represents an essential conflict between two ideas of art and the artist, the classic and the romantic. It was a theme that had guided a good deal of Mann's writing since he had established himself, at the age of 26, as one of the great German writers with *Buddenbrooks*, in 1901. And it was a theme that, as Mann considered his next book, he decided to return to, treating it this time in a much more comic way.

The Hans Castorp who sits so innocently in the train at the beginning of *The Magic Mountain* is therefore about to cross, as Aschenbach did, a whole series of frontiers that will separate him from his familiar universe. Like Aschenbach, he is going far, from north to south, work to leisure, Puritan and Prussian order to disorder, culture to nature, and from the world of normal health to the world of disease and death. Unlike Aschenbach, who deliberately seeks out the world of decadence, Hans is taking a journey that is to be physically and emotionally an ascent. As Mann was to explain to an audience at Princeton University, thirty years afterwards, when he was an exile in America, Hans is about to undergo a 'heightening process' in more than one sense. His train-trip is taking him out of the flatlands and into the uplands, out of the normal world of time into a new kind of time, out of daily duties into a place of abstract thought, and out of mediocrity into self-knowledge. His three-week stay will extend to seven years, and he will undergo a sequence of adventures – sensual, moral, intellectual and political – that would never have occurred in the world down below, though in time they will do much to explain the meaning of that world to him.

An episode in Mann's own life helped to provide the story. During 1912, his wife Katia contracted a lung complaint, and spent a period in a sanatorium at Davos very similar to the one in the novel. Just like the innocent Hans, Mann went for a while as a guest to the sanatorium, visiting her. There he developed a bronchial infection, was examined by the doctors, and advised to remain there for six months. Unlike Hans, though like Hans's uncle later on in the book, Mann rejected the advice. Instead he set out to write the story, drawing not only on his own but his wife's experiences. So the opening scene in the novel, 'Arrival', essentially transcribes Mann's own experiences as he departed everyday life and entered the 'upland' world of the sanatorium and the magic mountain on which it is set. Mann was interested in the ideas of Einstein, whom he came to know, and whose view of the 'space–time continuum' affected many thinkers in the prewar period. In the opening pages of the book, we can see space itself becoming a form of time. 'Space, like time, engenders forgetfulness,' the author meditates, 'but it does so by setting us bodily free from our surroundings and giving us back our primitive, unattached state.'

It is that primitive and unattached state that Hans will return to over the next seven years in the sanatorium. 'They make pretty free with a human being's idea of time, up here,' his cousin Joachim tells him when he arrives at the station in Davos. Indeed the different idea of time that prevails here – and so of all the things that are made from time, which include life and death, human consciousness, love, morality and art – is just what makes the mountain on which Hans finds himself a 'magic' one. 'One of the chief themes of *The Magic Mountain* is the mystery of time,' Mann told his audience in America when he lectured on the book. The critics who have tried to interpret it have rightly seen time as virtually a character in the novel, and observed that this is one of the things that links it with other major works of Modernism. Mann shared with Proust and others a deep sense of the difference between inner and outer – subjective and objective – time, and he considered the clock and the calendar as imperfect registers of human consciousness and the human spirit. But the 'hermetic' detachment from normal time that Hans experiences in the novel is not a way of separating him from the great events of his age. The mountain is not a retreat, and consciousness is by no means entirely subjective. Indeed Mann tells us that consciousness is communal and historical, and Hans realizes that we share the common experiences of our epoch. More than most of the Modernists, Mann is preoccupied with the

idea of time as history – and with history not just as a personal
memory, or a sentimental past, but as an ever-moving present im-
plicating all of us.

The Magic Mountain is thus a major historical novel. At the same
time it has an urgent sense of what lies beyond time – timelessness,
transcendence, 'the unmeasured', the 'eternal'. It is such matters which,
because they are so deeply brushed with death, the 'settled citizens'
and 'practised time-consumers' of the sanatorium are aware of, and
which change, for good and bad, their view of life in the 'flatland'
world. It is sometimes said that Mann separates his characters completely from that world, and that his book is a comedy of the hermetic
life of the mountain. In fact the two worlds are constantly played off
against each other, as everything is in this dialectical novel. Hans's
growing detachment from life down below becomes a challenge to
his mind and spirit, and his move to the sanatorium is a way of seeing
his life – indeed all life – under a new and more metaphysical gaze. In
the flatland Hans has seen his destiny as a practical one, 'helping to
bring the nations together through the development of commerce
and communications.' That innocent hope of the age is now tested
against the image of a dance of death, a dance that was as important
to the historical world itself as it was to the threatened citizens of the
sanatorium.

Thus it is appropriate that almost every chapter and section of this
long novel opens with some form of meditation on time: on its passage,
on the various ways we experience it, on the way it expands and
contracts around us, on the contrast between the static circlings of the
clock and the larger motions of the spirit, and on the way we tell
stories. For time is a challenge to novelists too, as Laurence Sterne
displayed in one of the earliest and greatest of novels, *Tristram Shandy*.
Like Sterne, Mann acknowledges that novels conventionally tempt us
to a chronological and hence very logical idea of time. Yet this limits
the potential of fiction. As he notes at the beginning of Chapter Seven
(the section is entitled 'By the Ocean of Time') time is the 'medium
of narration', just as it is the medium of life. 'But a narrative must
have two kinds of time,' he goes on. 'First, its own, like music, actual
time, conditioning its presentation and course; and second, the time of

its content, which is relative, so extremely relative that the imaginary time of the narrative can either coincide nearly or completely with the actual, or musical, time, or can be a world away.' And stories can practise 'a hermetical magic, a temporary distortion of perspective reminding one of certain abnormal and transcendental experiences in actual life.' Mann's book is constructed and located as it is in order to jolt us out of the realistic and logical view of fictional time. And that 'hermetic magic', that 'distortion of perspective', is just what Hans *and* his creator, the novelist, will find as a result of their move to the magic mountain.

2

It was one of the many ironies surrounding this most ironical of novels that time had a far greater effect on the book than Mann could ever have intended when he started the book so lightheartedly in 1912. For the book itself was to suffer the greatest dislocation the modern world has suffered in its public time. 'I began work on the book in 1912,' Mann later explained, 'but before it progressed far the First World War broke out. It did two things: put an immediate stop to my work in the book, and incalculably enriched its content at the same time.' Mann suffered the war painfully. He was a cosmopolitan writer and an intellectual. He was also a German patriot and an influential public figure, who had his own view of Germany's ideal culture and its historical destiny. He believed in an ideal Germanness, and wrote various essays supporting the war and seeing it as a way towards national purification and liberation. His brother Heinrich Mann, himself a writer, violently disagreed with what he saw as Thomas's instinctive, conservative and anti-democratic stand, and this forced Thomas into an agonized self-analysis. The outcome was his book *Reflections of a Non-Political Man* (1918), an endeavour to separate the cultural Germany, the Germany of music, poetry and philosophy, from the political Germany. Mann here emerges as the conservative defender of the bourgeois age – somewhat ironically, again, for his novels ever since *Buddenbrooks* had been concerned with the decay of the old burgher patricians and the conflict between the bourgeois and the artist.

It was as a result of this wartime conflict of beliefs that *The Magic Mountain* became an intellectual novel, a novel of ideas – particularly the ideas that had divided him and his brother. And it is also a novel of intellectual *crisis*, for the war profoundly changed Mann's thinking and his views of history. The wartime crisis fed the book, and was clearly evident to the minds of his readers when Mann presented it to them in 1924. 'It was in 1924, after endless intermissions and difficulties, that there finally appeared the book which, all in all, had me in its power for twelve years,' Mann explained. 'I conceived the idea as a humorous satire: the atmosphere was to be that strange mixture of death and lightheartedness I had found in the sanatorium.' But the brief, light-hearted story of Hans's encounter with life and death in his Alpine sanatorium had now been transformed into a vast novel, of over 700 pages. It remained a comic work, but now it became the comedy of a tragic historical transition. The changes, in fact, were so vast that one can fairly say they represent the transition from the early to the late Thomas Mann, and show his development from a late nineteenth-century to a Modernist writer.

They also express the transition from the pre-war to the post-war epoch, from the world of order and commerce to the world of political disorder and conflict, from one state of existence to another. This is what gives the book its exceptional stature and its importance. Time and history had upturned its narrative – more so, perhaps, than any other work of Modernism. They had pushed its story and its conflicts of ideas back into a distant epoch, an epoch which nonetheless had produced the crisis of the present tragic age. As Mann explains in the Foreword to the novel: 'The exaggerated pastness of our narrative is due to its taking place before the epoch when a certain crisis shattered its way through life and consciousness and left a deep chasm behind. It takes place – or, rather, deliberately to avoid the present tense, it took place, and had taken place – in the long ago, in the old days, the days of the world before the Great War, in the beginning of which so much began that has scarcely left off beginning. Yes, it took place before that; yet not so long before.'

So, it is very clear, Mann's twelve-year struggle with the book had to do with a good deal more than purely literary problems. For him, it meant the working out and the changing of deep-seated beliefs, and forced him to come to terms with events that had shattered the time of the world and transformed the responsibilities of artists and intellectuals. That is why Hans's departure from the flatlands and into the new time-scheme and the 'heightened' experiences of the Alpine sanatorium is no process of escape or detachment from real life or historical time. Hans's experiences during his seven-year stay are a personal growing up. But they are also the emotional, intellectual and political discoveries of an age, a prewar world itself obsessed with death and disorder, moving towards conflict. The 'heightening' is not just what has happened to Hans, but to the writing of the novel itself. Indeed it shaped the very form and method of the book, as Mann explained: 'It passes beyond realism by means of symbolism, and makes realism a vehicle for intellectual and ideal elements.' The characters all become more than themselves, 'exponents, representatives, emissaries from worlds, principalities, domains of the spirit.' Hans himself realizes that we experience life not just for ourselves, but communally, for our society and our age. The sanatorium is the world in its heightened form, and *The Magic Mountain* is a fable of the experience of Europe as it plummets towards World War.

3

When *The Magic Mountain* came out in the troubled Germany of 1924, Thomas Mann was already a very famous writer, the leading novelist of modern German literature. He took his representative role seriously. The Hungarian Marxist critic Georg Lukacs was to identify Mann as one of the major modern writers, and see him as the greatest German voice of his age. Mann, he said, was indeed 'representative', and in the key sense of being in tune with the march of modern reality and thought. Lukacs's interpretation of Mann is, of course, part of his own Marxist account of modern history as it moves from the bourgeois to the 'socialist' age. It also has a special interest because Lukacs is almost certainly a source for one of the characters in the novel, the Catholic and revolutionary Naphta. Mann had some important debates with Lukacs and we can understand the mutual interest of the two men. To Lukacs, Mann was *not* a Modernist writer, for he saw Modernism as largely an evasion of history, a retreat into private consciousness. Mann, on the other hand, saw the world 'as it was'. 'Thomas Mann presents a complete picture of bourgeois life and its predicaments,' Lukacs observes, 'but it is a picture of a precise moment, a precise stage of development.'

In fact Mann's work covered a dreadful series of such moments and developments. For the achievement of Mann's lifetime was the production of an *oeuvre* of major books that lead us from the earliest days of Germany as a nation through to the present postwar world, where Germany is not one state but two. Mann's first major book *Buddenbrooks* appeared in 1901, as the century started, and his last, *The Confessions of Felix Krull*, in 1954. Mann's lifetime therefore covered the growth of Germany from a confederation into a leading industrial and scientific nation, crossed with two World Wars and a double sense of defeat, and reached into the era of both German liberal democracy and German communism. And *Buddenbrooks* itself reached back three more generations, so that Mann's work effectively spanned the era from the age of Goethe to the age of Goering. His career began as a national writer who was challenging the twentieth-century bourgeois revolution from the standpoint of an older, deeper view of *Kultur* and spirit. It ended with Mann as an exile, driven from Germany by the rise of Hitler. The books of the great Nobel Prize-winner (he won it in 1929, after the appearance of *The Magic Mountain*) were burnt, and Mann fled to Switzerland and then the United States, a witness to what state modern ideas had brought the world. The writer of an ambiguous German conservatism had now become the spokesman for a modern humanism – in an era in which some of the troubling and deathly ideas that run through *The Magic Mountain* had become a terrible actuality.

Possibly, then, it is useful to describe Mann as a novelist of a bourgeois age, if we also say that it is that age in a succession of crises that particularly affected Germany but also the world at large. What is more, the term 'bourgeois' needs to cover the burgher age of the old nineteenth-century German and Hanseatic merchants, and the age of new science, industrialism, and imperialism, which went through almost all the conflicts and crises of modern politics and historical violence. That terrible epoch is at the centre of Mann's work. There are some very telling phrases in *The Magic Mountain* where Mann sharply sums up one of his essential preoccupations. He observes that, when the times seem to offer a hollow silence to all the questions a man puts, then a laming of the human spirit and indeed of the human body itself is likely to occur. 'In an age that affords no satisfying answer to the eternal question of "Why?," "To what end?", a man who is capable of achievement over and above the average and expected modicum must be equipped either with a moral remoteness and single-mindedness which is rare indeed and of heroic mould, or else with an exceptionally robust vitality. Hans Castorp had neither the one nor the other of these . . .' – and so he is the common or mediocre man, the representative of most of us. In his naivety he becomes an example of the way we suffer history in the time of the new industrial state, when old ideas and personalities begin to disintegrate under change, when reason wars with instinct, nationalism with inter-nationalism, the past with the future. These, of course, are just the battles that Hans Castorp encounters in his hermetic experience in the sanatorium, as his own needs and desires are debated by the gallery of international figures who, intellectually and erotically, fight for his soul just as the doctors seek to diagnose his body.

And, rather less naively, these are just the conflicts and problems that Mann was consistently attempting to deal with from the begin-ning to the end of his literary and public life. Mann was born in 1875, only four years after the incorporation of the German Empire, in Lübeck. His father was one of the great burghers of this old Hanseatic city-port on the Baltic – though after his death it was found that the family fortune was exhausted. With his mother, who came from a Brazilian background, and his brothers and sisters, Mann moved in

1893 to Munich, in Southern Germany, with its very different spirit. Here he attended the university, and resolved with a strong dedication to become a writer. While working as an insurance clerk he wrote some early stories in the spirit of Naturalism. Then his massive novel of some 1,000 pages, *Buddenbrooks: The Decline of a Family*, appeared in 1901. It was an enormous success, with the general public and with the intellectual community. 'Without any doubt we shall have to take note of this name,' wrote the poet Rainer Maria Rilke. It was in effect the story of Mann's own family, told over four generations. In many respects it was a classic realist novel, drawing on the spirit of Tolstoy and Flaubert, though also on the more Naturalistic and deterministic spirit of Zola and Fontane. Realism gives the book its solid, burgher density, but Naturalism gives it the scientific and medical detachment ('Now a typhoid infection proceeds in the following way . . .') and the analytical precision that was to become one of the great features of all Mann's work.

The classic realist novel has sometimes been called the 'burgher epic', and the term fits *Buddenbrooks* to perfection. The book is nothing if not solid, and it is the story of an apparently solid society, the saga of a great Lübeck merchant family over their rise and their fall. At the same time Mann shows a strange new spirit coming from the degeneration of the family – and it is nothing less than the fragile, individualistic, self-searching sense of art. The last Buddenbrook, the young Hanno, is an artist, in the modern decadent way. He is nervous, fragile, and exhausted, and he dies young of typhoid, almost as if he has willed it. As in much of Mann's work, great vitality often means a lack of spirituality, while the instinct toward the artistic is often destructive and deathly. The mismatch of physique and intellect is evident in Hanno, and clear in most of Mann's later books. With it goes a feeling of the conflict between the artist and bourgeois society. Equally there is the inner conflict of the artist between the needs for order and reason and for erotic and dangerous knowledge. These are the struggles of the heritage of nineteenth-century literature and philosophy, and Mann was a profoundly learned writer in the European tradition. Mann's artists – as he went on to portray them in his works that followed, such as *Tonio Kröger* in 1903, and then in *Death in Venice* – are drawn towards decay and disorder not just because they live in a world of historical decline, though that is important. They also live at the end of the quarrel between classic and romantic art, and need to know and understand the romantic dark underside of life, to ask what life in its scientific and spiritual nature is. Though Hans Castorp is no artist, he will inherit all these issues on his mountain.

Buddenbrooks is the start of these concerns, and though it is a typical work of nineteenth-century realism it shows that realism questioning itself under new concerns, producing new literary forms. Mann's later books, even the most metaphysical and fantastic, were to retain a quality of burgher solidity. They are dense in material and aim for an epic sweep. But they also challenge that material solidity, seeking a deeper mystery that art can unlock. The realistic aim quarrels with artistic desire, order quarrels with anarchy, the intellect with the passions, vitality with disease. The world and all ideas possess a Janus face, and the solid world secretes the aesthetic desire almost as if it were an inner sickness. This displays itself in Mann's form of art, which is fascinated with the grotesque, and constantly uses tragicomedy, irony and parody. It is significant that a book that preoccupied Mann for much of his writing lifetime was the story of Felix Krull the 'confidence man', the creator of illusions that deceive people with their reality. Mann treated the story of Krull several times, and was working on it when he died. Krull, the artist in deceptions, is partly a figure for the artist himself, and is able to create 'a compelling and effective reality out of nothing'. Like his creator, he also has a 'parodying nature'. From *Buddenbrooks* onward, Mann was to concentrate on the difficult task of modern art, and the difficult and dangerous venture of the modern artist.

Here then, was the main theme of a writer who was a clear-minded and analytic figure, with a strong romantic inheritance behind him, and it is a theme that links his work with the general spirit of Modernism. That conflict between the bourgeois, solid, material world which in its very vitality is indifferent to art, and the aesthetic world which in its very decadence questions and undermines the materialistic, instrumental view of life – all these things are persistent themes of

Modernist writing. Often this goes with a sense of profound cultural decline, a feeling that everything that had created the older culture, invested it with the values of the questing intellect, and made it stable, spiritual and mythical, has been defeated by the coming of the new. The new age is an ennervated age, weakened not simply by the material- ism and spiritual emptiness of bourgeois life but by the rise of the modern masses and the modern city. For some writers – in Germany this was clear among the Expressionist poets and dramatists – that new indus- trial city with its masses was itself an occasion for political and emo- tional excitement: this was what modernity was. For Mann – certainly the Mann of the prewar years who first conceived *The Magic Mountain* – it was also an antithesis to what he valued most, the older, spiritual Germany of philosophy and *Kultur*. Yet Mann admired Nietzsche, the great German philosopher of his day, and his vision of the need for artistic heroism in the new circumstances. Nietzsche held that the conflict of order and disorder was rooted in the foundations of social and cultural existence. He also celebrated the energies of the New, and the endless conflict of form and formlessness – one reason he so appealed to the Modernists. He asked for a new reconciliation of spirit and emotion, a new kind of will. And that search for the *modern* reconciliation is the great theme of Mann's work.

The artistic task was not to be easy, as Mann made clear in the novels and novellas that followed on from *Buddenbrooks*. The idea that in the material bourgeois world the artist becomes the superfluous man, exiled to explore spiritual knowledge on his own, is the great preoccupation of *Tonio Kröger* and *Death in Venice*. Thus Aschen- bach recognizes the paradoxical world in which art lives, and acknow- ledges that we poets 'by our natures are prone not to excellence but excess.' The modern artist must be bourgeois *and* artist, classic *and* romantic. These divisions of being, which Mann constantly explored, are evidently in part the product of his own nature. He was split two ways between the patrician and mercantile values of his father and the artistic temperament of his mother, between northern Lübeck with its chilly air and its Protestant ethic and southern Munich with its car- nivalesque and Catholic atmosphere, between an old, spiritual German conservatism and *Kultur* and a heady, dangerous sense of erotic delight in the ways of the new. But they were also the great dialogues of the German spirit and the dialectical opposites of the major German philosophers – the split between Goethe and Wagner, Schopenhauer and Nietzsche. And such oppositions, doublenesses, ironies and ambiguities were to become the stuff of Mann's fiction, which is as notable for its inner antagonisms as it is for its attempted resolutions.

And all of this is distilled in *The Magic Mountain*, one of those remarkable novels that seems to draw together all the deepest preoccupations of the author. Its hero, it is true, is not an artist, but his enforced residence in the world above the world presents him with the emotional, philosophical and political problems that might preoccupy the modern artist. *The Magic Mountain* turned into a work of enormous ambition. It has the epic sweep of *Buddenbrooks*, and something of its great physical solidity, its rootedness in place, atmosphere and character. At the same time it is a work that steps back from the world, into abstractions, ideas, dialogues, debates and duels, in the attempt to reconcile the adversarial needs of the age. Alas, as the events that happened over its writing were to show, that resolution could only be tragic. These dialogues about faith and humanism, reason and emotion, vitality and disease, are actually the very dialogues and conflicts that had brought Europe to war. As the end of the book suggests, Mann still hoped to transcend them, though 'the prospects are poor.' Mann closes, indeed, on a note of ironic indifference, refusing to concern himself about whether Hans Castorp survives the war or not. After all, he has experienced existence, and come to a dream of love. He has faced in his spirit the Nietzschean questions, though one more question remains, asked very sceptically in the very last lines: 'Out of this universal feast of death, out of the extremity of fever, kindling the rain-washed evening sky to a fiery glow, may it be that Love one day shall mount?'

4

At the beginning of *The Magic Mountain*, Hans Castorp is 23, a 'still unwritten page', a character of puppy-like comic innocence, who is ready to feel the ironic edge of Mann's pen. He is a typical hero of a familiar kind of German fiction, the *Bildungsroman*, the story of a young man's social, moral and intellectual education, though he is arrogant and absurd enough to suggest that the classic form will not simply be followed, but parodied. He comes from Hamburg, has a classic burgher education, and is a typical figure of his city and his age. There are, however, some signs that set him apart. There are the deaths of his mother and father, and the present illness of his cousin – all this suggesting that there is possibly some hereditary 'weakness' in the family. And then there is something just a little incomplete about his devotion to work, because it has evidently tired him recently. All this is one reason why his visit to the sanatorium might be of some good to Hans himself as well as a kindness to his cousin. Nonetheless he begins his stay simply as a guest, looking at the 'horizontallers', as the director of the establishment, the Hofrat Behrens, calls his patients, with a very critical and detached eye. They are an extraordinary international mixture, they appear grotesque, they are disorderly and decadent, and surprisingly engaged in an active erotic life, and they bring little of the dignity that Hans expects from those who are touched by the hand of death.

But already it is apparent that Hans is not as detached from them as he likes to think. He keeps having troubled dreams, feverish reactions, a troubling nosebleed, finally a serious cold. As Mann subtly indicates, these ailments are not exterior infections but an inward condition. Hans also finds that the feverishness affects his own erotic feelings. The great reminder comes when, after his nosebleed, he suddenly recalls a heated friendship he had had with a fellow-student at school. It was a brief episode, largely to do with the borrowing of a pencil, but it displays a new aspect of his nature. That there is something psychological or 'Freudian' about all this is emphasized by the fact that he now attends a lecture by the psychologist of the establishment, Dr Krokowski, who talks about how love can become displaced into a form of disease, and that love and illness are therefore closely linked. As, in a scene of marvellous comic symbolism, Hans listens, he finds himself unwittingly preoccupied by the white arm, the stubby gnawed fingers, and the visible spine of Mme Clavdia Chauchat, a Russian woman of a clumsy, chaotic and 'morbid' Slavic temperament. She has annoyed Hans, the lover of order and politeness, by banging the door every time she enters the dining-room. But a subtle attraction that could not have developed on the flatland now grows, and becomes the main preoccupation of the early stage of Hans's time in the sanatorium.

Hans is indeed ripe to become a patient of the place, and toward the end of his three weeks he goes to Behrens with his increasing symptoms. As Behrens explains to him, the mountain is not only good *against* disease. It is also good *for* it: 'it brings the latent weakness to the surface and makes it break out.' Hans is indeed ailing, and Behrens and Krokowski welcome Hans as someone with 'a talent for illness', 'one of us'. We are never to be entirely sure how ill Hans really is, and to what extent his seven-year stay in the sanatorium amounts to a chosen withdrawal from the world. But, as a friend he has made in the sanatorium, Herr Settembrini, an Italian humanist and 'windbag', who espouses the ideas of modern progressive liberalism, tells him, he appears to have an 'instinct for illness' – rather as Mann's earlier artist-heroes have. Coming into Hans's room and casting wide the curtains, in search of 'light', he warns Hans he seems to have chosen to be 'lost to life'. 'The spirit must protest in pride and anguish against the dictates of the wretched body,' he pronounces. Settembrini is a comic character, not least in the fact that he himself is ill and an inmate. But Hans is indeed falling out with the world of the flatlands, the world of practical moneymaking which he now starts to see as cruel and indifferent. Settembrini asserts the need for involvement, political and moral advance, and the need for the intellect to revolt against the dictates of nature and the physical body. 'I represent the world, the interest of this life, against a sentimental withdrawal and negation, classicism against romanticism,' he explains.

Settembrini claims his pedagogue's right to advise Hans on his illness, asking to be allowed to be beside him 'in your essays and experiments, and to exercise a corrective influence when there appears to be a danger of your taking up a destructive position.' Evidently Hans's mind and soul, as well as his body, are destined to come in for extensive diagnosis and treatment. His adventures, intellectual, physical and erotic, have begun, a series of adventures which will analyse the fundamentals of the modern self. And the fundamentals are what Hans will find when he is taken to the X-ray room. 'X-ray anatomy, you know, triumph of the age,' says the witty, chatty Dr Behrens, displaying to Hans the complex anatomy of the human body – the bony structure of the female arm, 'what they put around you when they make love', and the pulsing bag of the human heart. In a macabre moment, Hans is encouraged to look at his own hand through the screen, and sees 'precisely what he must have expected, but what is hardly permitted man to see, and what he had never thought it would be vouchsafed him to see; he looked into his own grave.' The skeleton beneath the skin is revealed: 'the flesh in which he walked disintegrated, annihilated, dissolved in vacant mist . . . for the first time in his life he understood that he would die.'

The patient who follows Hans into the room is Clavdia Chauchat, and the macabre but voluptuous relationship between them is extended. Clavdia, with her Russian decadence and passivity, is a figure for the chaotic and the formless, the world beyond order. The remarkable X-ray scene is shortly matched by another, in which Behrens shows Hans a portrait of Clavdia he has painted, and which hangs in his room. As the X-ray has portrayed the skeleton, so the portrait displays the flesh that clothes it, in all its erotic and its scientific complexity. Behrens discourses on the modern science of the flesh, and, acknowledging that to be interested in life one must also be interested in death, Hans begins a course of reading, in order to explore life's 'sacred, impure mysteries'. In one of the most remarkable passages of the book, Hans asks himself, on the strength of his reading, the question: 'What is life?' 'No one knew,' he realizes. 'It was undoubtedly aware of itself as soon as it was life, but it did not know what it was . . . It was a secret, an ardent stirring in the frozen chastity of the universal . . . conveyed and shaped by the somehow awakened voluptuousness of matter . . . the reeking flesh.'

Then, in an extraordinary vision, the image of life comes to him, blemished and impure, a 'living unit of a very high order', a monstrous multiplicity of breathing and self-nourishing individuals. This chapter is called 'Research', and the vision is learned – it merges anatomy and science, modern engineering and modern philosophy, atomic separation and inevitable disease. It is also profoundly and decadently erotic, as life reaches out to Hans and embraces him, and takes on the naked shape of Clavdia Chauchat. As Mann said of this scene: 'There grows in the young man, out of the experience of sickness, death, and decay, the idea of man, the "sublime structure" or original life, whose destiny then becomes a real concern of his simple heart. Castorp is sensuously and intellectually infatuated with death . . . but his dire love is purified, at least in moments of illumination, into an inkling of a new humanity.'

5

This moment of vision, less than half-way through the book, is surely the turning-point of *The Magic Mountain*. It establishes Hans as a modern hero, and the true kin of other Thomas Mann heroes – Tonio Kröger and Aschenbach before him, and Leverkühn in *Doctor Faustus* after him. It is the basis of his quest, the ground for his adventures, the justification for the seven-year pilgrimage on the mountain. In later years, Thomas Mann was to offer various accounts of just what Hans's quest is. It was, he suggested, a journey into decadence; but he also described it as his pursuit of 'the idea of man, the concept of a future *humanity* which has experienced the deepest knowledge of sickness and death.' The two notions are not entirely contradictory, but they can affect our view of the way we read *The Magic Mountain*. Like *Death in Venice*, it can be seen as a novel of romantic decadence, an ironic voyage to the heart of darkness. Or it can be read as a work of optimism in which a new hope for humanism and love is established. It can, in short, be interpreted as a diagnosis of the disease of the age, or the story of its cure. This double quality is familiar enough in the duplicitous works of Modernism. It is also a manifestation of Mann's very distinctive irony and ambiguity.

Hans himself is a difficult hero to grasp. He remains an innocent, and something of a mediocre young man. At the same time he is also 'life's problem child', experiencing and attempting to resolve, with a degree of dignity as well as a certain absurdity, the great problems of his time. He holds on to much of his stiff conservatism, and Clavdia, as their relationship complicates, describes him as a young man who loves order over liberty – '*Bourgeois, humaniste et poète – voilà l'allemand au complet.*' But he also becomes half in love with easeful death, and a pursuer of life's deep, decadent ambiguities. The conflict becomes clear in the scene called 'Walpurgis Night', the night of carnival and misrule, when the conventions break down. It echoes a scene in Goethe's *Faust*, from which Settembrini quotes as the sanatorium carnival begins. Here, despite Settembrini's warnings about the lure of irony, paradox and decadence, Hans begins to express his love for Clavdia Chauchet, switching from German to French, the language of erotic feeling, a language without responsibility which he can speak without truly speaking. She confronts his bourgeois instincts with the spirit of the decadent French poets, declaring that morality is found not in reason and discipline but in the dangerous adventures of evil. She brings back to Hans the image of the young student who had attracted him, and whose pencil he had borrowed; he now borrows Clavdia's. The scene of seduction is enormously comic, but it grows more intense as he learns that Clavdia is leaving the sanatorium the next day. Hans goes to Clavdia's room, 'possesses' her, and comes away with a token: her X-ray photograph.

This scene, which we do not see directly, is Hans's one completely erotic moment in the novel, for Clavdia goes the next day and their affair is never resumed. Settembrini retires to the village, his rational advice neglected. Hans is left to make sense of the knowledge he has gained, the decadent wisdom he has acquired. But an intellectual replacement for Clavdia soon arrives on the scene, an old intellectual adversary of Settembrini's, the strange, Jewish and Jesuitical Naphta. Where Settembrini stands for liberal and bourgeois progress, Naphta rejects the whole idea of individualism and libertarianism, and historical development through reason. These things have divided mankind from the common and unindividualized spirituality which he sees as the basis of life. Faith and not intellect is the source of knowledge, and where Settembrini is nationalistic and progressive, Naphta is mystical and fatalistic. Though trained as a Jesuit, he also expresses his sympathy with Marxist ideas of a revolutionary terror, believing that the triumph of the proletariat will sweep away moneymaking and individuation, and return mankind to the unindividualistic anonymity that will restore them as children of God. At once aristocrat and revolutionary, he is a voluptuary of thought who believes in the 'morally chaotic All'. As Settembrini says of him, his form is logic, but his essence is confusion. As for the question of health and disease, he takes a view that Mann himself sometimes expressed, believing that man voluntarily descends into disease, and that through this immersion in nature we can be led, by fanatics and true believers, back toward health.

The Magic Mountain is everywhere a comic novel. And Hans's two guides, Settembrini and Naphta, who dominate the next section of the book, are comic characters. Settembrini, the pedagogue, is always the windbag, full of an Italian flamboyance and excess. Naphta, the mystagogue, has a grotesque and sinister air, with his conspiratorial scholasticism. The ideas of both have a comic extravagance, but they are essentially serious, and represent a fundamental modern conflict that is to tease Hans's mind and soul. They reflect the conflicts between Thomas Mann and his brother Heinrich over the war. Settembrini, like Heinrich, believes in material progress and democratic liberty. Naphta, like Mann, distrusts the bourgeois soul, seeing it as materialist, lacking in spirituality, and destructive of culture. Settembrini is closer to the spirit of Rousseau, Naphta to that of Schopenhauer and Wagner. For all their excesses, they represent two lineages of European thought in conflict, and the battleground is Hans's soul. It is in effect the battlefield that Nietzsche defines in *The Birth of Tragedy*, the struggle of culture and nature from which civilization springs.

Settembrini represents the Apollonian principle, humanistic, classical, civilized, and Naphta the Dionysian, gothic, unruly and elemental. But this is also, of course, a version of the battle that, as Mann saw it, was to be fought across the battlefields of Europe over the period when he wrote the book.

The latter part of the story is that of Hans's attempt to 'take stock' and reconcile this weighty conflict. 'All this confusion must be reconciled,' he tells his cousin Joachim. Hans himself does not cease to be a comic character as he attempts to bring together the major problems of the world in his solemn and God-like way. 'True, down on the plain he had never been aware of them, nor probably ever would have been. It was up here that the thing came about, where one sat piously withdrawn, looking down from a height of five thousand feet or so upon the earth and all that therein was.' But it is now clear that his task has grown more serious, and his hunger to reconcile the abundant opposites of the novel – above all those between the rational and the irrational, between knowledge of life and knowledge of death – more profound. His great need to reconcile these ideas within his own spirit leads to another major scene of revelation, the chapter called 'Snow', which plays the same central role in the second half of the novel that the section titled 'Research' took in the first. It is one of the major scenes of modern literature, comparable with Mrs Moore's encounter with the panic and emptiness of the Marabar caves in *A Passage to India*, or Hemingway's crucial experience of the wound of war on the Italian front, which he then explored again and again in his fiction. It is a meeting with the nihilism that lies behind the world, the meaninglessness that lies behind the hope for human order. It also has a distinctively Germanic and European stamp.

Mann took the title as well as some of the key ideas of *The Magic Mountain* from Nietzsche: 'Now the Olympian magic mountain opens, as it were, to our view and shows us its roots.' In 'Snow' the magic mountain does indeed open to reveal its roots, as Hans puts his 'narrow, hyper-civilized breast' to the test of nature. Struggling to understand the conflicting views of life presented to him by his guides, he feels the need to immerse himself in the destructive element, and confront the limits of being. The great elements of nature on the mountain, where the 'deathly silence of the snows' prevails, seem 'a fitting theatre for the issue of his involved thoughts.' He feels one of the great romantic desires, *Liebestod*, a wish 'to carry the thrilling contact with these deadly natural forces up to a point where full embrace was imminent.' Against sanatorium rules, he buys skis, and sets off onto the mountain. Caught in a snowstorm, he is trapped for a time on the slopes. A vision, anonymous and communal, opens out to him − of a sunny Mediterranean classical harmony, evidently Nietzsche's Apollonian world of civilization. Then it shades into the Dionysian, into a vision of horror and human sacrifice. How could civilization then exist? 'Were they, these children of the sun, so sweetly courteous to each other, in recognition of that horror?' he asks. This is Hans's fullest vision of the Janus face of life and death, of the counter-positions that he has been confronted with throughout the book. Yet Man, he thinks, is the Lord of counter-positions, and will have to master them. This leads him to a key conclusion, which we may assume to be Mann's: 'I will keep faith with death in my heart, yet well remember that faith with death and the dead is evil, is hostile to mankind, as long as we give it power over thought and action. For the sake of goodness and love, man shall let death have no sovereignty over his thoughts.'

This is the most positive moment of the novel, but there is more dismay to come, as the world of the sanatorium changes, and the years pass on toward 1914. His cousin Joachim, the soldier, now returns, his illness worse, and he dies. The Dance of Death is clearly not over. An irritable lethargy now seems to come over the inhabitants of the Berghof, and Hans himself seems to weaken in will and purpose. Then, in the company of Clavdia Chauchat, who is deeply attached to him, a new teacher arrives, Mynheer Peeperkorn, a Dutch planter from Java. Peeperkorn is quite unlike Hans's two previous advisers, Settembrini and Naphta, whom he pushes to the sidelines. He is, for one thing, no pedagogue, and is incoherent, and often silent in the face of nature's mysteries. But he is a man of 'great personal weight, though incoherent', and a man who possesses 'the mystery of personality, something above either cleverness or stupidity.' Kindly, pagan and royal, a figure of majestic inadequacy, he is a cross between

Bacchus and Dionysus, an expression of the life-force and its mysteries. However he does not remain long in the scene. Suddenly he kills himself one night with a snake-like poison, and the mysteries he represents go underground.

Goethe had seen the world divided into four distinct epochs: an innocent age of poetry, an age when mysteries grow so complex as to produce an epoch of theology, a following age of philosophy, where reason dominates, and then an age of prose – the worst of the ages, when the attempt to apply reason to mystery forces it back into its barbaric state. Myths decline, fanatics arise, and scattered remnants of tradition are seized to guide men through an age of decline. Nietzsche too saw the coming of an age in which the intellect could not master nature, generating the tragedies of nihilism. The book ends on such a tragedy. The increasing rage in the sanatorium finds its expression in an embittered quarrel between Settembrini and Naphta. Despite Hans's attempts at reconciliation, they acknowledge that their principles are totally antagonistic, and insist on fighting a duel. Settembrini, claiming his right to act according to his reason, fires into the air. Naphta, calling for moral chaos, the anointed Terror that the age demands, turns his gun on himself, and shoots himself in the head.

These scenes prefigure the tragic and nihilistic end of the story. What philosophy cannot fulfil, the political and historical world does. After Naphta has gone, Settembrini falls ill, but into his voice there comes the sound of the eagle as well as that of the dove. The war-clouds that will divide Europe and make nonsense of the prophetic hopes and reconciliations of the upland world begin to sound the great *Götterdämmerung*. The historical thunderpeal fires the mine beneath the magic mountain. Hans is now freed from its enchantment, not by his own deeds and thoughts but by the acts of the historical powers. Like most of those in the sanatorium, he feels summoned away from the fundamental adventure of his life, the hermetic world of thought and discovery on the mountain, and down to the flatlands. He and Settembrini depart to fight on their different sides, and we last see Hans as one of a swarm of young men, soldiers, rushing through the smoke and mud of battle. He sings his favourite song, Schubert's 'The Linden Tree', a song itself of Germanic *Liebestod*, of love and death, and we are not to know whether he will survive. The nihilism of the age of prose is triumphant, and Hans's philosophical adventures and reconciliations end in this extremity of historical fever, a universal feast of death – out of which, just possibly, the principle of love might arise.

6

As we well know, love, the reconciliation of the mysteries, the marriage of reason with instinct, were not what survived from the Great War. The liberal reason of Settembrini remained in conflict with the prosaic residue of Naphta's irrational and mysterious dreams, and spawned a new age of totalitarianism. Mann himself hovered between Settembrini and Naphta, faith in reason and the cult of the compelling and demoniac mystery of existence which demands its tragic worship. In this he perhaps expressed, as he always had the power to do, the German soul. He looked backward to a great age of culture, depraved by modern history, and he tried to look forward to a new age of spirit. But in an age when the past was destroyed and the future of little promise, he found himself in the position of many of the great modern German thinkers, and became 'the ironic German', as he has been called. He nourished, for a time, the hope of a modern democracy in Germany, and the final and published version of *The Magic Mountain* comes from that period. But it was more than a novel of the German mind and soul. Indeed, though it was a novel of the prewar world, it was clearly a profound expression of the spiritual, philosophical and historical crisis of postwar times, times that were struggling with a sense of decline and nihilism.

The Magic Mountain takes a very German form in being a novel of ideas – a philosophical novel. It draws on a vast intellectual and cultural tradition and attempts to judge it in a new epoch. Yet the book is also profoundly ambiguous – as are many of the great modern novels – and it remains so to this day. Mann described the book as a search for

a Grail, a consecration, sought not only by his often foolish hero but
by the novel itself. 'It is the idea of the human being, the conception
of a future humanity that has passed through and survived the pro-
foundest knowledge of disease and death. The Grail is a mystery, but
humanity is a mystery too. For man himself is a mystery, and all
humanity rests on reverence before the mystery that is man.' Like
Conrad, a writer he deeply admired, and like many of his Romantic
German predecessors, Mann pursued that mystery to the end,
through the destructive element, the place where life becomes death
and individualized reason dissolves into anonymity or chaos. It returns
to the dark and often destructive vital energies, and yet, with Settembrini, it seeks reason and order, the desire for a humanism that
defeats and rebukes death and the nihilistic immersion in mystery for
its own sake.

Dark gods have continued to haunt the modern imagination,
challenging the enlightenment at every turn with the sense of neglected mysteries. Mann, in many ways a classical author, was perplexed
by them too, struggling to create a sense of reason that included and
enfolded the mysteries of life. Like Rilke, he sought to reconcile terror
and bliss through the means of art as vision. Like Freud, he sought to
portray the natural and unconscious energy that seems to work against
the survival of civilization, and generates its discontents unless the
energies can be repressed and sublimated. Like Nietzsche, who has
much to do with the nature of *The Magic Mountain*, he saw the conflict
of modern civilization as one between a flat, materialistic and profane
modern order and an 'upland' world that might afford transcendence
and offer something eternal within reality. That way might be by an
artistic and philosophical quest through the creative darkness of disease
and death. Man, Nietzsche had said, is '*the* sick animal'. And Thomas
Mann wrote of him: 'He well knew what he owed to his morbid
state, and on every page he seems to instruct us that there is no deeper
knowledge without experience of disease, and that all heightened
healthiness must be achieved by the route of illness.'

The Magic Mountain will no doubt remain the great novel of ideas
of the modern movement, ideas that retain their power for all the
spirit of comedy in which Mann displays their disturbing and un-

nerving import. But the book will continue to retain its double face –
as a portrait of the death-dance of a civilization in an epoch of decline,
and as a work that attempts a great modern resolution of our
underlying spiritual, moral and intellectual conflicts, and moves
toward a new humanism. As some critics have observed, the duplicity
is inevitable, because while the intellectual direction of the book is
towards the recovery of humanism, the historical thrust of it must
inevitably be towards the war which engulfed the modern Europe in
which Hans Castorp's mental pilgrimage occurs. We can read this
situation in different ways. Lukacs suggests that historical reality
undermines and ironizes Hans's hermetic life on the mountain. For
other critics, Hans's pilgrimage and Mann's attempt to reconcile
conflict is the crucial thing, and represents a possibility that has for the
moment been betrayed in the historical world. For yet others, it is
precisely the conflicts that evolve on the mountain that lead the European world to its tragic war. According to these different views, Hans
Castorp himself can be seen either as an always innocent and foolish
hero, or else as a young man who makes a profound moral and
intellectual discovery and, on the magic of the mountain, acquires a
great human dignity.

But, variously as the book can be understood in an age that still
battles with similar questions, there can be little doubt of its ambition, its
scale, and of course its greatness. It marked the beginning of a new
period in Mann's writing, and a line of great books followed – *Joseph and
His Brothers, Lotte in Weimar*, and the great treatment of the Faust legend
and its implication for the artist in the age of Fascism, *Doctor Faustus*.
There were also remarkable shorter works, including *Mario and the
Magician*, an earlier bitter treatment of Fascism. In 1929 Mann, seen as a
modern humanist writer, was awarded the Nobel Prize for Literature.
Four years later, this major German writer was driven into exile by the
rise of Hitler, and saw his books condemned in Germany, and his person
excommunicated. Living first in Switzerland, then in the United States,
he became one of the great figures of humanist courage, standing firm
against the Fascist movement. He took American citizenship, and described himself as a 'world citizen', condemning the terrible era of
German nationalism that had led onward to the Holocaust.

To the end something of the political and moral ambiguity that always marked his writing remained, revealed in part by his attitude to Communism in Eastern Europe. Both Settembrini and Naphta had spoken of their hope for a modern revolution, in Settembrini's case in the interests of human progress, in Naphta's in the interest of the Holy Terror. What had happened in Eastern Europe was closer to the second than the first, but Mann expressed some hope for revolutionary democratic socialism, less because it represented a triumph for the proletariat than as a prospect for the human spirit. He deplored the division of Germany, and he was dismayed by the McCarthy witch-hunts in America. In 1952 he moved again to Switzerland and settled near Zurich, returning to work again on an early theme, *The Confessions of Felix Krull*. In *Doctor Faustus* he had explored the notion that the commitment to art may become a demonic contract. In *Felix Krull*, more comically, he saw it as a form of the confidence trick, for it was not only a quest for the spirit but a magical attempt to deceive us into the truth of fictions. Art, Nietzsche had said, is always ambiguous, because it inverts life, and makes form its content. That comic yet dangerous ambiguity was the vision Mann finally felt the need to reassert. In 1954 *Felix Krull* was published, and in 1955 Mann died, at Kilchberg, near Zurich – only just out of sight of the magic mountain.

MARCEL
PROUST

I

From the small, innocent, provincial town of Combray, somewhere in the valley of the Loire southwest of Paris, two roads lead off in different and apparently quite opposite directions. One walk goes across the plain and by the blossom-laden hawthorn hedges towards Méséglise. It passes the park of Tansonville, the bourgeois house where Monsieur Charles Swann, the son of a wealthy Jewish stockbroker, lives with his wife and his daughter Gilberte. So this particular walk can be called either 'the Méséglise Way' or 'Swann's Way'. Though the people of Combray do not know it, M. Swann is a man of high taste and fashion who is highly regarded in the brilliant society of *belle-époque* Paris of the Third Empire, in these changeable years at the close of the nineteenth century and the start of the twentieth. He has, however, been the ardent lover of an elusive *cocotte*, Odette, and is now considered to have married beneath him. (Indeed his wife, and the mother of Gilberte, will prove in time to be that same Odette.) Thus 'Swann's Way' leads onward and outward from Combray – to Paris, its Jewish bourgeois world, which will be convulsed by the political tensions surrounding the famous Dreyfus case, the life of art and culture, literary *soirées*, and then onward into the world of smart society in which the well-connected Charles Swann can pass. But Swann's way also leads inward, into a psychological world of erotic desire, aesthetic appreciation, emotional dependence, and spiritual need.

The other walk goes along by the river to the ducal park and the chateau of the Guermantes family, one of the greatest and noblest families of France, descended from Geneviève de Brabant, who is in the legendary stories. This is the 'Guermantes Way.' The Guermantes way leads onward too, and upward – to Paris and its smart Faubourg

St-Germain, and into the great 'world'. The Duchesse de Guermantes, Oriane, is rarely seen in the village, but beyond her are figures yet more remote. The Prince and Princesse de Guermantes are at the very heights of society, at the pinnacles of nobility, rank and dignity. This Guermantes way therefore ascends toward the magical domain of wealth, power, rank and snobbery. But it too has its inside and its underside, for the aristocracy faces its own struggle for survival, has intimations of its own decline, and possesses its own forms of decadence. The cousin of the Duchesse, the Baron de Charlus, is a corrupt and decadent figure with homosexual tastes. Her nephew, the handsome Robert de Saint-Loup, will be destined to marry Gilberte Swann, and to die in the Great War which itself threatens and weakens this old international aristocracy. The two 'ways' thus represent very different things, different visions of social existence – not least a difference between the realm of art and culture and the snobbish and delicious fascinations of the *monde*, the social world. But both in fact belong to the flamboyant end of an era. The bastions of power and position held by the aristocracy are being infiltrated by the rising bourgeoisie. The *belle époque* itself will end with the war, and the entire map of society, manners and art will change. So these two worlds, apparently so different, are by no means disconnected from each other – as the marriage of Robert and Gilberte will suggest, and as the narrator of these different 'ways' and of the lives of their members will discover.

For the person who follows these two ways – first as a Sunday walk, and then as two versions or ways for living his own life – is the narrator of one of the greatest of all the modern novels, Marcel Proust's *A la recherche du temps perdu*. It is called *Remembrance of Things Past* in the famous English translation by C. K. Scott Moncrieff, lately marvellously redone by Terence Kilmartin to take in the changes that were made to the French edition of the novel when Proust's papers were re-examined. The English title chosen by Scott-Moncrieff comes from a Shakespeare sonnet ('When to the sessions of sweet silent thought/ I summon up remembrance of things past . . .') and remains evocative. But Proust disliked it, and it lacks the important emphases of the original – on the idea of loss, the idea of time, and the idea of *recherche*, or seeking again. For the novel is indeed a story of lost time – time lost in two ways. It is lost because it has gone, because its high moments have disappeared like a fleeing lover into the past, and its intensity seems beyond recapture. And it is lost because it has been wasted – in frivolous social activity, futile pursuits and irrelevances.

The narrator of these ways, these events, these hungry memories is unnamed, but later in his story he tells us we can call him 'Marcel', even though that is not his real name. He is, as it were, a close relation of Marcel Proust, while not quite being Proust himself. His indeed is a story of loss, but it is also an epic of rediscovery, of a life re-searched, re-examined and re-experienced. It is a life that starts in Combray, the seemingly innocent place of childhood summer holidays at the home of Marcel's great-aunt Léonie – where the peal of the bell at the gate, which heralds visitors, like M. Swann, and announces the Sunday walks along the two ways, starts an echo that sounds through the rest of his days. It starts too with a missing good-night kiss, as the visit of M. Swann deprives the young narrator of the attentions of his mother, so that here begins a history of emotional dependence and neurasthenic stress that will make his story a deep psychological narrative and a quest into the unconscious. It then leads onwards into the most complex areas of French high society and personal emotion. The two 'ways' – ways of walking, ways of life – form the basic ground plan of the novel, its social, its artistic, and its emotional geography. They give the book its underlying structure, for throughout it 'Marcel' follows one or the other of them to the distant destinations to which they lead, through art and frivolity, love and snobbery, until he too finds they end up in much the same place. But that psychological crisis of childhood, and the emotional desires and dependencies that come from it and shape Marcel's sense of need and vocation, will form its texture, its depth, its intensity, and bring about the resolution of the book.

Proust began the book in 1909, largely by following Swann's Way. He originally intended it to run to three volumes, and he published the first of them – *Du côté de chez Swann* (*Swann's Way*) – in 1913, at his own expense. The next volume, which followed the second way, and is called *Le Côté de Guermantes*, was already set in type when the

war came, delaying further publicaton. But this halt allowed Proust
to reconceive the whole book. He expanded it to three times its length,
from the original half million words to around a million and a quarter.
It was one of the great transformations of a literary idea, in some
respects even more remarkable than the impact of the war on Mann's
The Magic Mountain. Against the world of the *'jeunes filles en fleurs'*,
the young women of Marcel's youthful admiration and desire, could
be set the world of the modern Sodom and Gomorrah, of corrupted
love in a declining Society. The war itself pushed his memories even
further into the past, and set an irrevocable distance between the narrator and his emotional origins, driving the formative events of his
life down into deeper strata of existence. It halted much of the social
life, broke up the world of high society, and sent many of its members
to their deaths in battle or to emotional breakdown, like the breakdown in speech that afflicts the Baron de Charlus. It filled the story
with the symptoms of social anxiety, moral crisis, political division,
self-doubt and death. 'Combray' itself was occupied and fired on by
the Germans in the war. The book filled with more time, and death
now became a dominant preoccupation, intensifying the need for
memory and re-creation, *recherche.* Indeed Proust kept writing the
narrative up to the day of his own death in 1922.

So *A la recherche* . . . turned into a work of lifetime dedication, a
massive monument, like a cathedral, as Proust said himself, entire if
not perhaps quite completely finished. It is one of the great social
satires, and one of the finest of psychological novels. It is also a book
that, in its mass and its depth, lies essentially beyond summary – as its
author intended, for he meant it to be a novel of sensation and
emotion, not simply of record. One critic has put it perfectly: 'Proust
managed to make the pointless story interesting. He says: "Imagine,
dear reader, yesterday I was dunking a cake in my tea when it occurred
to me that as a child I spent some time in the country." For this he
uses eighty pages, and it is so fascinating that you think you are no
longer the listener but the daydreamer himself.' Proust meant the
book to be a total and enveloping world, a sensation which itself
explained the sensation of sensation. It is a work filled with more than
thirty years – overlapping and interfusing years, intricately threaded

with different stories and characters – of changing history and human existence. It is stocked with a massive society, Society with a capital 's' and a small one. It can, if we wish, be read as the major social satire of French life in the period of the *belle époque*, for, as Edmund Wilson said, Proust was 'perhaps the last great historian of the loves, the society, the intelligence, the diplomacy, the literature and the art of the Heartbreak House of capitalist culture . . .' It can be read as a work of an extraordinary analytical intelligence, looking at itself. As Joseph Conrad said: 'I don't think there has been such an example of the power of analysis, and I feel pretty safe in saying that there never will be another.' It can also be read as one of the most remarkable penetrations of inward psychology we have, a work of research into the deepest and darkest aspects of the mind and its process.

To understand the book, we need to respond to its brilliant social map, and the extraordinary comic and satirical portrait Proust gives us of the social, intellectual and artistic world of *belle-époque* France as the modern spirit and the modern movement came into being. We also need to respond to the erotic, the sensual, the psychological and the aesthetic intensity with which he forges this world and creates this novel. *A la recherche* . . . has produced two kinds of reader. There are those (including Angus Wilson, C. P. Snow and other modern British admirers who were themselves influenced by Proust) who have emphasized that Proust brought to the modern French novel a social awareness and intensity comparable to Balzac in the nineteenth century, or Henry James in the Anglo-American tradition. And there are those – they include Samuel Beckett and some of the French 'new novelists' – who emphasize that here is a novel of consciousness, new psychology and experiment much more comparable with the work of Joyce, Woolf, or Faulkner. Both books are there, for this is a rare kind of novel: an autobiography of human sensation which is not quite an autobiography, a satirical novel of society that withdraws from society, a novel of great geographical and physical materialism that dissolves space and place into the world of timeless time, a portrait of the modern artist who does not become an artist until he finishes his work of art. So if the book gives us, in the ground plan of the two 'ways', the book's world of society and its spatial dimension, something else provides its underlying form. And this is essentially Proust's idea of time – a modern idea, the idea of a contemporary of Einstein, of Freud, of Mann – and of the way we recover its mysterious operations, its inward duration, its fractures and its continuities.

2

'For a long time I used to go to bed early.' This is the first sentence of *A la recherche du temps perdu*, one of the shortest and plainest sentences in the book. The word 'time' is in the French title, it sounds in the first sentence and then again and again through the following sentences of the novel's opening, or its 'Overture', as Proust calls it, insisting on the book's underlying musicality. By the end of the first paragraph we are already in a confusion of time, not even sure when or where this opening scene takes place. 'I cannot understand how a man can take thirty pages to describe how he rolls over and over in his bed before he gets to sleep,' complained one publisher who rejected *Du côté de chez Swann* in 1913. The answer is that the state between waking and sleep is a state of heightened awareness of a kind that will dominate the sensibility of the entire novel and that this brilliant opening passage is not one scene but a hundred – for we are in no one time, no one place, no single narrative present, but rather being introduced to a general condition of being we would nowadays recognize as 'Proustian'.

In Proust's 'Overture', his sense of time and space, the measure and the motifs of his musical style, the beat of his cadence, the rhythm of his sensibility, are all stated for us. Our narrator, who is not only unnamed but strangely unplaced, closes his eyes in the second sentence. In the third, the thought that it is time to go to sleep wakens him from the sleep he is already in. Asking himself 'what time it could be', he begins reflecting on other sleepings and wakings, other rooms, other beds, other places of darkness. Most of this is written in the past continuous, that most ruminative of tenses, which lifts us out of chronology: 'I would ask myself . . . I would fall asleep . . .' The particular – even though Proust is a great novelist of particulars – is never quite particular. It turns into the general, into recurrence. These are all things he did 'for a long time'. Place turns to generalized space, the present moment turns into memory, and out of these things Proust constructs for us a dense and crowded cosmos.

Thomas Mann writes at the beginning of *The Magic Mountain*: 'Space, like time, engenders forgetfulness; but it does so by setting us bodily free from our surroundings and giving us back our primitive, unattached state.' But in *Remembrance of Things Past* one thing that space and time, working together, do *not* do is engender forgetfulness. In a brilliant little phrase in a brilliant little book on Proust, Samuel Beckett, who owed much to him, wrote: 'Proust had a bad memory . . . The man with a good memory does not remember anything because he does not forget anything.' Proust had a bad memory that was a million and a quarter words long, and would have been longer had there not been Death – though it is Death, as he is to make clear, that makes the search through the fragile past the essential task. 'When a man is asleep,' he tells us, 'he has in a circle round him the chain of the hours, the sequence of the years, the order of the heavenly bodies.' When he wakes, he consults all these things, and 'in an instant reads off his own position on the earth's surface and the time that has elapsed during his slumbers; but this ordered procession is apt to grow confused, to break ranks.' For sleep displaces place, and it de-clocks time. It also fragments consciousness, creating that half-waking sense that one does not know who one is. It does bring, therefore, Mann's 'primitive, unattached state': 'I had only the most rudimentary sense of existence, such as may lurk and flicker in the depths of an animal's consciousness.'

But what wakens is memory, which reconciles time and space. It is memory 'not yet of the place where I was, but of various other places where I had lived and might now very possibly be.' It comes 'like a rope let down from heaven to draw me out of the abyss of non-being, from which I could never have escaped by myself.' Memory is what constructs the space, shapes and confuses the room in which we lie, and gives things their names (Proust's original plan for his three-

volume book was to title them *The Age of Names, The Age of Words,*
and *The Age of Things*). Memory also reconstructs or recreates the
self, by estranging us from the world of habit. And it is involuntary, a
function of the body and the senses: 'Its [the body's] memory, the
composite memory of its ribs, its knees, its shoulder-blades, offered it
a whole series of rooms in which it had at one time or another slept,
while the unseen rooms, shifting and adapting to the shape of each
successive room that it remembered, whirled round it in the dark.'
The powers of this 'involuntary memory' are one of the great themes
of the book, and 'involuntary memory' is the trigger of many of the
key scenes and revelations of the novel. The most famous example of
them all is the madeleine – the small cake steeped in Marcel's tea –
which triggers so much of the world of lost time. Proust distinguishes
it entirely from voluntary memory – memory governed by intelligence and purpose, memory managed for proper inspection and
discussion, memory as collective agreement. For Proust memory is an
organ of being, not a remembered thing but an active process of
consciousness in motion. As Samuel Beckett says, involuntary memory
is an unruly magician which will not be importuned.

Involuntary memory is what makes the world strange, and turns
the familiar room into the unfamiliar, cracks open our sense of habit
and what we conventionally call reality. It dissolves and recreates the
room around us, turns it into all the rooms we have ever slept in and
all the sensations we have had in them. It links together the physical
sensations of our bodies with other past sensations of the same kind,
and is a sort of synaesthesia, a coming together of every one of the
senses. But, as one becomes 'well awake', it becomes something more
systematic. The 'good angel of certainty' locates us, and brings us into
this room (though we are not, of course, yet sure which one it is). So
the night thoughts take on more order, once memory has been set in
motion; 'as a rule I did not attempt to go to sleep at once,' he tells us,
'but used to spend the greater part of the night recalling our life in the
old days at Combray with my great-aunt, at Balbec, Paris, Doncières,
Venice, and the rest; remembering again all the places and people I
had known, what I had actually seen of them, and what others had
told me.' This is a more orderly kind of memory, and it opens out

into the novel proper. For next Proust will take us back to Combray, and to childhood, and the peal of the bell on the gate, and the way to the two ways – and the social world of the novel can begin.

And so memory turns not towards reportage but towards consciousness. Proust distinguishes carefully between involuntary memory and consciousness, and *A la recherche du temps perdu* is a novel of consciousness. Consciousness is the envelope of life in which we live and feel. It is also a creative state, a form of artistic discovery and composition. It is an alertness, an analytic power, a sense of the vividness of being, a search for revelation, an endeavour to shape and to frame – like the work of a painter. This whole matter of the nature of consciousness and psychology was the great preoccupation of his age, and one of the marks of the 'modern' vision of existence. That new vision deeply changed the form and construction of the modern novel, creating an art of subjectivity, inward perception and open form. In his preface to his early *Roderick Hudson* (1876), Henry James tells us that the 'centre of interest throughout . . . is Rowland Mallett's consciousness, and the drama is the very drama of that consciousness.' Such dramas of introversion came to abound in modern fiction – in James, Woolf, Joyce, Faulkner and of course Proust himself. Virginia Woolf would speak of consciousness as 'this, the essential thing . . . whether we call it life or spirit, or truth or reality . . .' For all these writers, consciousness was both a psychological and an aesthetic phenomenon – that is to say, it was not only a means of exploring the inner being and perception of their characters, but of opening out the actual form and structure of fiction, freeing it, as Woolf said, to be 'more itself'. Nonetheless, each one of these writers provides us with a different sense of what consciousness *is*, its nature, its anatomy, its impressions, its mechanisms of perception, its subjectivity. Proust's 'Overture' is a hymn to inwardness, a probing of the psychological world, *and* a process of aesthetic heightening – and *A la recherche* . . . is one of the most aesthetic of our novels.

So we could say that this idea of consciousness is the way Proust builds his bridge between memory, the ubiquitous amassing of re-collected and re-experienced sensation, and art. In this novel of difficult and closely examined ideas, that of art ('the most real of all things',

'Marcel' calls it) is probably the most difficult. In a famous phrase that
challenges the entire convention of realism, Proust writes: 'Genius
consists in the reflective power of a writer and not in the intrinsic
quality of the scene reflected.' Of course the scene Proust reflects to us
is itself vast and dense, but it too is filled with works of art, past and
present. Long passages describe the paintings of his Elstir, for instance,
and these descriptions are clues to Proust's own method in the novel.
It is also filled with artists and aesthetes: the connoisseur Swann, the
writer Bergotte, Elstir the painter, and the composer Vinteuil, whose
'little phrase' of music echoes through the book and helps give it its
form. These artists help Marcel learn many of the essential lessons of
art. At the same time the novel is set in the world where art and
society meet, in the Paris where the arts are cultivated, the new
movements flourish, and social life occurs at theatres, the opera,
musical *soirées*, the Paris which despite its great social conservatism
still saw over these same years the great explosion of the new arts,
from Impressionism and Decadence to Cubism and Abstraction.
Society itself is a form of art, an elegant, expressive artefact. It is also
its patron and sponsor, which is why a cultivated man like Swann is
cultivated by the aristocracy, and why Marcel himself finds a home in
Society and is divided between its various 'ways'.

Yet finally the story of *A la recherche du temps perdu* is the story of
the personal discovery of form, and of the growth of Marcel from
dilettante into artist. 'The human mind can never be satisfied unless it
can manage to achieve a clear analysis of what, at the moment of
composition, it produced unconsciously,' Proust wrote in an essay.
His book is an endless speculation on the form of art it is in process of
creating. It will acquire its wholeness as it goes along, and as it does
so the becoming of the book will be the becoming of the writer. On
the first page of the great fictional adventure, when Marcel falls asleep
without knowing he has done so, he has been reading a book – perhaps
a novel, or a work of history, or a musical score. When he wakes, he
realizes he has continued to think of that book while sleeping, and 'it
seemed to me that I myself was the immediate subject of my book.'
By the end of the book, Marcel is feeling old and ill. He has been in
sanatoria and feels a strong awareness of mortality. His fictional world

has aged, and his memories have taken on a new distance. Yet the task of his lifetime seems to have become clear, and the things that have taken him along so many ways have reached some sort of destination.

Swann's way and the Guermantes way, space and time, memory and consciousness, have begun to combine into one form. Indeed 'Marcel', by living through them, and Proust, by writing of them, have also begun to combine. All these things have led by their different routes to one common end that was not to be seen at the beginning. The book becomes a book, and that narrator who much earlier dreamed that he was the subject of a book now becomes the writer of one. The various ways and the lessons he has learned by taking them have brought him to his vocation: 'the true life, life at last discovered and illuminated, the only life really lived, is that of the writer,' he writes. In the end, this book, like so many other of the great modern novels, is a book about its own coming to existence, and the portrait of an artist. In a modernist paradox, Marcel ends the book starting the book he is in fact already finishing: 'In the awareness of the approach of death I resembled a dying soldier, and, like him too, before I died, I had something to write.'

3

A la recherche . . . is a book remarkable for its intensely autobiographical quality, and for the fact that the writing of it occupied much of its author's lifetime. Not surprisingly, the many critics who have explored this massive work have been much concerned with the question of whether the 'Marcel' of the novel and the author Marcel Proust should be considered as one and the same person. As his way of ending the novel shows, with 'Marcel' just beginning his book as Proust is finishing it, it was a question that Proust himself developed elaborately. T. S. Eliot pointed out how different is the man who experiences and the mind which creates, and Proust persistently makes the same point. As he said, writing about the great nineteenth-century social novelist Balzac: 'A book is the product of another self than the one we display in our habits, in our social life, in our vices. If we would try to comprehend it, we can do so only by seeking to recreate it within ourself at the very depth of our being.' The discovery of that 'hidden self' was the lifetime task Proust set himself. And there are many obvious differences between 'Marcel' and his author. Marcel is heterosexual, Proust was homosexual – though this particular piece of literary disguise has been common in literature, and the proclivities of the Baron de Charlus, whose homosexual tastes take him towards male brothels and bondage, are a part of Proust too. Marcel has no Jewish blood, while Proust did, and his divided heritage was important to him, not least in the matter of the Dreyfus case. Again the Jewish part of himself is present in the book, displaced into Charles Swann.

Thus it is possible to see *A la recherche* . . . as Proust's biographer George Painter does in his excellent and extensive life of him, as a work unique among the great novels because it is 'not, properly speaking, a fiction, but a creative autobiography'. What Painter argues is that Proust altered everything but invented nothing, and intended the book as 'the symbolic story of his life'. Painter is able to show us many close and mostly convincing identifications between actual people or events and Proust's many-sided and complex characters. Indeed we know that even when Proust became reclusive in his later years he would still set out, coddled in coats, to research some social detail, gathering information from the waiters at the Ritz, or visiting a duchess to ask her to show him her old hats. When he added new passages to the book, as he endlessly did, it was often to put in some new social trophy, like adding newly collected stamps to an album. Proust researched his world, a world he knew well, with a rare intensity and exactitude, and had an extraordinary dependence on realities, like the Naturalist novelists before him. Yet *A la recherche* . . . is also a revolt against Naturalism, a spirited rejection and refusal of realism. The lifetime task was not just to recover but to recreate, which meant reconstruct, the materials of the book, and the angular perceptions of art, the transpositions of creativity, are in fact an essential quality and a theme in the novel.

In some ways Proust's was a Romantic conception of art. Like Wordsworth he recollected in tranquillity, depended on the full creative visitations of the imagination, and drew on what flashed upon the inward eye, so very different from the eye that seeks to mirror reality. Indeed the whole task of the novel is to shift the centre of the novel from characters or reality to the creative mind of the novelist. More than any other novelist Proust broke open the French heritage of realism, with its language of clarity and certainty, its famous *clarté*, while having a profound respect for what has been so, for the 'true'. Proust moved the novel into what one French 'new novelist', Nathalie Sarraute, has called the 'era of suspicion', where we do not trust to the truth of a text. As another of those new novelists, Michel Butor, has said, all literature in France thereafter was changed by *A la recherche* . . . and its way of reflecting art in art. Proust's own biography therefore only takes us a certain distance into the book. Indeed we could almost say that in his later years he withdrew not just from life but from his own autobiography in order to become an artist.

Proust was born into a prosperous Parisian family at a terrible time. It was 1871, the year of the Franco–Prussian war when the Germans were besieging and bombarding Paris and the Paris commune began. The Third Republic was yet to be founded. Proust's father, Louis Proust, who came from Illiers, which would be Combray in the book, was an eminent doctor, surgeon and professor of medicine who held the Legion of Honour. His mother – the mother whose affection and attentions dominated Marcel's life, and on whom he became so dependent that when they separated once in Venice in anger the very image of that artistic city fell to pieces – was the former Jeanne Weil, daughter of a cultivated and wealthy Jewish family. Proust was born at the home of one of her relatives in Auteuil, near Paris, when his mother took refuge from the terrible events of the year. He would later trace his neurasthenic nature and his troubled, fragile homosexual inclination to the events around his birth and to his enormous emotional dependence on his mother, which lasted right to and beyond her death. This relationship is dramatized deeply in the novel, above all in that famous scene where Marcel attempts to remain awake in order to secure her goodnight kiss, a scene which has been described

as one of the most remarkable love-scenes in all modern literature. As
he says toward the end of the novel: 'It was the evening of my
mother's abdication which, together with the slow death of my grand-
mother, marked the decline of my will and of my health.'

Proust's ailment, asthma, declared itself at the age of nine and was
to recur for the rest of his life. It had another great dramatic effect. It
prevented him from returning in the summers to Illiers, his
'Combray', with its pollen-rich hawthorn hedges, and so made of the
town today called Illiers-Combray the lost kingdom of childhood and
origins which he set out so fully to recapture. Neurasthenic illness
troubled Proust for the rest of his life, and the crucial relationship of
illness and art is as crucial a theme of his novel as it is of *The Magic
Mountain*. Like Mann's Aschenbach, though also greatly under the
influence of his admired Ruskin, he loved Venice, and other parts of
his fictional landscape – Cabourg in Normandy (Balbec in the novel)
and various spa towns – reflect the geography of his ailment. Illness
and psychology were indeed a family speciality. Proust never read
Freud, for the French translations came too late, but he belonged to a
world of medicine and science that knew him, and to literary circles
that were deeply fascinated by modern psychology. The psychological
novelist Paul Bourget is thought to be the original of his fictional
novelist Bergotte. Michel Butor has said that Proust and Freud pursued
the same researches in parallel, and that each of them helps make sense
of the other; in this there is much truth. Proust describes his novel as a
diver's search into the unconscious, and *A la recherche . . .* is in part the
quest for the origins of a psychic and somatic malady begun in
childhood, which in its time leads to the 'sublimation' of art.

Proust's interest in art developed early, and the books and magic-
lantern shows of childhood led him to 'a more than ordinarily
scrupulous examination of my own consciousness'. His penetration of
the magic circles of society was in part the pursuit of a life lived
according to the rules of art. Growing up in Paris, he went to the
Lycée Condorcet, took an interest in the rising 'Decadent' movement,
from which many of his artistic ideas arose, and showed the first signs
of both his homosexuality and his habitual snobbery (very apparent in
his voluminous letters). His father encouraged him towards a diplo-

matic career, but he preferred the role of man-about-town, and entered the social-literary circles of the day. He attended lectures at the Sorbonne, and especially those of his relative Henri Bergson – the powerful philosopher of creative intuition, of the metaphysics of time, of 'involuntary memory,' and of the flowing line and the flowing mind. By the 1890s, as we have seen, the idea of Naturalism, so firmly established by Zola, was beginning to die in Paris, and a new spirit of aestheticism, decadence and symbolism dominated. The psychology of consciousness, the 'impression' of art, were emphasized. In 1884 J.-K. Huysmans had published his decadent novel *A rebours* (*Against Nature*), about an aristocratic hero who retreats into sensation and art, into the ivory tower of existence, in a revolt against the modernizing world. Its hero was said to be modelled on Count Robert de Montesquiou, into whose circle Proust now came, and the Count acquired the troubling distinction of being the reputed original for Huysman's Des Esseintes and for Proust's own Baron de Charlus.

Often dressed in two overcoats to keep out the cold, Proust was a familiar figure in the fashionable boulevard cafés as well as *salon* society. To Debussy, whom he admired, he was 'long-winded, precious and a bit of an old woman', but he fought a duel, impressed his seniors, and won a literary reputation as a dandy and a decadent of the *fin du siècle*. In 1896 he published his first book, *Les Plaisirs et les jours*, a collection of poems, stories and sketches in the Impressionist manner. By now he had already begun his first novel, *Jean Santeuil*, which he discarded, but which was retrieved from his papers and published in 1953. This book already contains much of the narrative substance of *A la recherche* . . ., and is an obvious source of the later project. It is a pleasing enough book in its own right, but what it inevitably shows us now is the original materials from which Proust started off on his great quest, which was not simply for an interesting narrative but for a radical and original form of art. The steps onward were slow. He began a translation of Ruskin, greatly helped by his mother, who did a literal transcription of the text into French and took him to Ruskin's city of Venice. She attended him in all ways, taking her unmarried son to spas when he became ill, and supporting him in his elaborate and dilettante social life.

Then in 1903 Proust's father died, and, more crucially, in 1905 so did his mother, falling ill while taking her fragile son on a cure to Evian. Her death, in his thirty-fifth year, was a profound crisis, generating a terrible guilt and self-accusation. After a period in a sanatorium, he moved to the family apartment in the Boulevard Haussmann, where he fitted out the famous cork-lined room, into which he was increasingly to retreat. For many years he continued to travel quite extensively, particularly to Cabourg. He maintained his profound interest in the arts – for example, in the Russian ballet of Diaghilev, which took Paris by storm in 1910. He was a member of the artistic scene that included Ravel and Apollinaire, André Gide and Cocteau, and he responded to the new scene in painting, among the Post-Impressionists and the Cubists, acknowledging, as he does in the book, the fascinations of abstraction. He maintained a succession of homo-sexual affairs, most importantly with Alfred Agostinelli, who became his secretary, and is often identified with the 'Albertine' of the novel.

He also wrote journalism, and began another book which he aborted, an interesting critical study called *Contre Sainte-Beuve*, also retrieved from his papers, and published posthumously in 1954. It is a writer's challenge to the critics who fail to see the nature of the creative process, or understand the writer's 'hidden self' – specifically to the critic Sainte-Beuve for his biographical interpretation of Balzac. The preface mentions the importance of 'involuntary memory' and indeed calls up some of the images – the madeleine steeped in tea, the Japanese paper flower that opens out in water – so central to *A la recherche* . . . He also wrote a number of parodies of great French writers, testing and challenging the concept of style, another crucial act of preparation (there is an important parody of the work of the Goncourt brothers in the later pages of *A la recherche* . . .).

But Proust's own self was becoming more hidden, as he began to step away from society and into solitude, into the world of art and illness. He coddled himself, constantly having his room fumigated, resisting offensive scents and noises. He walked the streets by night and occasionally attended parties, but now this was *recherche*, material for the book. This process seems perhaps less strange if we recall that many of the decadent authors had commended an art of nerves, a dependence on the fragility of the self, the need to withdraw into art's ivory tower to create the world of correspondences from which art might be created anew. It also belongs with that profound modern association of disease and illness that Mann had explored and Nietzsche had observed. It was a physical version of that expatriation, inward and outward, that has so marked the modern movement. It was not an exclusion of the world, but a changed relation to it, a creative detachment from the world's frivolity, a fastidiousness of being that illness itself helped to justify. Proust's brother was a doctor, and Proust had plentiful access to treatment, but he frequently refused it; this rejection was to prove the cause of his death.

But essentially it was a retreat into art and the making of the one great book. In a sense Proust had been writing that book ever since the 1890s, when he embarked on *Jean Santeuil*. But his mother's death became the starting-point for a new approach to it. By July 1909 he had began working systematically on the manuscript, and by 1912 a three-volume version was done, which forms, in effect, the outer frame of the book we have. The first of these three appeared in 1913, but the war interrupted further publication, allowing Proust to go back into the writing of the work. It now turned into a lifetime task, multiplying endlessly from within as Proust added new passages, new themes, and new episodes deriving from the war itself. It took on new meaning as Proust's own health declined, and as, increasingly, he recreated through art what was being lost from life. In 1919 publication was resumed, and he won the Prix Goncourt for the second volume. Now he was suddenly a writer of the 1920s, very much in the postwar spirit, and he enjoyed his new fame. Delicate, self-protecting, fortified with adrenalin, he still maintained some social life, and took a great interest in the new arts that flourished in the postwar mood – in the paintings of Picasso and the cubists, who gain a mention in *Time Regained*. But now the book and its culminating sense of self-creation was his one task, and he saw it through to almost the very end. He felt the intimations of death, and even spoke of himself as dead. But the additions, or rather the multiplications, went on relentlessly, right up to the end, through every proof stage, as he stuck in new material that cascaded in sheets from the already printed copy. The grim theme of the later volumes, with their own premonitions of death and their struggle towards the completion of art, was enhanced by his own physical decline and by a kind of deliberate self-neglect.

On the day he died, 18 November 1922, he summoned the maid at three in the morning to dictate some further additions – appropriately enough, to the scene of the death of his own writer, Bergotte. After his death, the volumes continued to appear up to 1927, making thirteen in all, representing the seven parts of the book. Some of the later volumes were put together from imperfectly assembled proofs, so a finely edited text did not come until 1954, with the French *Pléiade* version, which is followed by Terence Kilmartin in his recent English re-translation. In the last volume, entitled *Time Regained*, what began to dissolve in the very first sentence is put together. We have seen the first sentence, and this is the final one:

> But at least, if strength were granted me for long enough to accomplish my work, I should not fail, even if the results were to make them resemble monsters, to describe men first and foremost as occupying a place, a very considerable place compared with the restricted one which is allotted to them in space, a place on the contrary prolonged past measure – for simultaneously, like giants plunged into the years, they touch epochs immensely far apart, separated by the slow accretion of many days – in the dimension of Time.

4

So Proust did, in effect, complete the work which is one of the most monumental books of Modernism. As the German critic Walter Benjamin observed: 'The conditions in which it was created were extremely unhealthy: an unusual malady, extraordinary wealth, and an abnormal disposition. This is not a model life in every respect, but everything about it is exemplary. The outstanding literary achievement of our time is assigned a place in the heart of the impossible, at the centre – and also at the point of indifference – of all dangers, and it marks this great realization of a "lifework" as the last for a long time.' There were, indeed, other works of an extraordinary dedication, not least Joyce's *Ulysses* and *Finnegans Wake*, but few that have possessed their authors so completely, demanded so complete a self-dedication in order, as it were, to justify the achievement, or that so profoundly constructed a modern religion of art. The quest from Combray to the world of the 1920s is an extraordinary one – lit at every stage by a quality of strangeness, by an endless vivid observation, both microscopic and telescopic, as Proust would put it, by an extraordinary, learned, considerate analytical intelligence, by an unremitting historical and psychological curiosity, and by that profound intensity of erotic desire and emotion that each attentive reader finds in this vast book.

A la recherche . . . thus turns from being a certain kind of memoir to being a major artistic achievement, and perhaps the heart of the novel is that section of the last part, *Time Regained*, when this begins to happen. The war is over, and Marcel has been away in a sanatorium. He returns to Paris in a state of creative despair and dejection, his imagination failing to bring life to anything he sees. The world he has known seems very far away, an epoch far apart, but he is invited to a musical *soirée* at the new house of the Prince de Guermantes on the Avenue du Bois. Various reminders of the past meet him on the way, not least a brief meeting with the very ailing Baron de Charlus, who is suffering from aphasia, a dislocation of speech. Then, suddenly, the 'only door which one can enter' opens suddenly of its own accord:

> Revolving the gloomy thoughts which I have just recorded, I had entered the courtyard of the Guermantes mansion and in my absent-minded state had failed to see a car which was coming towards me; the chauffeur gave a shout and I just had time to step out of the way, but as I moved sharply backwards I tripped against the uneven paving-stones in front of the coach-house. And at the moment when, recovering my balance, I put my foot on a stone which was scarcely lower than its neighbour, all

my discouragement vanished and in its place was that same happiness which at various epochs of my life had been given to me by
the sight of trees which I had thought that I recognized in the
course of a drive near Balbec, by the sight of the twin steeples of
Martinville, by the flavour of the madeleine dipped in tea, and
by all those other sensations of which I have spoken . . .

The past comes back to him, saying: 'Seize me as I pass if you can,
and try to solve the riddle of happiness which I set you.'

The passages that follow this moment on the paving-stones are the
story of an artistic regeneration, as the Japanese flower of memory
opens in its right medium, and with a fresh sense of purpose and
understanding he begins to revisit again the old sensations. The touch
of a spoon against a teacup brings back the peal of the bell at the
garden gate in Combray, the feel of the napkin with which he wipes
his face takes him back to Balbec. As 'Marcel' begins to analyse these
impressions he has a sense of diversity and multiplicity, a realization
that 'a uniform depiction of life cannot bear much resemblance to the
reality', and that the essential moments of life are in a variety of sealed
vessels, are situated 'at the most various moral altitudes and give us
the sensation of extraordinarily diverse atmospheres'. Any work – he
now begins to see that he can write – must therefore need to be
executed in a variety of different materials. These materials had something to do with happiness, and therefore he also judges that the
moment of essence is both past and present, and to be found 'in the
one and only medium in which it was likely to exist and enjoy the
essence of things, that is to say: outside time.' What follows is a great
unifying of the disparate experiences that the book has explored for
us, under that timeless gaze. The 'inner book of unknown symbols'
begins to take its shape.

The book, 'Marcel' acknowledges, cannot be a work like any
known book, and we have to discover it. 'In this conclusion I was
confirmed by the thought of the falseness of so-called realist art, which
would not be so untruthful if we had not in life acquired the habit of
giving to what we feel a form of expression which differs so much
from, and which we nevertheless after a little time take to be, reality

itself,' he writes, expressing a truth that still has fully to enter the modern novel. So, in a massive, fascinating passage of literary speculation and abstraction, unusual in any fiction, Marcel stands in the Guermantes's library and conceives – emotionally, critically, intellectually – the subject and art of the book we are reading, and the central experiences of which it must be made. The scene is followed by a shock. Marcel has become timeless indeed, but now he joins the guests at the party – to feel that he has entered a masquerade at which each person of his acquaintance has put on some disguise, whitened the face, powdered the hair. The party is a great puppet-show of the aged, a peepshow of the years, a mockery of society and love. Age mocks them all, including Marcel himself: 'I had made the discovery of this destructive action of Time at the very moment when I conceived the ambition to make visible, to intellectualize in a work of art, realities that were outside Time.'

In the extraordinary and grotesque spectacle that Proust creates of this scene, his Dance of Death, the entire social and erotic world of the book is questioned. And when finally he does turn towards his book, it is not just in a desire for timelessness but with an overwhelming intimation of mortality. With this double vision he can return to the peal of the bell on the garden gate at Combray – the moment when, he says, 'I existed.' Now he knows that it still adheres to him, and can be found again. The circle of the novel becomes complete, but into the circle has come the discovery of the artist's vocation and an idea of the book as a totally original form – that of the 'inner book of unknown symbols', symbols and hieroglyphs that are discovered in the unconscious just as a diver stumbles against rocks in water. The book is not a memoir, not an autobiography, not a formless thing, but a work that has grown into shape from within, like the Japanese paper flower that opens in the water and takes on form. It is not simply a personal book, as Marcel explains: his task is, he says, 'to interpret the given sensations as signs of so many laws and ideas, by trying to draw forth from the shadow what I had merely felt, by trying to convert it to its spiritual equivalent. And this method, which seemed to me the sole method, what was it but the creation of a work of art?'

5

A la recherche du temps perdu, for all the melancholy of its last scenes at the Guermantes' *soirée*, is one of the most positive of the works of the modern movement. The book finds its form not out of fragments but in a sense of wholeness. It ends on a profound vision of mortality, but also on a feeling of spiritual renewal, and a belief in the power of art to dispute with as well as to explore Time. Proust really believes in the magic lantern of art, which shines its pictures across the walls of the domestic and familiar bedroom and opens life out towards lost domains, other worlds – to the glitter of the sea beyond the hotel bedroom or the wonder of the night at the opera as the Guermantes come into their box. To this extent he was more of a Romantic and an Impressionist than most of those writers we call modern, and his profound veneration for the world of polite society he portrayed so profoundly and comically, and so much from the inside, is something most other writers have found the need to suspect. Proust's modernity comes from the great withdrawal he made into the intelligence, the sensuousness, the synaesthesia, the psychology of art. He is one of the great *creators*, even though it seems as if he did not create at all, but just lay there and remembered. Indeed for the French novel he created the entire possibility of a great novel after realism, and conducted an entire and necessary revolution all on his own. As he said, 'What we have not had to decipher, to elucidate by our own efforts, what was clear before we looked at it, is not ours.'

It could fairly be said that once *A la recherche* . . . had appeared the future of the modern novel lay in the heritage that was divided between Proust and Joyce. The two met only once, in May 1921, when the British novelist Stephen Hudson invited them to a party for Stravinsky, Diaghilev, Picasso, Proust and Joyce. It must be thought one of the better social occasions, and who cannot be sorry to have missed it. It was, of course, assumed that Proust would not come, but he did. Joyce came late and the worse for wear, and only approached Proust as he was departing. Proust complained of his stomach, and Joyce complained about his eyes. 'I regret that I do not know

M. Joyce's work,' said Proust. 'I have never read M. Proust,' said Joyce. A great moment of literary history passed, as such moments so often will, in imperfection. By the time *Ulysses* appeared the following year, Proust was engaged in his final race against death. The two generations never did quite meet, and it was left for successors like Samuel Beckett to see the connection. So it has gone on, each leaving their powerful trace. As Michel Butor says, even in the era of the 'New Novel' we have still not fully learned to read the complex book of Proust, the great work of self-creation, and the task will undoubtedly reach on, into the century still to come.

JAMES
JOYCE

James Joyce was not always a giant of modern literature, though it is hard now to remember the time when he was not. Like Proust, he is one of the essential representatives of the idea of the modern in the novel, and if the movement has any one single folk-hero, Joyce must be that figure. He was a writer who came to suggest that in many respects the task of literature had been completed, the great modern text achieved (after all, his remarkable last novel *Finnegans Wake*, seventeen years in the writing, was nothing less than a 'history of the world'). Yet he has more clear successors than any other modernist writer in the English language – though this last great novel was not so much in that language as in some new, punning global tongue. Most of the major modern, or indeed postmodern, writing that has followed since his death in 1940 has flowed in one way or another from him. And if *Finnegans Wake* was in its way the wake not just of Finnegan but of modernism, the work with which the whole great episode seemed to end, there has indeed been much life after the wake. *After the Wake* is the apt title of a study by Christopher Butler which examines the experimental tradition in writing since the appearance of that book, and it suggests the enormous spread of his influence, the extraordinary domination that the very idea of Joyce has exercised over modern views of literary style and form.

Joyce is an influence, direct and indirect, that few of us could or would deny. His own contemporaries saw him as central. The appearance of *Ulysses* in 1922 was an apparently obscure event, for the book came out in Paris from an American bookshop, in a limited edition of 1,000 signed copies, and was set with many errors, long to be perpetuated, by a Dijon printer, only then to be excluded from Britain and the United States for its immorality. Yet the book radiated everywhere, and was the stimulus for much of the experimentalism that followed through the rest of the twenties. Virginia Woolf thought his work 'underbred', but *Mrs Dalloway* would not have taken the shape it did without the pressure and the premises of his great novel. The same may be said of the work of John Dos Passos in *Manhattan Transfer* and *USA*, and the great experiments of William Faulkner, in books like *The Sound and the Fury*, in the later 1920s. By the end of the twenties and the thirties, he was the Grand Old Man of European literature, and established and new writers clustered in Paris to find him.

And, when the novel after the Second World War took a marked change in direction, because Joyce had in effect finished the task of modernism, he was still there. Samuel Beckett, the fellow-Irishman who was for a time Joyce's translator and friend in Paris (Joyce acknowledged his book *Murphy* in 1938 with, appropriately enough, a limerick), developed his absurdist and minimalist form of postwar fiction in direct descent from the master. Malcolm Lowry, the still underestimated author of *Under the Volcano* (1947), saw himself as 'Joyced with his own petard.' Anthony Burgess, who defers to few, defers to him, and has pronounced *Ulysses* the greatest single work in the English literature of this century, a view in which he is not alone. Nearly all novels of any ambition written today acknowledge his reconstruction of language and of the tactics of modern myth, his transformation of fictional time and consciousness. Much modern criticism would scarcely exist without him, and depends heavily on his view of the task of modern writing and the crisis of the modern word. Joyce explained when he was asked what *Ulysses* was about: 'I've put in so many enigmas and puzzles that it will keep the professors busy for centuries arguing over what I meant, and that's the only way of ensuring one's immortality.' To date, he has been proved perfectly right.

What makes Joyce's work seem so essentially modern? In his book *The Struggle of the Modern*, Stephen Spender constructs a fascinating distinction between two lines he observes running through twentieth-century writing. One is the line of the 'contemporaries', the other that of the 'moderns'. The 'contemporaries' are writers like H. G.

Wells, Arnold Bennett, C. P. Snow and many more – writers who on the whole have accepted the processes of the modern world, and been sympathetic to the forces for change running through it, and in their work have maintained an attitude of realism, rationality, and positivism. The 'moderns' are writers of the kind we find in this book, writers like T. S. Eliot and Pound, Proust and Virginia Woolf, who have generally taken a different view of their age – have distrusted its historical direction, doubted its progress, felt dislocated from its past and been intensely conscious of the anarchy of modern life and culture. So they have tended to withdraw into the stronghold of art, and make it more modern by constructing radical orders of their own: fragmentary, disjunctive orders that express modern life and consciousness. Spender suggests that a great deal of modern literature has actually derived from the trade *between* the two lineages – the work of Thomas Hardy, E. M. Forster or Thomas Mann, for instance.

But if we were to wonder where to put, say, D. H. Lawrence, there would be no doubt where to put James Joyce. He would most certainly be a modern, a distinct and central case. The view would depend particularly on *Ulysses* and *Finnegans Wake*, published in 1939: two books that clearly express the element of 'decreation' that Spender identifies with the modern. They imply a collapsing tradition, a lost connection, a broken mythology. At the same time they pursue a religion of art, a desire for an artistic revelation and an epic synthesis that creative form might provide, even if life itself somehow does not. *Ulysses* in particular is the great modern example of the 'decreative' novel, a work that moves our attention away from its realistic subject into its language and its form. It makes an epic approach to us – calling up Homer in its title and its structure – and it also functions as an anti-epic. For the wily Ulysses is now Leopold Bloom, a seedy Jewish advertisement canvasser, his ten years of mythic wandering are telescoped into eighteen hours of a single day, 16 June 1904 (now known as 'Bloomsday') and his great deeds are reduced to commonplace, lowlife incidents told in a mockingly naturalistic way. In *The Odyssey*, journeys are heroic, the founding or preserving of nations has historical meaning, and bravery and chastity and honour are venerated. In *Ulysses*, all this grandeur is undercut and parodied.

History is not a cause but a nightmare from which Ireland, Leopold Bloom and Stephen Dedalus are in their different ways trying to awake. And none of the conventional acts of heroism are performed though a whole new form of heroism is conceived, that of the small ordinary man trying to live his life in the ironic commonplace world of modern times.

In that world, the old myths may have crumbled. But what we see in *Ulysses* is a new myth in the very process of its creation. How, it asks, do we give sense to the random, daily, trivial world of our age? *Ulysses* is a commonplace book – or rather a book of the commonplace – in which trivial things acquire a pattern and a mythic function. Leopold Bloom's most ordinary and intimate actions – at the lavatory or the bath, the bar or the brothel, his masturbations and seedy contemplation of girls – are an essential part of the story. So are his wife Molly's menstruations and micturations, her soiled dreams and sexual fantasies. Bloom's low bourgeois life, his apparently aimless wanderings round the city, his cuckolding by his Penelope, the earthy Molly, all too ready to accept her suitors, his brothel encounter with his Telemachus, Stephen Dedalus, and his return to the shrine of domesticity, the jangling and untidy bed – all of this both mocks and reconstructs the form of epic. It equally plays with the more modern attitude of Naturalism, with its basic assumption that we should meticulously record the details of life because they represent the material truth of experience. No one could be more meticulous than Joyce in his massive recording of Dublin, and to this day the dedicated Joycean can wander through the described landscape and cityscape of the novel. But, as the presence of Stephen Dedalus in the novel constantly reminds us, the task is larger. It is the task of finding what is transubstantial in the substantial, and it reaches beyond the material existence of the city to the search for new languages and forms. Joyce's naturalistic methods, then, are not simply there to give the firm substance of reality in lowlife Dublin, though that is of very great importance. They are the basic, base material of life, which art and technique may transmute into something more whole and complete.

And transmutation and transubstantiation are in fact the business of stately plump Buck Mulligan and his friend Stephen Dedalus, as in the opening pages of the novel they start off their day with mock-religious blessings, using Mulligan's crossed mirror and razor. All this is appropriate enough, for Stephen Dedalus is a failed priest who has taken to a new religion, that of art, which itself requires ceremonies and revelations. Stephen is Joyce's 'Marcel'. He is 22, an Aristotelian and an aesthete, whose Parisian expatriation has been interrupted when he has been called back to his own provincial Dublin because his mother is dying. He lives with Mulligan in the Martello Tower at Sandycove, and teaches at a private school; he walks the beach beside the snotgreen, scrotum-tightening sea, a son in quest of his own Irish history. For Ireland is provincial indeed, a land whose history has been suppressed, and whose art resembles the 'cracked looking-glass of a servant'. How might one change it, or write about it? 'Hellenize it,' suggests Buck Mulligan, and indeed Stephen, or the author of this book, whom he represents, duly will.

Stephen's aims, from the start, are both clear and complex. As an artist, he is searching for transcendental meanings behind the material world, the 'ineluctable modalities of the visible': 'Signatures of all things I am here to read.' Yet the rigidness and insolation of Irish history, in hock both to the British Empire and the Italian church, seems to rob him of a subject: history is, he says, 'a nightmare from which I am trying to awake.' Nonetheless he teaches the subject at a private school, and Mr Deasy, the Nestor of the novel, reminds him of some prime, if false, historical facts, as does Buck Mulligan too. Ireland, it seems, might arise from Greek origins, and it has never let in the Jews. Gradually we move into the Protean interior monologue of his thoughts as he engages with his own sensations and ideas, experiments with his problems of bad sight, which causes the form of things to change. Language, too, is equally volatile, multiplying into a chaotic sing-song as the vernacular rhythms of talk and chatter, philosophy and theory, gossip and popular songs, merge in the flow of his mind. Passing impressions merge with inward sensations. He feels guilty that he has not returned to the faith as his dying mother has begged. Perhaps Ireland is his mother and the nation will give him a succouring myth. Perhaps he is himself a son without a father, an artist without a book. 'Where is poor dear Arius to try conclusions?

Warring his life long on the contransmagnificandjewbangtantiality.'
In the gathered sensations and jumbled phrases of the first three chapters
are most of the underlying ideas of *Ulysses*, the stuff of an extraordinary
new myth of a book. Yet 'Who ever anywhere will read these written
words?' he wonders.

Meanwhile at 7 Eccles Street another breakfast takes place, another
style of writing commences, another inner monologue and process of
the mind begins, another quest starts. There are, after all, two quests
in the *Odyssey*, that of Telemachus for his father, and that of Ulysses
for his home and wife. Evidently the second quest is more corporeal.
'Mr Leopold Bloom ate with relish the inner organs of beasts and
fowls. He liked thick giblet soup, nutty gizzards, a stuffed roast heart,
liver slices fried with crustcrumbs, fried hencod's roes. Most of all he
liked grilled mutton kidneys which gave to his palate a fine tang of
faintly scented urine.' Leaving his wife in bed, the Jewish Mr Leopold
Bloom – there *are* Jews in Ireland – goes out through the complex bazaar of the streets to buy his kidney, returns to hand over the
mail, scald the tea, hand breakfast to his wife, still in bed, and go to
the jakes. As with Stephen, his thoughts, condensed and captured in
the mind at the point before they are expressed, flow freely. They are
in a grosser mould, less about art and myth than sentiment, crude
romance, food and potted meat. They move from the problems of
constipation ('Hope it's not too big bring on piles again') to popular
songs and newspaper advertisements, from domestic problems – a
daughter's letter, the death of a son recalled – to such abstract matters
as the problem of defining metempsychosis, the transmigration of
souls: 'Reincarnation: that's the word.' Later, in the carriage on his
way to Paddy Dignam's funeral, he catches a brief glimpse of Stephen
Dedalus. Two ways of seeing, of thinking, of living, two ways of
knowing Ireland, cross for a moment, and as they do we feel the idea
of the novel coming to birth. At its simplest, *Ulysses* is the story of
two men whose lives meet in Dublin on 16 June 1904.

2

There are two important dates to do with *Ulysses*. One is Bloomsday, the one long day-and-night out of which James Joyce did indeed manage to construct his own modern myth. The other is 2 February 1922, Joyce's fortieth birthday, the carefully chosen day on which the book was published. Its fame had gone before it, and it was at once hailed by fellow writers and serious readers as the great postwar novel. In a famous review T. S. Eliot observed the book's remarkable modernity, and its equally remarkable and complex method, which was, he said, 'a way of controlling, or ordering, of giving a shape and a significance to the immense panorama of futility and anarchy which is contemporary history.' The book therefore took on much the same importance as Eliot's own *Waste Land*. It became acknowledged as the novel that seemed most to express the experimental, international spirit of postwar Paris, and was taken as an essential example of the new 'Revolution of the Word'. It was a great international novel, a novel of the modern city, one of the great achievements of modern exile. It was a work of new method, above all the methods of what were called 'interior monologue' or 'stream-of-consciousness'. And not only did it display the flow of artistic consciousness, the flickering impressions of a writer's mind, but it reached down into under-consciousness, to the unconscious, and Molly Bloom's great reverie at the end of the novel came to seem the great statement of the inner nature of the human mind.

Yet the novel was also an historical novel, set nearly twenty years earlier. It dealt not with the world of postwar crisis, but with a city on the European fringes which drove many of its writers into exile. Between the time of the story and the time of the book's publication, the world had changed. There had been a great European war which had turned the bohemian expatriation of the author into a more troubled form of exile. In Ireland too there had been a revolution, and the Irish State had now been founded. The spirit of aesthetic revolution to which Stephen Dedalus responded – the spirit, very largely, of the Celtic Twilight and the Celtic Revival – seemed to lie in the past. And the book itself displayed its own long sense of distance, a distance of time and geography. The book ends with the famous last words of sexual and emotional acceptance of Molly Bloom: 'yes I said yes I will Yes' But they are not quite the final words, for they are followed by a few more of equal importance, the dateline 'Trieste–Zurich–Paris, 1914–1921.'

Like many works of Modernism, then, *Ulysses* built a complex bridge between the prewar and the postwar worlds, two ages of modern writing. And we may therefore well ask why Joyce – who started the book in 1914 in Trieste, just a short time before the war started, and wrote most of it in Switzerland during the conflict – should have chosen to set his story back in 1904. The reasons were of great importance, for 1904 was Joyce's crucial year, a year of choice, creation, and indeed of exile itself. Just like Stephen Dedalus in the novel (he is a very autobiographical hero), Joyce was then in his twenty-second year. He had grown up in a middle-class Dublin family whose own fortunes, rather like those of the city itself, had declined, as his father, whom he adored, squandered the family in-heritance. His mother was a devout Catholic who made sure he was educated by Jesuits, and he had nearly taken up the vocation of a priest. He had then gone to University College, Dublin, and become drawn to another vocation, that of the author. He had begun to write, and while still at college published his article on the topic of Ibsen's new drama. Then had come his famous *'non serviam'*: 'I will tell you what I will do and what I will not do. I will not serve that in which I no longer believe, whether it call itself my home, my fatherland or my church; and I will try to express myself in some mode of life or art as freely as I can and as wholly as I can, using for my defence the only arms I allow myself to use, silence, exile, and cunning.'

He said this in the predecessor to *Ulysses*, the book called *A Portrait of the Artist as a Young Man*, which was published in 1916, though he wrote it very much earlier. Here he tells the story of his early growing up, his Jesuit education, his aesthetic ideals and his aim of becoming an artist. Joyce was prepared to give to art the same sense of devotion demanded of the priest, and that idea of a total dedication has much to do with his choice of name for his autobiographical hero – the name of 'Stephen Dedalus.' Dedalus in legend built the labyrinth at Minos, and then escaped on wax wings he had constructed. In the novel Stephen calls up the image of this 'fabulous artificer', the hawklike man who flies above the sea, and he becomes 'a symbol of the artist forging anew in his workshop out of the sluggish matter of the earth a new soaring imperishable impalpable being.' His own task, like that of Dedalus, is to voyage into the unknown arts, and the novel ends with Stephen making his own flight, to Europe and art, with the words: 'Welcome O life! I go to encounter for the millionth time the reality of experience and to forge in the smithy of my soul the uncreated conscience of my race.' He then adds: 'Old father, old artificer, stand me now and ever in good stead.'

The revolt into art that Joyce describes in the book took place in 1902, when he himself departed for Paris to study medicine and write. Then in 1903, just like the Stephen we see again at the beginning of *Ulysses*, he had been called back to Dublin because of his mother's illness, which led to her death from cancer during the year. The return brought back again the whole question of artistic duties and responsibilities, and encouraged him to larger literary tasks. Indeed 1904 was to become for Joyce a year of major creation. He produced the poems of *Chamber Music*, the collection of verse that was published in 1907. He began a group of linked short stories about the paralysed city of Dublin that would eventually make up the volume called *Dubliners*, published in 1914. One of these stories was to be called 'Ulysses', and deal with a Jewish Dubliner called Hunter, the first direct indication we have of one basic idea of his great novel. And he also began the first draft of his autobiographical tale of Stephen Dedalus; this is the version which is called *Stephen Hero*, and was posthumously published in 1944. *A Portrait of the Artist . . .* is the revised, distilled and mature version of this, and it was when he completed that story of artistic dedication in 1914 that he turned to the 'sequel' that became *Ulysses*.

So 1904 was the year of Joyce's own adventure into the unknown arts, the time when he ceased to be the artist as a young man, the real beginning of his whole enterprise in creative discovery. But there was one further reason for setting *Ulysses* on its chosen day of 16 June in

1904. For it was on that day that Joyce first took out Nora Barnacle, the young chambermaid from Galway who was to live with him as his common-law wife – they married formally only in 1931 – and who has every claim to be regarded as the original of Molly Bloom, though she suggested that Joyce did not know a very great deal about women. 'Nora Barnacle, she'll stick to him,' said Joyce's father, and indeed she did. In October of that year the two left for Europe on an artistic exile that was to become a lifetime affair. They duly settled in Trieste, where Joyce taught English at the Berlitz school, where the projects begun in Ireland in 1904 were largely completed, and where, in 1914, the text of *Ulysses* was begun. It was in 1904 that there began the devising, the constructing, the voyaging, the mature vocation, the business of an artist for a lifetime.

As all this suggests, *Ulysses* shares something in common with many of the major works of Modernism; it is very much the story of its own act of creation. It was born first in a Dublin that, as Joyce frequently shows us, was a great literary talking-shop. It was a Dublin filled with the spirit of the Irish literary revival that had been active in the 1890s. It lived on the memories of Shaw and Wilde, and the ideas of W. B. Yeats, James Stephens, George William Russell ('A.E.'), and Oliver St John Gogarty – the original of Buck Mulligan, with whom Joyce indeed shared the Martello Tower. Joyce, just back from Paris, may have thought it provincial and paralysed. But the Dublin–Paris link was well established, Dublin took in all the latest artistic news, was constantly in search of artistic revelation, and it craved the modern spirit. In his marvellous record of his friendship with Joyce in Zurich during the First World War, *James Joyce and the Making of 'Ulysses'*, Frank Budgen records him describing Dubliners as the most hopeless, useless and inconsistent race of charlatans. But Joyce also believed – he has the Citizen say it in the 'Cyclops' episode – that the Irish have stamped on a language not their own the mark of their own genius, and compete for glory with the civilized nations: 'This is then called English literature.'

In his distinctive, already half-exiled way, then, Joyce picked up on the artistic ideas that flowed like gossip through talkative, literary Dublin. He was at his most theoretical, his most susceptible, at this time. He was also concerned with the newest spirit in the arts, and responding to the two main international literary movements that had developed during the 1890s, Naturalism and Symbolism. Naturalism, as we have seen, particularly meant Ibsen. Joyce, as his early essay on Ibsen's drama shows, was a great admirer, and he always held that Dublin was more a Scandinavian than it was a Celtic city. It also meant the vast, deterministic, social narratives of Emile Zola, and when he began work on the stories of *Dubliners* he described himself as an Irish Zola. 'My intention was to write a chapter of the moral history of my country and I chose Dublin for the scene because the city seemed to me the centre of paralysis,' he wrote in a letter about the book. 'I have written it for the most part in a style of scrupulous meanness and with the conviction that he is a bold man who dares to alter the presentment, still more to deform, whatever he has seen and heard.' The stories of *Dubliners* share the Naturalist feeling that we live in a determined and conditioned world, which art must treat with meticulousness and radical frankness. We can see this spirit not only in Joyce's sexual explicitness, which led to the volume being refused publication in 1906, but in the extraordinary exactness and detail of his record of Dublin life. 'Are Aungier Street and Wicklow in the Royal Exchange Ward?' he wrote home from Trieste. 'Can a municipal election take place in October?' That meticulous detailing, and the 'scrupulous meanness', are essential stuff in *Ulysses*. As Joyce said, he wrote the book in such a way that if Dublin were to be destroyed it could be reconstructed from the novel.

But the other movement of the times that excited him was Symbolism – the French movement that had been so powerfully supported in Britain by W. B. Yeats and Arthur Symons. Joyce's debts to the *fin de siècle* were great, not the least of them being that he saw art not as a plain report on the world but an active work of creation and moving consciousness, a story of the artist. His version of Symbolism perhaps comes out most clearly in the various arguments that Stephen advances, both in *Stephen Hero* and *A Portrait of the Artist . . .*, about the inner luminosity and the transcendent beauty of art. And above all there was the famous idea of the 'epiphany' – the transcendental revelation which Joyce took from religion and applied to art. 'By an epiphany he meant a sudden spiritual manifestation, whether in the vulgarity of speech or of gesture or in a memorable phrase of the mind itself. He believed it was for the man of letters to record these epiphanies with extreme care, seeing that they themselves are the most delicate and evanescent of moments,' we are told in *Stephen Hero*. In *A Portrait* . . ., where the notion is somewhat changed, Stephen endeavours to become 'a priest of the eternal imagination, transmuting the daily bread of experience into the radiant body of evolving life.' His task is to create art out of life, and means the artist must rival the God of creation Himself, filling everything with intangible aesthetic life. 'The mystery of aesthetic like that of material creation is accomplished. The artist, like the God of creation, remains within or behind or beyond or above his handiwork, invisible, refined out of existence, indifferent, paring his fingernails.' *Ulysses* is the book where these ideas are reconciled, the great work both of meticulous social recording and aesthetic expression. The relating and blending of Naturalism and Symbolism was thus essential to the great novel to come. Again, they take us back to the years around 1904. Some of Joyce's most important artistic ideas were already formed before he carried them off with him into his European exile.

Yet *Ulysses* is a work made out of exile. Exile, as we have seen, has been profoundly important in creating the 'unhoused' spirit of modern art. Certainly it mattered greatly to Joyce, whose only play, written somewhat in imitation of Ibsen, was given the title of *Exiles*. And exile is the other major imprint that was placed on the novel. Ulysses, Odysseus, was the great exile among the Greeks, wandering homeless but homeward after the Trojan war. Bloom is a version of the wandering Jew, who has Hungarian origins but has married Molly Tweedy and settled in Dublin, changing his name from Virag. Stephen is himself a literary exile with a Latin Quarter hat. As for the book itself, that clearly displays the experience of a writing life that was always in process of constant movement and displacement – from Ireland to Trieste, Trieste to Zurich, Zurich to Paris. *Ulysses* itself was for a long time to be an exiled book, found outrageous in its own Dublin, and long banned from Britain and the United States because of its naturalistic detail and its sexual explicitness. It was exile that helped the Dublin of the book to become the timeless, everlasting, modern city it appears in the novel. Exile brought home to Joyce his sense of separation from the established literary tradition, its rules and ways with language; and it encouraged his outrageous fluency, his verbal display, the high linguistic self-consciousness that was in time to become one of the marks of Joyceanism. Thus it was exile, too, that gave *Ulysses* perhaps its most modern quality – its texture of linguistic displacement, its spirit of universal parody, its air of having access to all the available varieties of literary style, and devoting itself to no single one of them.

As Frank Budgen, the painter who became Joyce's confidant in Zurich during the First World War, has said, the cosmopolitanism of that city is present in *Ulysses*, just as Dublin is. If Dublin was the second city of the British Empire, as Joyce stressed, Zurich was the second city of psychoanalysis. It was also, as any fan of Tom Stoppard knows, the city where during the First World War it was possible to find Jung and Joyce, Lenin and Tristan Tzara – the founder of the absurdist artistic movement called Dada. There is little doubt that writing the book there created a space between the work's form and its subject which we can still read in it. So *Ulysses* became the great modern story both of place and placelessness, of allegiance to one's literary origins and enforced artistic separation from them. It was a story of enormous cultural specificity; it also undermined the entire idea of honest naturalism. Like some great compendium of the possibilities of writing, it multiplied the modes of telling, acquired a multiplicity of voices and linguistic registers. Each chapter was told in a different way, paralleling and upturning not only the original myth of Homer, but the many languages and forms of art that exist in the great kitty of narrative.

Twenty years therefore went into the writing of *Ulysses*, a book that was made like the layers of Troy. Certainly we could say there are three versions of it. One is the Naturalist *Ulysses*, the dense tale of life in the British Empire's second city, the life of its streets, its pubs, its hotels, its cab-stands, its shops, its newspaper offices, its maternity hospital, its brothels. The book is clearly a work of enormous social and historical registration, told with an extraordinary sense of fact and an extraordinary love of detail. Another is the Symbolist *Ulysses*, the book that could be described in just the way that Samuel Beckett described *Finnegans Wake*: 'Here form is content, content is form . . . His writing is not about something, it is something itself.' A third is the parodic *Ulysses*; many critics have described the book as the ultimate work of modernist parody, a novel in which every device seems to be inverted, every literary assertion becomes an enigma and a puzzle, and every perfect sentence has its own touch of self-mockery. It is the plurality of *Ulysses* that has made it the great literary text of the times. Dense with naturalist reality, it also revolts against realism. Committed to symbolism and an art of transcendental revelation, it also teases the symbol, and parodies the revelation. And it was because of all this that the long narrative of eighteen hours in distant Dublin so excited and upset the literary world of 1922.

3

It is not surprising that a book so richly and cunningly made should have become the modern writer's book – a great compendium of creation, a glorious exploration of the potential of literary language and the inordinate variety of modern styles. But it is also important to stress that *Ulysses* is also a wonderful reader's book, and mainly because the story it has to tell is in many respects intensely human, and very direct. As one of the best of all the Joycean critics, Richard Ellmann (he wrote the great life of Joyce, recently revised), has said, it is essentially a story of the discovery of life's affirmation – the affirmation found in Stephen's realization, as he confronts the image of his dead mother, that the word known to all men is 'love', that is displayed in Bloom's circular return to the domestic and connubial bed, and that is declared in Molly's 'yes I said yes I will Yes' It might be called the myth of a male return to the mother or the wife who is life itself. It is a social and political story because a nation is a mother too, though a mother who can breed rage, jingoism, vulgarity and virulent hatred. It is a religious story because a church, too, is a mother, and though

Bloom is an atheistic Jew and Stephen an atheistic Christian the redemptive imagery of the church and its message of love is crucial to
both of them. It is a sexual story because it is amid erotic and often
perverse desires and fantasies, among squalid couplings and adulteries,
that the great human ritual of birth, copulation and death takes place.
It is a story of journey because Bloom, though his travels are largely
local and domestic, is indeed a wandering Jew in search of home. He
has been separated from his partner by the sexual abstinence that has
begun eleven years before, when relations between them ceased after
the death of their son Rudy at the age of eleven days. Bloom thus
travels, like another Fisher King, through a land of often sterile and
squalid adventures, which are the essential adventures of human life.
He finds Stephen, who recalls thoughts of his son, returns home with
him, and takes his husband's task again, accepted back into Molly's
cunning, promiscuous and yet finally tender affirmation.

The reader has to accept the enormous scale of the original invention that Joyce put into the writing of the book. He told the story
of the story to Frank Budgen, the former sailor who became a painter
and was then in the British commercial consulate in Zurich during
the war, and who followed Joyce's work on the book there attentively.
'I am writing a book,' Joyce told him, 'based on the wanderings of
Ulysses. The *Odyssey*, that is to say, serves me as a ground plan. Only
my time is recent time and all my hero's wanderings take no more
than eighteen hours.' It was to be a book, he said, about a modern
Ulysses who is an all-round man, a complete man – an everyman,
who is son and father, husband and lover, companion in arms to
friends, a good man with some frailties, a figure who can be seen from
many sides. The episodes of the *Odyssey* would structure the story,
and each episode would be treated in a different literary style – from
the dramatic monologue of the 'Cyclops' chapter in the tavern to the
hallucinatory surrealism of the 'Circe' chapter in the brothel, from the
question-and-answer comic catechism of the 'Ithaca' chapter, where
Bloom and Stephen return home to Eccles Street, to the interior
monologue of the 'Penelope' scene, when Bloom is back in bed with
Molly, who freely reflects on her past, uses the chamber pot, and
seems to respond sexually to Bloom at last.

The plan was massive, and Joyce set it out as a great schema. As he told Budgen, it was also a book about the parts of the human body, each section being related to a particular bodily organ – the kidney that we see Bloom cooking at the beginning of his story is not put into the pan by accident, any more than the eggs for breakfast he requests at the end. Each section was associated with a particular art, so that Stephen's broodings on theology as he talks to Buck Mulligan are again there for a thematic purpose. Each section also was associated with a particular symbol and a particular colour, and set at a particular hour. But the extraordinary thing about the book is the way in which all these abstract and often learned notions – the idea of the jingoistic Fenian Citizen as the giant Cyclops, windy, loud-mouthed and monstrous, for instance – are always naturalized, brought to the human and commonplace level. We might well find it helpful to know that Molly is intended as the equivalent of Homer's Penelope, or that the graveyard scene is set in Hades. But this intellectual and literary skeleton does not have to be exposed in order for us to experience these characters and actions as recognizable and humanly valuable.

In *Ulysses* (far more than in *Finnegans Wake*) we do penetrate beyond the language to the life. We suffer with Bloom's persecution as a victimized Jew, with his feelings as a cuckold, laughed at by his fellow-Dubliners because even as he walks the city his wife is having a tryst with 'Blazes' Boylan, her musical manager and 'the worst man in Dublin'. We can even sympathize with the suspicion that he has deliberately permitted the tryst to occur, and that his wanderings are to let it happen, and with his own attempts to find satisfaction, by the correspondence he conducts under the name of 'Mr Henry Flower', and above all by his visit to the brothel in the 'Nighttown' scene. For in the surreal atmosphere we are made aware of his fantasies both of humiliation and power, as he thinks of himself as Lord Mayor of Dublin ('I'll stand for the reform of municipal morals and the plain ten commandments . . . Electric dishscrubbers'). We recognize his feelings for his dead son, his kindness to Stephen, his complex Jewish heritage and its meaning for him. Likewise we can identify with Stephen's own crisis – the agony of conscience he feels about his mother's death and his failure to please her with an expression of faith (his 'agenbite of inwit'), his mixture of physical and spiritual desire. We can recognize Molly's fallibility and gross sensuality, her love of sentimental physical pleasure and her own sense of loss.

Indeed the book is a great human comedy – and first and foremost *Ulysses* surely *is* a comedy, in the great tradition of the novel, the tradition that goes back to Fielding, Sterne and Rabelais. In my own view it is precisely the scale and variety of the comic method that holds the novel together, and makes it much more than the sum of its parts. From the moment when the mock-religious dialogue starts between stately plump Buck Mulligan and the listless Stephen, *Ulysses* reveals itself as a work of profound wit. Bloom is certainly Joyce's 'complete man', but he is also a comic character. The use of the 'interior monologue' may be a great literary invention and a new key to the exploration of consciousness, but it is also a means for generating a metaphysical wit by juxtaposition, allowing heterogeneous images to be yoked by violence together. And the story of the novel may be vast in its epic scope, but it can also be condensed down to one simple newspaper advertisement:

What is home without
Plumtree's Potted Meat?
Incomplete.
With it an abode of bliss.

Surely enough, there is potted meat in the conjugal bed when Bloom returns to it.

Joyce's comedy is a very verbal comedy, but it also comes out as scatological reference and gross slapstick. A jangle of cod songs and dirty jokes runs throughout the tale ('when I makes tea I makes tea, as old mother Grogan said. And when I makes water I makes water'). The extent to which the book is built on boys'-school jokes about upside-down sex and sodomy is something that not all the learned scholars have been prepared to admit. The surreal and hallucinatory effects of the brothel scene, in which Bella is the temptress Circe, who strikes men moon-mad and turns them into beasts, are also elaborate, slapstick comic effects, built out of a sequence of gross and dirty puns.

The associative flow of Molly Bloom's thought is based on the associative wit of the unconscious, carefully honed. And the flamboyant allusions to Homer's epic function not only as serious underpinning – of course they are that too – but as a parodist's display of his virtuoso technique. Indeed the brilliance of Joyce's comedy comes out most strongly in the parodic methods of his writing. Parody tells us that all writing is rewriting, both a comment on an original and a flamboyant new enterprise of its own. Joyce's book is a multiplicity of voices, both honouring and undermining some original source or literary technique, or mocking and satirizing some convention or sentimentality. It is a form of mastery of language – Joyce always had that – and a teasing of its limits.

There is no better example than the 'Ithaca' episode, near the end, where the method of catechism, of question-and-answer, is used to manoeuvre Bloom and Stephen back into the house, and then Bloom into bed. The technique allows almost everything. We learn an inordinate amount of information, from the means by which water is got from Roundwood reservoir in County Wicklow ('through a subterranean aqueduct of filter mains of single and double pipeage constructed at an initial plant cost of £5 per linear yard') into Bloom's kitchen tap, to the contents of Bloom's house and of the books in his room. We learn his migrant history and his theories of life. Indeed the catechism provides a mechanism of memory as complex as that of the interior monologue soon to come. We have a vision of the stellar universe, followed by urination. Dialogue between Bloom and Stephen is conveyed, and they reconstruct an exotic history of human speech and writing, which is followed by a song which is reprinted visually for us on the page. Then the method manoeuvres Bloom/Ulysses back into the marital bed with Molly/Penelope, in far lower circumstances than in the Homeric original:

Bloom's acts?
He deposited the articles of clothing on a chair, removed his remaining articles of clothing, took from beneath the bolster at the head of the bed a folded long white nightshirt, inserted his head and arms into the proper apertures of the nightshirt,

removed a pillow from the head to the foot of the bed, prepared
the bedlinen accordingly and entered the bed . . .
What did his limbs, when gradually extended, encounter?
New, clean bedlinen, additional odours, the presence of a human
form, female, hers, the imprint of a human form, male, not
his, some crumbs, some flakes of potted meat, recooked, which
he removed.
If he had smiled why would he have smiled?
To reflect that each one who enters imagines himself to be the
first to enter whereas he is always the last term of a preceding
series . . .
What preceding series?
Assuming Mulvey to be the first term of his series, Penrose,
Bartell d'Arcy, Professor Godwin, Julius Mastiansky, John Henry
Menton, Father Bernard Corrigan . . .

And so on, to Hugh E. ('Blazes') Boylan. After all, Homer loved
lists. And so Bloom kisses Molly's rump, stirs sexually, engages in
another dialogue of catechism with her about Stephen, and then 'He
rests. He has travelled.'

The rich mockery of discourse is not, of course, the final mood of
the book. Molly's monologue follows, an extraordinary achievement
of fictional creation. The thirty-eight pages fall into only eight sentences and go from an initial to a final 'yes'. The extent to which
Molly in this section accepts Bloom, and Bloom in turn resumes a
normal genital relationship with her, is uncertain – an issue left for
modern scholars to tease their minds with. But the rhythm of the
section – from the beginning, where Bloom has clearly reversed the
roles we saw near the beginning of the novel, and has asked to have a
breakfast of two eggs served to him in bed – to the comparison she
makes between Boylan and Bloom, and settles in Bloom's favour,
implies that he may not only have travelled but arrived. Molly
Bloom's dreamy soliloquy is, as the psychologists have said, a remarkable exploration of the unconscious, an extraordinary enterprise
in psychic retrieval. But it is also a great, coarse, comic speculation on
fertility, and a form of Rabelaisian fertility itself. Whether what Molly

accepts is in the past or the present we are not sure, but it is one of the most extraordinary of fictional endings, an open embrace that shows that Joyce is a master not just of conceptual but of densely erotic writing.

That last chapter of *Ulysses* is in every sense a seedbed – the birthplace for what was to follow. What followed for Joyce was *Finnegans Wake*, where the central figure of Anna Livia Plurabelle is unmistakably an extension of Molly Bloom, now turned into a universal image of flow and fertility. Joyce began the book in 1922, almost as soon as he finished *Ulysses*, and it bears the same relation to that novel as *Ulysses* does to *A Portrait* . . . – an extension which is also a completely new conception. And probably no book has ever been more ambitiously conceived. It was intended to be a history of the world, the book of here comes everybody; it sought to construct a modern meta-language, an Esperanto for the art of fiction. 'I could not . . . use words in their ordinary connections,' Joyce noted, as he struggled, his sight failing, with the great work-in-progress that became the great work-in-expectation of the 1920s and 1930s, a dream-work that attempted to assimilate all myths while at the same time monumentalizing and memorializing the difficulties of constructing them.

Finnegans Wake at last appeared, exactly seventeen years after *Ulysses*, on 2 February 1939. War came later that year, and Joyce left Paris once more for the old home of his exile, Zurich. Two months later he died there of a perforated ulcer, and we were left in the world after the wake. Modernism seemed completed and over, but indeed it was not. *Finnegans Wake* was the book that spoke abstractly to the great Modernist task both of breaking down an old language and myth, and constructing a new and self-made one that made the art of fiction the art of language itself. To that we owe much, including a good many new literary experiments, and much of our modern linguistic anxiety. But to *Ulysses* we owe more, a sense of modern creative ebullience in the form of a comic as well as a cosmic possibility. It became part of the onward spirit of modern writing, and we recognize its presence everywhere. *Ulysses* was a seedbed indeed.

T. S. ELIOT

I

There is a well-known poem which warns us just how unpleasant it was to meet Mr T. S. Eliot,

> With his features of clerical cut,
> And his brow so grim
> And his mouth so prim
> And his conversation, so nicely
> Restricted to What Precisely
> And If and Perhaps and But . . .

The view seems uncharitable, so perhaps it is fortunate that the subject of the poem and the author of it were one and the same person. This typical piece of self-mockery was one of Mr Eliot's own 'Five Finger Exercises', a group of playful verses in the 'Minor Poems' section of Eliot's *Collected Poems, 1909–1935*. This volume, which first came out in 1935 and went through many reprintings, was probably the most important British or American verse collection of this century. Certainly, in the hands of several generations of readers, it did more than any other to change our idea of what modern poetry is or might be like.

And, if the book had its minor, playful poems, it also had its major ones. There was, for example, *The Love Song of J. Alfred Prufrock*, which opens the book as it opened Eliot's extraordinary career – establishing through the timid, hesitant figure of Mr Prufrock a spirit of mannered irony new to Anglo-American verse. There was the religious poem *Ash Wednesday*, and there was *Burnt Norton*, which proved to be the first of Eliot's *Four Quartets*, a group of profound meditative poems which represented the mature and contemplative poet of later years just as *Prufrock* represented the early fireworks. And somewhere in the middle of the volume, and the middle of the career, there was the most famous poem of all, *The Waste Land*, a poem in 433 lines, and five sections. It covered 17 pages, and there were seven pages of added notes, which have kept the scholars busy for many years. These are, it has been noticed, probably the most heavily studied pages in all modern literature, and *The Waste Land* itself has been called the greatest poem of the twentieth century. Certainly it is the poem from which most modern verse in English, and indeed a good many other languages, has flowed – the poem every poet today finds in his or her path, the poem that once and for all changed our idea of what to expect of a modern poem and a modern poet. In one way or another most of us meet Mr Eliot, or some version of his influence.

And in fact – as I discovered on the one occasion when I did encounter him – it was extremely pleasant to meet Mr Eliot in the flesh. I met him in the middle of the 1950s, when as a young critic I was writing something on *The Criterion*, the major magazine he edited between 1922 and 1939 (*The Waste Land* appeared in its opening issue). He agreed to see me in his publisher's office at Faber & Faber, in Russell Square, London, and I found him warm, courteous and friendly. He was generous in his judgements on the many younger poets, British and American, he had introduced, both as editor of the magazine and as the main publisher of verse in Britain. He was also very disinclined to talk about his own work. But this was to be expected; he was also a formal, reserved, gentlemanly figure, and a great believer in the mask of the poet, the separation between the man who suffers and the mind which creates. By this date he was the most important living British poet, the major literary critic, and a successful West End playwright who had led the postwar revival of verse drama. He had won the Nobel Prize for Literature in 1948, and been awarded the British Order of Merit. This was unusual in an American-born poet, but by this time Eliot was, in his own famous phrase, 'classicist in literature, royalist in politics, and anglo-catholic in religion.' He had been received into the Anglican Church five years after publishing *The Waste Land*, and taken British nationality about the same time. His accent was British, his features were indeed of clerical cut, his conversation was scholarly, and his manner almost studiously unpoetic.

Being young at the time, I therefore found it hard to relate this pleasant but retiring figure to the moment of outrage and transformation he had created two decades before, when *The Waste Land* was published. 1922, the year it appeared, was a year of major Modernist events, the moment when the pent-up experiments that had developed over the First World War broke out and set the tone for what followed. Even so, the poem produced a sense of shock, a feeling that the poetic tradition was being upturned. There was the matter of its difficulty; there were those who found it totally obscure, and others who found it arid and dessicated, grim and prim – as some people found Mr Eliot himself. One influential critic of the day, F. L. Lucas, attacked it by saying that 'Among the maggots that breed in the corruption of poetry the commonest is the bookworm.' Lucas's massive misjudgement was understandable enough, for the apparatus of parody, pastiche, and recondite allusion gave the poem a formidable look – intensified by the fact that Eliot added seven pages of notes to the book version, not, he said later, to explain the poem, which explains itself, but to fill the volume out to book size. Nonetheless Lucas, and other critics, missed much: the fact, for instance, that the learning is not simply pedantry but a complex method for interweaving old and modern poetic cadences, and the fact that the dry bones called up in the poem were not so much an expression of the aridity of the poem or the poet himself, but a profound critique of the culture of the time.

But other like Edmund Wilson recognized *The Waste Land* as the culmination and fulfilment of the modern movement in poetry that had been developed since the 1870s, a work that belonged with the achievement of Joyce in fiction, Picasso in painting, Stravinsky in music. If *The Waste Land* was a great poem, it was not simply because it was learned or difficult, though it was both. It was because it built an extraordinary bridge between the great poetic and mythic achievements of the past and the poetic necessities of the present, because – like other great works of Modernism – it was both a great undermining and a new beginning. To Edmund Wilson, writing in *Axel's Castle* in 1931, it was a work that dealt authoritatively with postwar despair,

spiritual drought and anarchy, the work of a complete poet who had
'enchanted and devastated a whole generation' able to recognize, as
their elders did not, a vision that belonged to them. The postwar poets
of Eliot's own generation were also shaken by the poem, and some
found it a profound challenge to their own view of modern poetry.
'To me especially it struck like a sardonic bullet,' the American poet
William Carlos Williams confessed later in his *Autobiography*, 'Critically Eliot returned us to the classroom when I felt we were on the
point of escape to matters much closer to the essence of a new art
form itself – rooted in the locality that should give it fruit.' Like Eliot,
Williams had been influenced by Pound. But he wanted the new
poetic spirit to emphasize nationality and not cosmopolitanism,
optimism and not decadent despair. Yet, much as he resented the
new classroom, he felt, like most of his serious contemporaries in
poetry, the scale of the achievement, and its monumental importance.

The *Waste Land* indeed placed itself at the centre of the tradition of
the new. As Eliot has declared himself, in his essays, no poet has his
complete meaning alone, and by each new work the tradition is
slightly altered; at the same time the ideal poet is fully aware of the
tradition. *The Waste Land* both extended and dislodged the tradition,
being a break with Romantic and Victorian poetry, a return to the
tradition of Metaphysical wit and Shakespearean flamboyance ('O O
O O that Shakespeherian Rag'), a homage and a sacrilege. Equally it
questioned the habitual idea of the poet, above all the Romantic view
of him as public prophet, seer, voice of nature and true feeling. In the
tired prophet Tiresias, and the pierhead clairvoyant Madame Sosostris,
the wisest woman in Europe, two figures at the centre of the poem,
Eliot seemed to mock the visionary mode in verse, and what visions
there are in the poem are those of dismay and despair. When,
somewhere close to the start of the First World War, Eliot began his
initial work on the poem, he gave it a title from Dickens: 'He Do
The Police In Different Voices.' It was a title well chosen to describe a
poem of parody and pastiche, a poem that sought to relate the great
poetic cadences of the past to the vernacular intonations and speech
patterns of the present. We are, of course, fortunate that he finally
dispensed with this title in favour of one that seemed itself to sum-

marize the state of the postwar world. Nonetheless, that lost title summed up a great deal about Eliot's work.

2

Ezra Pound called Eliot 'Old Possum', after the most cunning of animals, and the name was apt. For Eliot poetry was no Whitman-esque song of myself, an assertion of the poet, a spilling-over of emotion or a great incorporation of experience. He was a masked poet, a poet of mocking disguises, a dramatic poet, a poet not of one but many voices. No doubt this was partly a matter of temperament. He was reserved, withdrawn, the poet as bank clerk. He had no fondness for public display, no desire for direct self-expression. Poetry he regarded not as an expression of emotion but an escape from emotion. The self-mocking Prufrock is a natural mask for such a poet; he prepares a face to meet the faces that we meet, he is not Prince Hamlet nor was meant to be, and his love-song is not a love-song at all but a fastidious separation from feeling. The very guise of the poet requires a disguise. But, whatever the temperamental source, the important achievement lay in the new poetic tone this produced. Eliot's poetry broke with the traditional voice, intonation and cadence of previous verse. His new tone was angular, difficult, complex – as angular as a Cubist painting, filled with the same sudden surprises of wit. It was also a voice that constantly modulated between lyricism and irony, feeling and intelligence. As one critic said, his thoughts move not through majestic curves, but like live thoughts in live brains.

The reader of *The Waste Land* – and even more of the entire repertory of *Collected Poems* – will soon begin to respond to the Eliotic tone. There is a the voice of the fastidious ironist, the voice of the troubled snob. There is the voice of the international traveller who has been too far and seen too much, as in the poem 'Mélange Adultère de Tout.' The title comes from the French symbolist poet Tristan Corbière, and is, like so much in Eliot, a mannered quotation: the poem is written in French, and is an image of the modern rootless traveller in an internationalized and adulterated world ('En Amerique, professeur; / En Angleterre, journaliste . . .'). This and most of the early poems take us hopping through a world of fragments, a world of chatter, chance collisions, noise and syncopations, office blocks, turning gramophones, dusty back lots. The task of the modern poet in such a world must be different, and Eliot constantly summons it, doing the police in different voices. Indeed *Collected Poems* ranges from the dandyish irony of Prufrock, the speaker of the first poem, hesitant witness to events always greater than himself, who feels he 'should have been a pair of ragged claws / Scuttling across the floors of silent seas,' to the many-voiced drama of *The Waste Land*, and then on to the meditative voice of the later Eliot.

Which, then, is the 'serious' poet, the real Eliot? The answer lies in the variety itself, and the way Eliot builds his extraordinary bridges between the voices, the tones, the dramatic levels. The serious poetic gesture proves to be an allusion or a quotation. The tragic tone – and tragedy underlines much of Eliot's poetry – modulates, by some sudden cut, into buffoonery. *The Waste Land* is unquestionably a poem of tragic vision, but it is also a comedy, a parody, a mockery of as well as an expression of literature. Feeling is always subject to intellect, lyricism to scepticism, and the old charismatic priests and prophets of traditional poetry are constantly being resisted. Each poem constructs its own connection between irony and seriousness and from this comes a third tone, the tone of the witty modern poet. Playful as all this is, it is also part of a coherent theory. For one reason Eliot is a great poet is that he is always seeking to define what kind of creature the poet of modernity might be. He is always concerned with what Frank Kermode once called 'the ruinous and exhausting task of writing the major poetry of the age.' The word Eliot gave to the spirit in which he wrote was 'classicism,' a term he took from his teacher at Harvard, the anti-Romantic philosopher Irving Babbitt.

Of course we always ask our poets to be the custodians of the imagination, and there is a good deal of the spirit of Romanticism in Eliot, not least in his often lyrical response to modern fragility ('I am moved by fancies that are curled / Around these images, and cling: / The notion of some infinitely gentle / Infinitely suffering thing'). Nonetheless it was 'classicism' that controlled such fancies and presented them with detachment, 'classicism' that gave Eliot his famous doctrine of poetic 'impersonality', and the 'objective correlative' – the image outside ourselves that allows poetic creation to distil. From Flaubert onwards, the notion of the separation of the artist from his work had been important to Modernism. James Joyce – whose career overlapped and interlocked with Eliot's in many ways, *Ulysses* and *The Waste Land* being published almost simultaneously – explores in *A Portrait of the Artist as a Young Man* the need for creative detachment, as the artist stands apart from his work like the God of creation, creating a 'luminous silent stasis' of aesthetic pleasure. As Eliot similarly explains, in his essay on his French poetic contemporary Paul Valéry, poetry is 'impersonal in the sense that personal emotion, personal experience, is extended and completed in something impersonal.' Eliot acknowledged that the separation can never be complete. Indeed we know – thanks in part to Peter Ackroyd's brilliant biography of Eliot – that his poetry is filled with personal traces. But the way it *becomes* poetry is through an act of separation and angularity, and it was in this way that Eliot became the masterful modern poet.

3

Where did the idea of the responsibility of the modern poet and his exceptional task come from? Eliot himself traced it to Charles Baudelaire, the French symbolist poet of the mid-nineteenth century who was both the offspring of the Romantic movement and the first great anti-Romantic. Like his successor, Arthur Rimbaud, with his famous dictum – *il faut être absolument moderne* ('it is necessary to be absolutely modern') – Baudelaire believed in an art of modernity. Like Walt Whitman in America, he considered that in the modern world the entire poetic convention had collapsed, and needed to be re-invented entirely. But, unlike Whitman, who believed that the solution lay in attaching poetry to America's hopeful, democratic, expansionist, optative mood, Baudelaire saw poetry as dwarfed by the past and the unpoetic nature of the modern world, a world of historical decay and frail urban sensibility. Poetry was forced inward, into the world of the imagination, where all faculties, all arts, all connections and correspondences, could meet and combine to produce 'the sensation of newness'. And, as Eliot said in an essay on Baudelaire, it was his decadence, his famous 'unhealthiness', that allowed him to distil the essential gift of a major poet, a sense of his own age. Baudelaire's sense of fragmentation, of the fragile sensations that came from modern life and the modern city – '*Fourmillante cité, cité pleine de rêves*' – and his power of incorporating this into poetry was the way to a poetry of the modern metropolitan, self-alienating world.

The Symbolist movement was to have a massive impact on the new, anti-Victorian poetry that developed in the early part of the century both in Britain and in the United States. The book that transmitted the message was Arthur Symons' study *The Symbolist Movement in Literature*, which appeared in 1899. Both Eliot and Pound read it while still at college in the United States, while in London the major poet of the Celtic Twilight, W. B. Yeats, passed the news onward. Symons's book made it quite clear that the 'decadence' of the late nineteenth century was a good deal more than a group of cynical mannerisms, 'unhealthy' attitudes, Latin Quarter trilbies, and a pervasive disordering of the senses and of language. It was a new and different way of viewing the universe, the arts, the poetic role, the nature of poetic form and language. Baudelaire's 'sensation of newness' extended into Théophile Gautier, Paul Verlaine, and Stephane Mallarmé, who in various ways broke with the romantic tradition and attempted a subjective reconstruction of language. And above all it reached into the fragile dry irony of Tristan Corbière and Jules Laforgue, the two late Symoblist poets who were most important to the young and increasingly anti-Romantic Eliot as he began his early poetry.

It was the development onward from the late Romanticism of the decadent 1890s through toward what one critic has called 'the new poetic' of the early twentieth century that shaped the Modern movement in poetry – a movement towards a poetry that was, as Pound said, drier, harder, nearer the bone. The apocalyptic feelings of the decadents – the feeling of fragility, despair, of historical decline and cultural loss – and their commitment to modern sensation and urban impressions were part of the essence. So was the figure of the poet as the ironic dandy; Eliot did not invent all of this himself. Much of the best modern poetry was to become an ironic testing of Romanticism, and shaped by the desire to rewrite poetic history. Modern poetry would belong to the age of the city, the machine, the rise of the crowd, the growth of popular culture. It would be most abstract, and, as the philosopher T. E. Hulme put it, find 'beauty in small dry things.' Hulme wrote a handful of poems that Ezra Pound would use as major examples of the new spirit when he tried to draw it all together into a movement he called Imagism. Pound had arrived in London from the United States in 1908, and he attempted to co-ordinate the new spirit in poetry, accumulating Symbolist ideas, publishing manifestos and magazines. Imagism started in 1912, according to legend, in a Kensington teashop, when Pound, Hilda Doolittle ('H.D.'), a fellow-American, and her British husband Richard Aldington agreed on a number of principles, designed to confront the exhausted Victorianism that still persisted in Georgian poetry and cure the 'ailments' of poetic language.

The Imagist principles were clearness itself, as well as being a statement on behalf of clearness:

1. Direct treatment of the 'thing', whether subjective or objective.
2. To use absolutely no word that does not contribute to the presentation.
3. As regarding rhythm: to compose in the sequence of the musical phrase, not in sequence of a metronome.

The new poetry Pound looked for was therefore condensed, un-adjectival, centred on the object. It would be composed in the sequence of the musical phrase, which normally meant some form of 'free verse' – though, Pound said, no verse is free to the poet who does a good job. The aim was to break with the romantic tradition of lushness in poetry, and produce a new verse as radical as Cubist painting, the

Russian ballet, or Stravinsky's music. But Pound evidently had difficulty in finding a poet who embodied all the principles of his various
manifestos. 'H.D.' wrote verse of a timeless, Hellenistic kind, but
Pound hoped for a more direct confrontation with the modern world.
William Carlos Williams, James Joyce and D. H. Lawrence contributed to the Imagist anthologies, but they were visitors rather than
committed Imagists. Many of the early Imagist poems were small
elegant objects that look more like teaching examples than major
poetic innovations. One was Pound's own concentrated, Japanese-
influenced two-liner 'In a Station of the Metro':

> The apparition of these faces in the crowd;
> Petals on a wet, black bough.

This showed a basic technique Pound called 'superpositioning'. Two
images are set in equal relation, neither being subordinate to the other.
The aim was concentration, an explosion of linguistic energy from
fragments. But these examples did not show how Imagism might
construct a poetry of scale or epic intention, or deal with the problem
of the age.

Imagism was in effect a question to which many young poets were
trying to find an answer. But it is clear that the movement would
never have had the impact it did had it not been for a peculiar chance.
In the summer of 1914 Pound was watching Imagism slip away from
him, the anthologies having been hijacked off to the United States
by the cigar-smoking American poetess Amy Lowell. He moved on
with Wyndham Lewis to the movement of Vorticism, but that was
essentially a movement of painters rather than poets. However that
summer a young American philosopher – Thomas Stearns Eliot, from
Saint Louis, Missouri – who had intended spending his time at
Marburg in Germany moved instead to London, en route for Oxford,
where he was going to work on a thesis on the philosopher F. H.
Bradley. His intellectual education and literary interests were extensive, his critical gifts outstanding. He also had poetic aspirations
and had, quite independently of the Imagists, come to many of the
same ideas, largely derived from the later Symbolists. Indeed in some

ways his views were more solidly and firmly based, and the few poems he had written under the influence of Laforgue and Corbière were totally assured and remarkable. He was shy where Pound was flamboyant, precise where he was extravagant, pedantic where he was voracious. He was attracted more than Pound was to British culture itself, and over the year he married, as Pound had, a British wife. He was also glad to come under Pound's exciting tutelage and draw on his influential support. Of all the many young writers whom Pound assisted, he was the most assiduous, and the most impressive. It was he, indeed, who turned the Anglo–American experiments of 1890–1914 into a serious modern poetry, and along with Pound he established the poetic Tradition of the New.

4

Even in 1914, when he arrived unexpectedly in London, it was hard to imagine that the formal Mr Eliot had grown up, like Huckleberry Finn, on the banks of the Mississippi, the great rolling river that drains the heartland of America, and had come from Saint Louis, the city that rightly regards itself as the gateway to the West. The Mississippi River was to find its place in a number of Eliot's poems, most especially *The Dry Salvages*. And Saint Louis itself, he once suggested, was the original city of *The Waste Land*, 'upon which that of Paris and London have been superimposed.' It was the '*fourmillante cité*' that directed his attention to Baudelaire and the urbane sensation in poetry, and it was urban rather than frontier Saint Louis in which he grew up. In any case the Eliots always looked back East rather than West. They were originally New Englanders, part of the American intellectual aristocracy who went back to the Puritans (their ancestor Andrew Eliot had migrated from East Coker in Gloucestershire) and the Unitarian ministers of the nineteenth century, who had so much to do with civic duty and reform. Eliot's grandfather, the Reverend William Greenleaf Eliot, carried echoes of the New England con-

science in his very name. Like many other New Englanders, they had
come West with missionary purposes, and they still summered back
East.

It was said of the Unitarians that they believed in at most one God,
and prayed to whom it might concern. Eliot was a frail and serious
child, much influenced by his grandfather, and his notions of civic
service. The Eliot name still meant much at both Harvard and Yale,
and it was suitably to Harvard that he went for his college education
in 1906. His interest was philosophy, and it was no time to become a
poet. The 'Genteel Tradition' of Longfellow, James Russell Lowell
and John Greenleaf Whittier, the American Victorian sages, still
remained as dominant in American verse as it had in the mid-
nineteenth century. 'Whatever may have been the literary scene in
America between the beginning of the century and the year 1914, it
remains in my mind a complete blank,' he wrote later. 'The only
recourse was to poetry of another age and to poetry of another language . . .' Eliot indeed was chiefly interested in philosophy, though
he read avidly in literature – Virgil and Dante, the Elizabethan and
Jacobean dramatists, Shakespeare, the Metaphysicals, the French Symbolists, and, of course, Arthur Symons. Like Ezra Pound he was the
product of a capacious and comparative education, and intellectually
cosmopolitan from an early stage.

There is little doubt that Eliot turned to poetry in revolt against the
Eliot tradition of public service, as others of his generation did. He
read Swinburne and the decadents, and the Japanese poets. His earliest
poems drew on their manner, as the posthumously published *Poems
Written in Early Youth* (1967) reveal. But he was soon adopting an
ironic, Laforguian tone, and wandering the new *'fourmillante cité'* of
Boston. Its back streets, lighted doorways, its one-night cheap hotels
and sawdust restaurants with oyster shells became the stuff of his
poems, along with the more formal, genteel Boston of maiden aunts
and readers of the *Boston Evening Transcript*. These poems show his
own solitude, sexual anxiety and preoccupation with the darker side
of the city world, and his sense of the aimless chattering noise of
urban life. New England had a great deal to do with the spirit of
Eliot's writing, and even with the spirit of his expatriation. For it was

part of the New England tradition to develop one's academic and literary education in Europe, and in 1910 he went to Paris to hear philosophy lectures from Henri Bergson (just as Proust had) and write verse in the Laforguian manner. The best of these poems, which he finished in Munich the next year, was about an *homme moyen sensuel* who stands as a spectator in front of a tantalizingly empty but exotic world. With a Laforguian irony, he acknowledges his own modest role in this modern, sensual universe: 'I am no prophet – and here's no great matter; / I have seen the moment of my greatness flicker, / And I have seen the eternal Footman hold my coat, and snicker, / And in short, I was afraid.' J. Alfred Prufrock had been born – though he went into a drawer for several years.

For now Eliot returned to Harvard to study and teach philosophy, beginning work on the thesis on F. H. Bradley, author of *Appearance and Reality*, who gains his place in the footnotes to *The Waste Land*. In 1914 he set out on a Sheldon Travelling Fellowship from Harvard to a summer school at Marburg University in Germany, only to find war-clouds gathering, and moved on to London sooner than expected, en route for Oxford. So came the crucial meeting with Pound, running the poetic revolution from his flat in Holland Park. The relationship of the two is one of the fundamental relationships of modern poetry – formalized in the dedication Eliot added to *The Waste Land* 'For Ezra Pound, *il miglior fabbro*,' the better craftsman, the dedication Dante gave to Arnaut Daniel. The poetic revolution was at its height, and Pound was involved in the Vorticist manifesto-magazine *Blast*, a massive, Futurist-style explosion against the dead Victorian past and the dulled commercial present. He was also engaged with the magazine *The Egoist*, and was 'foreign correspondent' for the Chicago little magazine *Poetry*, which was printing new verse, much of it influenced by Symbolism and Imagism, from the new poetic generation that had wonderfully emerged in the *avant-garde* spirit of the immediately pre-war years.

It was therefore not surprising that, when Eliot showed him *The Love Song of J. Alfred Prufrock*, Pound recognized a poet who displayed the true spirit of the revolution he hoped to effect. He knew exactly what to do with the poem, and sent it to Harriet Monroe, the editor of *Poetry*, describing it as the best poem he had seen from an American: 'He has actually trained *and* modernized himself *on his own.*' Harriet Monroe knew exactly what to do with it, and tried to cut the poem, hardly her kind of Modernism; fortunately the danger was averted. At last, and rather despite her, *Prufrock* appeared in the magazine in 1915 – a lucky publication, for Imagism, for Modernism, for Pound and for Eliot himself. For, in a time of new poetic excitements, *Prufrock* was an extraordinary poetic debut. Several other of the outstanding new poets *Poetry* magazine had attracted indeed showed the influence of Symbolism and the Decadents. There was the outstanding Wallace Stevens, for example, another product of Harvard, who wrote initially in the pierrot-style manner, often gave his poems French titles, and signed his first submissions 'Peter Parasol'. Others, like William Carlos Williams and Marianne Moore, were clearly responding to the Imagist influence, and all of these would advance the spirit of modern poetry throughout the next decades.

Even so, *The Love Song of J. Alfred Prufrock* was different. It was, indeed, no love song, and its lyric feeling is spent on urban contrasts, between the one-night cheap hotels, and the cat-like fog in the streets, and the formal, dead drawing-rooms where the women come and go, talking of Michelangelo. It declared itself in an opening of startling power

> Let us go then, you and I,
> When the evening is spread out against the sky
> Like a patient etherised upon a table

that was to exemplify the new methods. As Craig Raine has said, this was the first of the modernist trumps – superpositioning triumphant, as the second image forces its way back on the first, turning the familiar poetic idea of the reddened night sky into a complex, surgical, intensely modern figure which leads us into a poem of moderated lyricism. The poem is as fragmentary as the modern city itself, and yet it has a structure, like its streets, which 'follow like a tedious argument / Of insidious intent / To lead you to an overwhelming question . . .' The question is never asked directly, the complex scenes and images of the poem providing an ironic answer. The person who raises the question is Prufrock, almost at times the fool, who cannot quite become the lover or the hero. It is a poem of failed emotions, lyrical tragedy, of visions, revisions, and endless indecisions. The 'overwhelming question' is never put, and the poem ends both on a lyrical evocation of emotion and Prufrock's separation from the emotion: 'I have heard the mermaids singing, each to each. / I do not think that they will sing to me.' It was a work of remarkable assurance from an unknown poet: it established Eliot's reputation, and the authority of the modern spirit of Imagism.

5

Prufrock's indecisions were thus to become the basis of many of the major decisions that Eliot himself took over the next few years, as his poetic and literary life now took shape. London in the wartime years grew increasingly gloomy – a gloom that penetrated the large new poem he now started, and that would become *The Waste Land*. But he chose to settle there, giving up his work at Merton and working as a schoolteacher and as assistant editor on *The Egoist*, thanks to Pound's patronage. He had married a British wife, the fragile Vivien Haigh-Wood, and he liked the orderliness of British life. He grew friendly with many of the main figures of the literary scene, not only among the expatriates around Pound, but among the Bloomsbury Group. He also began to emerge as a major critic. Indeed, over the next years he became – especially after the publication of *Prufrock and Other Observations* in 1917, and then of his first collection of essays, *The Sacred Wood*, published by Leonard and Virginia Woolf at the Hogarth Press in 1920 – both the leading poet and the leading critic of his generation. Just as his poetry was to shape the sensibility and feeling of the immediately postwar generation, his criticism was to guide many of its literary judgements and its critical standards, revising the general sense of the literary tradition and the academic practice of literary studies.

In his criticism, Eliot was in fact to perform an extraordinary task. Not only did he clear the ground for a new modern poetry – most specifically his own – but he constructed a new critical attitude that reshaped judgement in general. Like the great critics of the past – Dryden, Dr Johnson, Matthew Arnold, Sainte-Beuve, on whom he wrote – he spoke both with a broad judiciousness and with the engagement of the practitioner. His essays were substantial and finely conceived. He was formidably well-read, firm and philosophically exact in his judgements. He wrote as assuredly about the poets of the past as he did of those of the present, and like Pound he saw the task of the modern poet-critic as nothing less than that of reconstructing literary history, creating a new usable past. The task, as he said, took very great labour, but it was a labour he was uniquely able to perform. His sense of the past was cosmopolitan and capacious, and his tone measured; he saw criticism not as contention but clarification, a 'common pursuit of true judgement', and the outrageousness of his views – his large dismissal of Milton, for example – was tolerable because of the clarity and composure of his argument.

One essay, 'Tradition and the Individual Talent', did more than most to establish his critical attitude. Here he stressed that each new poet altered the tradition slightly, but needed in turn to be learned *in* the tradition. As for what the new tradition might be, Eliot made that clear. He looked back beyond the Victorians, and the 'dissociation of sensibility' that he said had set in during the seventeenth century, and was exemplified by Milton, to the Elizabethan, Jacobean and Metaphysical poets – Donne, Marvell, Herbert, Crashaw – and their 'wit'. A famous passage about Donne set the critical tone, and established one of his most famous notions, that of the 'dissociation of sensibility' that had divided intellect from feeling in British verse:

When a poet's mind is perfectly equipped for its work, it is constantly amalgamating disparate experience; the ordinary man's experience is chaotic, irregular, fragmentary. The latter falls in love, or reads Spinoza, and these two experiences have nothing to do with each other, or with the noise of the typewriter or the smell of cooking: in the mind of the poet these experiences are always forming new wholes.

Typically, Eliot's ordinary man was less ordinary than most. But the important point was the implied need for the modern poet to retrieve a wholeness of sensibility, a modern 'wit', where thought and feeling are reconciled. He was thus equally explicit about what modern poetry required. 'We can only say that it appears likely that poets in our civilization, as it exists at present, must be *difficult*,' he explained elsewhere, 'the poet must become more comprehensive, more allusive, more indirect, in order to force, to dislocate if necessary, language into his meaning.'

6

If these were important general ideas, they were also something more. They were pointers for *The Waste Land* – the great poem that, like so many of the major works of Modernism, began in wartime and was completed in the psychological slump that followed. In 1919 Ezra Pound finished his most notable work, *Hugh Selwyn Mauberley*, a depressed postwar farewell to London and its collapsed culture, and he thereafter took off for the more exciting cultural laboratory of Paris, setting to work on his own major modern enterprise of *The Cantos*. Both works showed that a major new poetry could be written using the imagistic, fragmentary methods Pound had celebrated before the war, methods that now had a greater significance in an era of Spenglerian despair about Western culture. Major poems in their own right, both can be regarded as important precursors of *The Waste Land*, a poem that was to some degree the fruit of a Pound–Eliot collaboration, for it was Pound's guiding hand over the text that brought the poem to concentration. But where Pound left London and became one of the gurus of Parisian modernism, Eliot remained in the city, becoming a bank clerk in Lloyd's Colonial and Foreign

Department. In 1921 he was asked to become the editor of a new review, *The Criterion*, a step that would eventually make him a full-time publisher.

1921 was a year of drought in London, when no rain fell in the city for six months. It was also a year of crisis for Eliot. Pressed by his work at the bank, the vast task of starting a major magazine in his spare time, money worries, the growing mental disturbance of Vivien, and his own feelings of emotional emptiness – he would come to call it *aboulie* – he suffered a nervous breakdown. He took three months' leave from work, and retreated, first to Margate, and then to a sanatorium in Lausanne. He also began intensive new work on his poem, completing it at the sanatorium. We can read traces of all these experiences in the text of *The Waste Land*: the psychic crisis that is not simply personal but belongs to the troubled age, the great drought, the glimpses of Margate ('On Margate Sands. / I can connect / Nothing with nothing') and Lausanne. That year he was also reading, with intense admiration, the draft of James Joyce's *Ulysses*, which he praised to Virginia Woolf as the book that showed the futility of all the English styles, and which shared with his own poem a strong sense of parody, a dramatic form, and an awareness of the collapse of traditional myth and ritual, coupled with a desire to reconstruct it.

Then there was the crucial advice from Pound, to whom he twice showed the manuscript. Whole sections disappeared under Pound's skilful surgery, including much exposition ('Don't try to bust all records by prolonging it three pages further,' Pound warned), some parodies, of Pope, for instance, and the section that became the separate poem *Geronton*. In all, Pound reduced the poem to about half its length. The clear if difficult structure that survives, with its shape from 'April is the cruellest month . . .' to 'Shantih, shantih, shantih,' is largely Pound's. As a result, when *The Waste Land* appeared in 1922 – first in his own magazine *The Criterion*, then as a book – its significance if not necessarily its meaning was fairly clear. As Pound, who had contributed so much, put it in a letter, in genuine admiration: 'It is after all a grrrreat littttttttterary period.'

As all this suggests, much went into *The Waste Land*, from difficult personal experiences to complex aesthetic ideas. It was born from the pain of the postwar world and the personal crises and anxieties of the major period of its writing. It was also the product of the literary and indeed the military battlefields of the years immediately previous, when the war itself seemed to justify an art of fragmentation and cultural despair. It was a fulfilment of the critical ideas Eliot had been and was still exploring. It was 'difficult', and indeed the difficulties were of such a kind as to fascinate the scholars ever since. It was fragmentary – 'these fragments I have shored against my ruins' – though it sought to draw the fragmentary into a new coherence. It was modern, a poem of the modern city, filled with typists and young men carbuncular, the swarming crowds who daily crossed London Bridge with their eyes down to go to work in the City, just like Eliot himself. Indeed London, which is coalesced with all the cities of past and present in their apocalyptic decline, is the *'fourmillante cité'* of Baudelaire in its new form as the 'Unreal City'. It established both its relation to and its separation from the tradition, by massive allusion, quotation, pastiche, and parody. It was a work of wit and irony – the wit that comes from the need to reconcile feeling with intelligence, the irony of a lowered time that can no longer aspire to the great achievements of the past, but desires its own redemptive myth. If there is a profound subjective feeling in it – something the critics have emphasized greatly in recent years – it was also objective and impersonal, and certainly no Whitman-like 'Song of Myself'. It was rather a dramatic work, like *Ulysses*, done in a variety of separate scenes in a widely conceived set of poetic styles which are then modified, amended, teased and transformed, so that indeed it did the police in different voices.

Eliot himself was later to suggest, when he became the religious poet and playwright of his later years, that the poem was somewhat chaotic, and contained an element of personal grouse. But this was not how it functioned in 1922, and certainly not the reason for its impact – any more than the personal traumas of Scott Fitzgerald afford an explanation of the power of *The Great Gatsby* or *Tender is the Night*. *The Waste Land* was a poem for its times, the immediately postwar years. It created a dark and agonized vision of spiritual loss which belonged not to a single individual but to contemporary culture, the modern city, and the postwar world. Its fragments may have been part of an inward fragmentation of spirit; they also expressed the fractures of the modern city, and they explored further the methods of superpositioning that had developed from Imagism. Fragments are the essence of *The Waste Land*; it is made of fragments of poems, the fragments of captured speech, the fragments of lives, and the fragments of culture. The method of fragmentation was a way of relating the past to the present, the mythic and religious sensibility to the world of the mundane, the history of art to its contemporary task – working like a painter's collage or a compendium both to make abstract and to clarify the artistic possibility. Above all it permitted Eliot a system of poetic modulation, as he captured the intonations of the major poets and dramatists of the past – from Shakespeare to Goldsmith, Dante to Pope, Webster to Browning – to provide the underlying lyricism, the poetic echo, for his modern scenes and settings.

The Waste Land is a poem of modern anti-climax, of contemporary sterility, and it is therefore tempting to read all its many poetic echoes and allusions as a series of parodies, where the poetic dignities of the past are mocked by the vulgarities of the present. Thus the lyrical impulse is set there to create its opposite ('O the moon shone bright on Mrs Porter / And on her daughter / They wash their feet in soda water'), and Eliot imitates the great effects of previous poetry only to undermine it. Yet the pattern of the poem is evidently more complex. Several of the five sections start from a high literary point, drawing upon and making a pastiche of the literature of the past. They then move on into a variety of scenes from the modern world, displaying modern despair and sterility. So the great speech of Enobarbus in *Anthony and Cleopatra* is adapted for the vivid opening of Part Two, 'A Game of Chess'. It then leads us, through a sequence of modulations, first to the empty exoticism of the lady of fragile nerves, then to 'rat's alley,' and then to the public-house scene where the 'sweet ladies' discuss abortion. But within this are the lyric arrests, the evocations of modern fragility, pain and suffering, and the endless presence of deathly anxiety, the sense of the skull beneath the skin. Indeed at many points in the poem Eliot becomes the great lyricist of the fragile sensitivities of the present. He should also be taken seriously in his declaration that the modern poet should reconcile intellect and feeling and create new wholes from disparate awarenesses. Tiresias, the old man with wrinkled dugs, the blind seer, is there to serve this function, bringing together past and present, male and female, the relation of things long foretold to the events of the time.

The Waste Land is a poem in which many things meet, a *mélange adultère de tout*. It condenses and connects past and present, showing the decline of history but also its unity, exploring the detail of one modern bourgeois city, London, but also of all the cities of world. It can be read as a work of postwar despair, but equally as a universal cry for faith, a search for a lost wholeness of being. Its despairing sense of spiritual loss and emptiness comes from a vision of the fragmentation, materialism and vulgarity of the modern city, but it is also a state of the soul. The structure of the poem is not a consistent narrative, but a large emotional curve, taking us from the collapsing empires of Europe, and the routines of urban life, through to the vision of a quest through sterile lands towards a possible salvation, while the cities fall. If the detail is difficult, the underlying myth of a search for fertility and redemption is not hard to see. In welcoming *Ulysses*, Eliot had spoken of its continuous parallel between antiquity and contemporaneity as 'a way of controlling, of ordering, of giving a shape and significance to the immense panorama of futility and anarchy which is contemporary history.' He added that, thanks to modern psychology and anthropology, it was possible to use a 'mythical method' which would be a step 'toward making the modern world possible for art'. It is clear that the comments have some appropriateness to *Ulysses*, but they apply even more fittingly to *The Waste Land*.

7

Today, thanks in part to the massive scholarship (some of it, in Eliot's view, quite superfluous), and our growing familiarity with the rhythms of modern verse, the structure of filmic cutting and scene-changing, and the merging of languages from high and popular culture in art, *The Waste Land* is no longer the difficult poem it once was. Nonetheless, we can still dispute about its meaning and importance. For some it is indeed the greatest poem of the century, for others a work of indulgent despair. Ezra Pound came to call it 'the justification of the "movement" of our modern experiment since 1900.' To many, it not only focused modern verse, but represented a supreme moment of associated poetic sensibility when the British and the American traditions of poetry united, internationalizing both. To others like William Carlos Williams, it was 'the great catastrophe in our letters'. Eliot had made the modern a place of cosmopolitanism, parody and dismay. Williams wished it to be a place of Americanism, optimism and hope, and in time he produced his own Modernist poem of American locality, *Paterson*, the modern epic of fecundity that nonetheless shows Eliot's trace. Similarly Hart Crane wrote *The Bridge* in a spirit of modern romanticism, challenging the classicism of Eliot's poem. Yet again the significance of Eliot could not be displaced completely, and Crane expressed his own doubts about whether a poet today could achieve an epic of total modern cohesion. For Pound and Eliot, the fragmentary nature of modern poetry was an endeavour both to express and to heal the fragmentation of the modern psyche and modern culture. For Williams and Crane, it was a way of revealing the fecundity of objects and myths themselves, a modern form of Whitmanesque inclusiveness. But this means excluding the dismays and erosions of modern history, as Eliot and Pound did not.

Thus, after *The Waste Land*, modern poetry divided and quarrelled, particularly across the Atlantic Ocean. Both Pound and Eliot remained in Europe, though in time their ways divided too. Pound explored the modern cultural crisis to the point where he identified with Mussolini's Fascist solution to its problems. Eliot remained in Britain, took British nationality and British religion, and became a convinced believer and a voice for continuity. His influence was international, for he was after all an international poet, a true contemporary of Rilke and Valéry. But he especially influenced the future of British poetry. Though they shared neither Eliot's politics nor his classicism, the social poets of the 1930s, above all W. H. Auden, Louis MacNeice and Stephen Spender, drew on his ironic and critical vision of modern culture. During the 1950s some of their successors revolted against the Modernist spirit as such, and looked behind it to the work of Hardy and Hopkins. The influence of Williams passed onward to American poets like Charles Olson and Robert Duncan, whose pursuit of the modern image and the free verse line went with a lyrical, even a shamanistic, attitude to poetry. Yet through all these divisions and revolts Eliot's influence somehow remained pervasive, and it persisted. Particularly it was the influence of *The Waste Land*, a poem he came to think less well of as he grew older. He died in 1965, and after her husband's death his second wife Valerie declared that 'He felt he had paid too high a price to be a poet, that he had suffered too much.' *The Waste Land* is a poem of that suffering, but it is vastly more. As the critics on both sides have said, modern poetry could not be the same without it.

LUIGI PIRANDELLO

I

'When an individual plays a part he implicitly requests his observers to take seriously the impression that is fostered before them,' writes the sociologist and psychologist Erving Goffman in his brilliant study of *The Presentation of Self in Everyday Life* (1959); 'They are asked to believe that the character they see actually possesses the attributes he appears to suggest, that the task he performs will have the consequences that are implicitly claimed for it, and that, in general, matters are what they appear to be.' Goffman is writing about the theatre of everyday existence – where, if society is to function as a society, each one of us has parts to play, roles to perform, masks to put on. That daily drama we call real life. But supposing we transfer such an awareness of so-called real life to the theatre itself? Now the individual who plays the part is an actor, the task he performs is a performance, and the sense that matters are what they appear to be is a theatrical illusion. After all, a play is a game and a fiction, a flamboyant copying of existence, performed by people who are paid to tell lies about themselves, and are called the acting profession. Supposing then we return again to the world of the real, everyday life. It might then seem that there was truth in the theatrical masks, and that we ourselves are wearing them on the street and at home. As Goffman shows, all the world is indeed a stage, and all the men and women merely players. We might think now we can *never* leave the theatre – especially if we have just been to a play by Luigi Pirandello.

Let us remember again the theatre of Ibsen, especially Ibsen the Naturalist. The set is solid and utterly familiar, a conventional room where, perhaps, old portraits hang, reassuring us of the past of the characters and their society. Here actors can speak words and perform actions so like our own we quickly acknowledge their reality. When they address problems like the conflicts of modern marriage, or the transmission of a congenital disease, these too make the drama real for us, for we can go on discussing them in our own world and our own lives. When they talk about the social events of the world outside – the coming of the railways, for example, or the moral problems of private and public life – we are moved by this, as we are when they have misfortunes, because we recognize the nature of the world and the kind of life they are after. Naturalism has been described as theatre removing the fourth wall from reality, and letting us see it. But of course we could remove *more* walls, perhaps all four of them, just leaving us with the unfamiliarity of the stage itself. We would then be back in the theatre of Pirandello.

Consider how a play is made. A set is designed and built, and a stage manager appointed. A director auditions and rehearses the actors, who may or may not have some similarity to the characters they will play. In any case, the actors will be disguised – costumed, made-up, and, in some forms of theatre, masked. The characters they impersonate in the theatrical game they are about to play can be people of their own time and their own kind, or kings and princes, people of another culture, another sex, or none at all, or animals, gods, trees or machines. They are normally part of a play already written, so that they are scripted, spoken for, and asked to perform relationships and conflicts which will form a dramatic unity. So they will be guided by a director, who will ensure the illusion is total, the vision all of a piece. All this goes on on one side of the curtain; an audience comes to the other. When the curtain rises, the masks should be on, the parts learned, the illusion complete. But if we were to see that illusion before it is complete, before the stage manager has left the stage or even before the playscript is finished, then again we might be in the theatre of Pirandello.

The steady undermining of Naturalism, the insistence on revealing just how it is that art creates its illusions, the belief that the very making of art's fiction is its proper subject – all of this, we have seen, is one of the deepest themes in Modernism. Joyce's *Ulysses* is set in the Naturalistic world of Dublin, but the form of the book, the half-mocking and parodic voices of the narrative, remind us we are reading a text, and watching the composition of a fiction. Like many modern novels, *Ulysses* is a self-concious novel, or a meta-novel. This does not mean that because its characters are fictions, constructs of words, and because the narrative technique is mocking and parodic, we fail to grant the story an inner reality. But we certainly depend on building a collusory relationship with the creative process, as it goes about the business of creating or forging that reality. In the same way there is a meta-theatre, which, because of the special relation between the illusion of theatre and the illusion of real life, can take on even more self-awareness. Again, the playwright who most clearly laid this bare for us, and most deeply explored the modern metaphysics of theatre and theatrical illusion itself, is surely Luigi Pirandello.

Meta-theatre has played a major role in modern drama, from the 1890s onward. The first glimpses are there in Ibsen's late plays, and like most modern playwrights Pirandello paid his homage to Ibsen: 'After Shakespeare, without hesitation, I put Ibsen first,' he said. But it owed even more to what came out from under Ibsen's shadow, the new theatre of the turn of the century – Alfred Jarry's mocking, grotesque *Ubu Roi* in 1896, or Auguste Strindberg's *A Dream Play* (1901), which followed from Ibsen's revolution and developed it into a new conception of theatre by both exaggerating and mocking the illusory space in which the theatre is performed. Meta-theatre (theatre that insists it is theatre, and not life, and which is in process of testing each aspect of its own illusion) surrounds us today, in the strange, half-undermined world of the plays of Tom Stoppard and Harold Pinter, Samuel Beckett and Eugene Ionesco. And it unlocks the illusion not only of theatre but of life itself, revealing its inauthenticity and absurdity – so that meta-theatre is often also a form of the theatre of the absurd, a theatre based on a vision of the human condition. Again, all this finds its illusory and disturbing centre in the drama of Pirandello.

When the audience enter the theatre for a performance of Pirandello's most famous play *Six Characters in Search of an Author*, which is subtitled 'A Play In the Making', they find the curtain up and the stage unset, or rather set informally as for a play rehearsal. It has been said that this entry into the 'empty space' of the 'real theatre' was the moment that truly heralded the Modern movement in drama. Certainly when the play had its premiere in Rome in May 1921, it caused a near-riot, and there was a whole audience in search of the author, who had to take refuge in a taxi. 'There is no set and there are no wings; [the stage] is empty and in almost total darkness,' say the stage directions. 'This is in order that right from the beginning the audience shall receive the impression of being present, not at a performance of a carefully rehearsed play, but at a performance of a play that suddenly happens.' This has been described as a stripping away of the theatrical illusion. In practice it is the opposite, for what Pirandello does is to construct that theatrical illusion for us, right in front of our eyes, meanwhile suggesting we too live in a similar world of illusion. 'Let us begin with the thing that illusion makes for each of us, with the construction that each person makes for himself through the work of illusion,' Pirandello wrote in his critical book *On Humour*, the work that reveals him most completely. 'Do we see ourselves in our true and genuine reality, as we are, or rather as we would like to be?'

In exploring the theatrical illusion to its most complicated and deceptive depths, Pirandello always knew he was primarily concerned with the illusions that govern our 'real' life and our human existence. It is important to remember that this great playwright of modern masks believed there were realities to unmask, and that theatre was a fundamental image of existence which offered access to the contradictions and profundities of life. The masks and mirrors of his plays are means for breaking the *boundaries* of illusion – for crossing the line, fracturing the mirror, touching the limits of identity, of reason, of certainty, and entering the world of double vision in which life is lived. 'Whoever understands the game can no longer fool himself, but if you cannot fool yourself, you can no longer derive any enjoyment or pleasure from life,' he said. 'So it goes. My art is full of bitter compassion for all those who fool themselves. But this compassion cannot help but be succeeded by ferocious derision of a destiny that condemns man to deception. This, succinctly, is the reason for the bitterness of my art, and also my life.' That bitter humour, that dark laughter, is another essential legacy left to us by the plays – and indeed by the life – of Luigi Pirandello.

2

'I am the son of Chaos,' Pirandello once wrote in an autobiographical fragment, framing a pun that was always of great importance to him. For this writer whose work contains all the shifting uncertainty, anxiety and formlessness of modern identity and existence was born in 1867 in Sicily, in the region between Agrigento and the sea still called by the name given it by the Greeks who colonized it with their temples and amphitheatres: Kaos. His house still stands in the area, and his ashes are kept here, as he wished, on the edge of the blue-clay plateau overlooking the African sea. In Fascist Italy, Pirandello kept his dark humour to the last. He knew that his remains, the remains of Italy's one surviving Nobel prizewinner for literature, would not disappear without trace, but would probably be buried in the Fascist black shirt. 'Burn me,' he therefore wrote, just before his death in 1936, 'and as soon as my body has been burnt the ashes must be thrown to the winds, for I want nothing, not even my ashes, to remain. But if this cannot be done, the funeral urn must be taken to Sicily and walled into some rough stone near Agrigento, where I was born.' The black humour he applied to his death he also attached to his birth. He came into the world, he recalled, during a cholera epidemic, which brought on his premature birth and gave it an odd importance in the atmosphere of disease and death. 'I believe people will think it inevitable that I should have been born there rather than anywhere else and at that moment rather than any other,' he said, adding typically, 'although I must admit that I myself have no views on the matter.'

Pirandello seems always to have felt he led life as an illusion, and that there was a constant doubleness to his (and everyone's) identity. 'Yes, I laugh sometimes, as I watch myself playing this self-imposed role,' says his character Gala in *Each In His Own Way*. But that sense of illusion derived from a strong regional heritage. In an Italy divided into different cultures, an Italy that only became a nation around the time of his birth, Pirandello was born in its most feudal as well as its southernmost part. As Sicily's greatest contemporary writer, Leonardo

Sciascia, still stresses today, that complex heritage, which mixed the Roman, the Greek and the Arab, lies deeply in Pirandello's work. He wrote many of his stories and novels about Sicily, and often in the Sicilian dialect. The strict codes of honour and shame that ruled in this feudal, fatalistic and peasant society shape the early fiction and are often recreated in the later plays. The hot, ancient and unchanging landscape, the grotesque aspects of life, the awareness of the inexorable power of the family, the very sense of theatre and of human comedy and tragedy – these basic features of his writing have much to do with his Sicilian birth. Just before it, Garibaldi and his redshirts had landed on the island, and his own father had fought for the cause. Over the next years the Italian 'Risorgimento' took place, and Italy was unified into a nation and a kingdom. But Sicily remained different, poor and feudal, and Pirandello grew up in the era of disappointed idealism that followed.

Pirandello's father owned a sulphur mine dug deep into the dramatic and volcanic Sicilian landscape. He was a passionate, violent man who at one point crossed swords with the Mafia. His wealth gave the young Pirandello the benefits of a good bourgeois upbringing which allowed him to pursue artistic interests, even though he was expected to enter the family business. He was withdrawn, detached, observant, and held the liberal opinions of the age. He supported the Sicilian peasant revolt of 1894, for example, and its failure had much to do with his later commitment to Fascism, which he thought would renew the country and give it the national reinvigoration and unity it still needed. But from early on he rejected the romantic idealism of his near-contemporary Gabriele D'Annunzio, who became not just man of letters but flamboyant man of action, leading armies and celebrating his Nietzschean and his sensual energy. Pirandello was always the withdrawn intellectual, not at home in the world of action, and aware of the endless conflict between thought and the flux of life. His sense of living through the death of the heroic age was reinforced by the general world-weariness of the *fin de siècle*. He felt he lived in a world where the lamp of God had gone out, and the lamp of identity flickered only faintly; seeing around him contradiction, absurdity, negation, cosmic irony, he felt displaced from life. 'When you end up without an ideal, because when you look at life it seems like an enormous puppet show, without ever any connections or explanations . . . you will be a wayfarer without a home, a bird without a nest,' he wrote as a student in 1886.

The sense of homelessness in a world which is a puppet show, a fictional construct of which we attempt to make sense, was there from the beginning, and it came to dominate his writing. It was what made him a great modern ironist and a precursor of more recent explorers of the fictionality of things, like Italo Calvino and Umberto Eco, as well as of the saddened, self-questioning clowning of the film-maker Fellini. He started writing early – poems, short stories, and an early play (though his deep fascination with drama would come only later). He began to establish himself in the 1890s, publishing his first novel, *The Outcast* (about the dramas of popular Sicilian life, like many of his books) in 1893. He was a studious author, who after three months in the family sulphur business went to the University of Palermo to study law, and then, in 1887, moved to the University of Rome to study Italian literature. He quarrelled with his teachers and moved on to Bonn, on the Rhine, where he did a doctorate, writing a philosophical dissertation on the Sicilian dialect, and remained there for a time as lector in Italian. Then he returned in 1891 to Rome, and began a career of enormous literary productivity. He was one of a group of regionalist writers concerned with Naturalism, *verismo*, and local colour, though he was also deeply interested in new literary aesthetics and the dominant new ideas of the time – Nietzsche's influential theories of art and energy, Bergson's notion of the *élan vital* and creative intuition. An unwavering intellectual gaze is apparent in all his work: 'One of the novelties I have given to modern drama consists in coverting the intellect into passion,' he was later to say.

Being and seeming, the gap between art and life, self and others – these were the concerns even of his most Naturalistic writing. He always considered his existence was somehow mirrored, doubled: 'There is someone who is living my life, and I know nothing about him,' he once noted. His troubled life confirmed this view. Nothing more revealed his Sicilian heritage than the form of his marriage. In 1894 he agreed to his father's wish for an arranged match with the daughter of one of his business partners, whom he scarcely knew. Their early years were happy and three children were born, but in 1903, when the sulphur mines flooded after a landslide, his patrimony and his wife's dowry were lost. He became dependent on teaching and writing to earn a struggling living, and his wife fell into a lifelong psychological illness, which turned to persecution mania and pathological jealousy of her husband. He now lived permanently in the company of madness, and with the prison of his wife's delusions about him, until she was hospitalized in 1919. Only then did he return to himself, and to his greatest writing. His sense of conflict, of false accusations and delusions, his awareness of the world as a place of disguises and masks upon masks, his feeling for the fragility of human identity, his grotesque realization that all life is lived on the rim of madness – all this he carried over into the world of theatre, where he found himself again.

If the idea of the double is a major theme of modern literature and modern drama, it was thus a practical fact of Pirandello's existence. Even his career was a double one, for his work falls into two distinct eras – one before the Great War, one after. Like all else in Pirandello, they stare at each other in the mirror, sometimes passing through the glass to meet directly. The first Pirandello was the writer of *verismo* and Naturalism, always powerful in Italy, and especially strong in regional writing; the second Pirandello was the philosophical, relativistic Modernist, whose work nonetheless drew on the foundations of that earlier Naturalist writing. The first Pirandello was essentially a regional writer, a disciple of the great nineteenth-century Sicilian novelist Giovanni Verga; the later Pirandello wrote for an international audience in the *avant-garde* spirit, making his greatest reputation outside Italy. The early Pirandello was above all a writer of fiction, producing many short stories (at his death he was still trying to write a short story for each day of the year) and four important novels; the late Pirandello was the dramatist and the transformer of the entire spirit of modern theatre. But the early writer provides endless material for the later (the plays often drawing on older stories), and the later writer constantly looks back to an intense sense of life that has been left behind.

But what particularly links the two writers is the spirit of irony, strongly present in some of the early stories, especially those dealing not with peasant life but with the bored bourgeoisie. Like the brilliant novelist Italo Svevo, writing in Trieste at the same time, Pirandello was exploring unheroic heroes, chracterless characters, men without qualities, ironically self-aware of their own social and historical impotence. Indeed Pirandello was working towards an art of ironic tragedy of a kind he explored in his book *On Humour*, a major statement about modern form in the arts. In it the two Pirandellos meet, for he worked on it twice – once for an edition of 1908, then for a revised version in 1920, just before he began *Six Characters in Search of an Author*. It is a celebration of the double vision that has been so fundamental to modern writing, a way of seeing everything in the light of its opposite. Pirandello calls this 'the sense of contradiction', or 'the sentiment of the contrary'. Humour arises in contemplation of a world where every yes becomes a no, and is a spirit of unmasking, a way of seeing life if not naked, said Pirandello, then in its undershirt.

For Pirandello, humour is that which sees the conflict between ideas and life, between idealism and the flux of existence, which 'seeps under the dykes we build, beyond the bounds we have imposed in an attempt to order our consciousness and construct a personality for ourselves.' Thus man creates his mask as best he can, the mask he wears in public, 'but within each of us is another, which often contradicts the external one. Nothing is true. Oh yes, the sea, a mountain, a rock, a blade of grass – these things are true. But man? Always wearing a mask, unwillingly, unwittingly . . .' So man constructs himself, is a self-created fiction: 'He invents so much and creates so many parts for himself which he needs to believe in and take seriously.' Humour observes this, but differs from comedy in having an identity with what it sees. Pirandello explains this with a famous example:

I see an old lady with her hair dyed, dyed and completely smeared with some horrible ointment, all made up with rouge and dolled up like a young girl. I begin to laugh. I can see she is the opposite of what a respectable old lady should be. I could stop here, at this superficial comic reaction. The comic is exactly this, an awareness of the opposite. But I may at this point reflect that perhaps this old lady does not like dressing up like an exotic parrot, and that perhaps she is distressed by it and does it only because she pitifully deceives herself into believing that like that she might be able to hold onto the love of her much younger husband. Then I cannot laugh at her as I did at first . . . I have made myself pass to a *feeling* of the opposite. That is the precise difference between comedy and humour.

So, like Cervantes in *Don Quixote*, the humorist must penetrate the fictions of the soul, and mix the comic and the tragic. In fact the definition closely resembles that of Thomas Mann, who wrote in his preface to Conrad's *The Secret Agent* that 'the achievement of modern art is that it has ceased to recognize the categories of tragic and comic or the dramatic classifications "tragedy" and "comedy", and views life as tragicomedy.'

This is the vision of Pirandello's major drama, for which his central image was the mirror. When a man lives, he said, he does not see himself, but put a mirror before him and make him see the act of living and: 'either he remains astonished and dumbfounded at his own appearance, or turns away his eyes so as not to see himself . . . If he had been weeping, he can weep no more; if he had been laughing, he can laugh no more . . . there arises a crisis, and that crisis is my theatre.' The crisis is part of the drama itself, which in Pirandello constantly mirrors its own mirroring. When Pirandello collected his plays together, he found the perfect title: *Maschere nude*, or *Naked Masks*. He also found a perfect if perplexing definition for his drama: 'a farce which in presenting a tragedy included its self-parody and self-caricature.' It was a true modern drama, which writers from T. S. Eliot to Jean-Paul Sartre and Eugène Ionesco have since seen as opening the way to the fundamental methods of modern theatre. It passed onward, to Beckett and Ionesco, Pinter and Stoppard, and all the modern playwrights and novelists who went on to write the dark comedy of an age that seemed one of self-alienation and irredeemable exile, of separation between the individual fiction and the larger fiction of reality. Pirandello's meta-theatre, with its pitiless investigation of everything, was the beginning of that spirit of modern tragicomedy we have come to call the Theatre of the Absurd. For, said Albert Camus, 'The divorce between man and his life, the actor and his setting, truly constitutes the feeling of Absurdity.'

3

'Mine was a war theatre,' Pirandello once wrote. 'The War revealed the theatre to me. When passions were let loose, I had my characters suffer those passions on stage.' Thus, like so many modern writers, Pirandello was released into his major and most experimental period of writing by the upheavals that shook the old European world between 1914 and 1918. For Pirandello, the war marked the great break from the old and static world of nineteenth-century Sicily, in which he had grown up, and the new world that the war shook into political, social and moral change. His own image for modernizing change was four generations of the lamp: oil, paraffin, gas, electric light. Now an well-established writer of fifty, who had written under all these lights, he declared it all too much; it ruined the eyesight and the mind too. In fact the new light, power and energy of the dynamo age, the acceleration of consciousness by the speed of the modern machine, the need for a new action and energetic violence – these are all the messages of Futurism, the Italian modern movement that swept through artistic life in the years before the War, and exulted in its coming. Marinetti, the leading spokesman, demanded an outright destruction of the banished old museum of the past, and exalted 'aggressive action, the mortal leap, the punch and the slap.' The Futurists challenged Naturalism, and the idea of an art based on the human figure. They asked for an art of speed, abstraction, energy, spontaneity, improvisation and contemporaneity.

The reflective, cerebral Pirandello was no Futurist, but he was sure of the need for theatrical innovation and the evolution of modern forms which exposed the ambiguous nature of modern identity.

Under the pressure of new ideas like those of the Futurists, the largely moribund Italian theatre was now opening its doors to new methods and possibilities, new attitudes to production and a wider sense of theatricality. It looked to its own traditions of grotesque theatre, masquerade and *commedia dell' arte*, and sought to make them new. This was the atmosphere in which Pirandello began to see new possibilities for an art form he had largely disdained as a lesser and more limited form of narrative. He now began to see theatre as a total form, an image of being, a fundamental arena for the exploration of the theatrical impression and his own sense of life as a metaphysical crisis of identity and disguise. It was in 1915 (when, as it happened, James Joyce tried to introduce his work to the British public) that he began to look seriously to theatre. In 1916 three plays were produced, including a delightful Sicilian comedy, *Liola*. In 1917 came the first play of the 'new' Pirandello, a play of the distancing and perspective we have come to know as his method and spirit. It was called *Right You Are (If You Think So)*, and deals with two people who each consider the other mad, and who have both constructed 'a world of fantasy that has all the substance of reality itself', which cannot be destroyed 'because they live and breathe in it'.

The upheavals of war and the upheavals of Italian theatre had much to do with Pirandello's new drama; but so did the upheavals of his own domestic life. His two sons enlisted in the army after Italy entered the war against Austria and Germany, and one was taken prisoner. Now his wife's paranoia increased; she grew desperate in her accusations, claiming that Pirandello had committed incest with his own daughter. The daughter attempted suicide, and left home, and he was left to live with the madness which dominated his life. He had now, he later said, become two people – the self he knew and the self his wife saw, 'a sad phantom, whose every look, smile, gesture, the very sound of whose voice, the sense of whose words were transformed in her own mind. The other man came to life and lived for her while he himself no longer existed.' He too lived in a world of fantasy that had all the substance of reality itself, endlessly doubled in the mirror of his wife's madness, which could not be contained or indeed disguised from others. In 1919, when the sons returned, it was decided to commit his wife to a sanatorium. This act was itself both a release and the entry into a new prison, of empty solitude. 'She was my nightmare, but she filled the house for me,' he wrote. 'I feel that my life is devoid of meaning and I no longer see any reason in the acts I perform or in the words I say, and it astonishes me that other people can move about outside this nightmare of mine, that they can act and speak.'

The plays from *Right You Are (If You Think So)* onward were thus plays that came from the sense of relativity and multiple identity that had been so profoundly sharpened by these events, just as the theatre now became the one home for this increasingly homeless writer of fifty whose domestic world had gone. Pirandello's drama, like so much other modern writing, was a drama of exile, an exile in part from reality itself, with the theatre affording the freedom to explore the illusions of existence. *Right You Are . . .* is thus the story of a marriage seen from two viewpoints, and told to prying neighbours who wish to know the 'truth'. The husband says his mother-in-law is mad, because she will not admit that her daughter has died and that he has remarried. The mother-in-law says the husband is mad, for he thinks his first wife has died and that his present wife is his second, when she is still the same woman. When the wife herself appears, the mystery appears to be close to a solution. But she is veiled, and tells the neighbours 'I am just who you think I am.' The inner story is told naturalistically, but to it Pirandello adds a device from the *commedia dell' arte*, the clownish narrator Laudisi. His derisive laughter mocks the whole quest for truth – indeed the very notion that any one of us has a single identity. Looking at himself in the mirror, he remarks that it is only our mirrored social selves that others ever see. His 'humour', his sardonic sense of contradiction, dominates the play, and his use as a device for interrupting the 'reality' of drama is a foretaste of the use of the 'empty theatre' of the great play that would develop out of this and other similar plays written just as the post-war world began, *Six Characters in Search of an Author*.

Six Characters . . . may not be Pirandello's greatest play, but it was the play that made Pirandello world-famous as the major *avant-gardiste* of theatre, and the play that has done more than any other to shape the future of modern drama and theatre itself. Out of it new theatre came, just as forty years earlier a whole new era of drama had been opened by the international production of Ibsen's *Ghosts*. The premiere in Rome caused outrage, with the members of the audience fighting the actors onstage and threatening the wisely elusive author. In Milan it was better received, and the scandal itself helped spread the news of this new approach to drama. A new idea of experimental theatre was now springing up internationally in the world after the war, and *Six Characters* . . . became the great example of the break away from Naturalism and into a theatre of modern anxiety and identity. It was staged widely, reaching London in 1922, the year of *Ulysses* and *The Waste Land*. Though restricted by the Lord Chamberlain's regulations to a private production, it was recognized as the dramatic equivalent of the change taking place in the novel and poetry. As T. S. Eliot would put it, Pirandello had shown all modern dramatists how to penetrate 'realism' in order to arrive at reality. The Paris production by Pitoeff in 1923 was the most famous premiere of the age of Dada and Surrealism, establishing Pirandello as the major influence on the subsequent history of French theatre right through to the present. 'The entire theatre of an era came out of the womb of that play, *Six Characters*,' one post-war French critic declared, while Jean-Paul Sartre, when asked who was the most important modern playwright, replied 'It is most certainly Pirandello.' The production (which caused Pirandello to revise his entire staging of the play) brought the six characters seeking their author down from above on an old scenery elevator, like gods or ghosts from an empty, barren, theatrical sky. So it went on; when the play was staged in the United States, where the new theatre of Eugene O'Neill and Elmer Rice was also opening up the stage, a larger theatre had to be hired and the playtext sold 500 copies a week.

Pirandello was now a world dramatist, and the most famous figure in Italian theatre. The plays multiplied, 28 in five years, some of them written in a few days. The dimensions of theatre Pirandello opened with *Six Characters* . . . were explored more and more fully in work after work. In 1924, Pirandello controversially became a member of the Fascist Party, and a supporter of Mussolini, hoping for a new national '*Risorgimento*'. He was far from alone, for Mussolini seemed committed to the new arts, and many of the Futurists took the same path. This allegiance was later to turn sour, and had much to do with the homeless and exiled character of Pirandello's later life. But his support was warm, and he won his reward by being made director of the Teatro d'Arte in Rome, where he could stage his plays himself. This company made a famous international tour in 1925, with two major performers, Ruggio Ruggieri and Marta Abba, for whom Pirandello was now writing many of his best roles, and Marta Abba became, in effect, his Muse. He now worked with and accompanied the cast, directing the rapid-fire pace of the production and the balance of naturalism and the grotesque. The group came to London in 1925, performing their remarkable versions of *Six Characters . . .*, the equally important *Henry IV*, and also *Right You Are (If You Think So)* and *Naked*.

Pirandello in effect became theatre, and everything about theatre became part of his work. The Teatro d'Arte ended in financial failure, but he became world-famous, winning the Nobel Prize for Literature in 1934. Nonetheless he resisted all definitions, insisted on formlessness. 'Henceforth I live in the vast world: the hotel is my home and all my worldly possessions consist of a typewriter . . . My beautiful dream of a patriarchal existence in the bosom of my family has faded away into thin air,' he observed. The hero of the late play *When One is Somebody* is a famous poet simply called ★★★. Fame has imprisoned him, and 'At night in my study I feel as if I were a puppet seated in part of my desk, in the light of the lamp, with wig, wax face, wax hands, lifeless eyes and motionless figure.' It is a self-portrait of the writer killed by success and by public and political reputation. It is reported that when the theatrical company visited Germany Pirandello was approached by the great explorer of relativity, Albert Einstein, who told him, 'We are kindred souls.' They were indeed, for Pirandello was undoubtedly the Cubist of theatre, the explorer and breaker of the frame of time and space, and the great theatrical relativist, whose relativism and scepticism extended even to his own very self.

4

'What author can say how and why a character is born in his imagination?' Pirandello asked:

> Several years ago my imagination had the unfortunate inspiration, or maybe it was just caprice, to bring a family into my house. I don't know where it fished them from, but apparently I should be able to find in them the subject for a magnificent novel . . . I found them before me, alive – you could touch them and even hear them breathe – the six characters now seen on the stage. And they stayed there in my presence, each with his secret torment and all bound together by the one common origin and entanglement of their affairs, while I introduced them into the world of art, constructing from their persons, their passions and their adventures a novel, a drama – or, at least, a story.

This is how Pirandello explained the origin of *Six Characters* . . . in a famous preface he later wrote for the play. The very idea of an author visited by 'real' characters is strange and vivid, for it is an idea close to the centre of fictional creation, a fable of literary genesis. Many writers speak of being 'taken over' by their characters who then guide the work that comes into existence. But Pirandello tells us that he was not in fact interested in these characters for a story, since he is a philosophical and not a naturalistic writer and could see nothing of universal value in them, 'so I concluded it was no use making them live and did all I could to forget them.' In any case, as he makes clear, their story lay close to the recent events in his own household. But as he wrote in a letter to his son in 1917, the story of a story that will not be composed itself makes a composition.

'I suddenly saw a way out of my difficulty,' Pirandello explained in his preface, 'why not present this highly strange fact of an author who refuses to let some of his characters live . . .? In the struggle for existence they have had to wage with me they have become dramatic characters that could move and talk on their own. So, I thought, let them go where dramatic characters should in order to live, onto a stage. And let's see what will happen.' Pirandello's preface makes it clear that this 'stage' is a double one. It is firstly the stage of his own creative imagination, on which the drama of an art in the making happens. And it is secondly the empty stage of a theatre, where that story can be told, interrupted, examined, from many perspectives, and where a 'whole complex of theatrical elements, characters and actors, author and actor-manager or director, dramatic critics and spectators (external or involved) present every possible conflict.' Thus Pirandello came to one of the most remarkable of modern literary concepts, that of writing a play in the making, giving us the sense not of something already complete, but of the double process of literary creation, composition and theatrical improvisation. He could have said, as Vladimir Nabokov said of his own work later, that the heroes of his work are not characters but methods of composition.

It is therefore appropriate that story is set at a rehearsal – and even more that the play being rehearsed is an earlier piece of Pirandello's own, *Rules of the Game*. The crew begin constructing the set, the actors come, and the Director begins trying to explain to them the rather annoying spirit of Pirandello's intellectual drama, with its conflicts of reason and instinct, form and life. Then the six characters appear, a Father, a Mother, and four children, legitimate and otherwise. They are surrounded by a 'tenuous light', the 'faint breath of their fantastic reality'. Pirandello provided his script with careful stage directions about how they should look, because although they are in fact actors they must be distinguished from 'actors'. They wear dark clothes (the actors wear coloured ones) as if in mourning. They have stiff stylized masks to emphasize that they are artistic constructions, though they must appear 'not as phantoms but as created realities'. 'The drama is in us, and we are the drama,' says the Father. But they are scriptless, unauthored, and they need both to recreate and to find the universality of their story, in which each one defends his or her own version of that story against the accusations of the others.

The story the six characters seek to perform and perpetuate is sensational and melodramatic. The Father has sent his wife away to live with another man, by whom she has had three children. He has met his own Stepdaughter in the brothel of Madame Pace: in the family rivalries, a boy has shot himself. Such a story, told naturalistically, would make a limited and provincial melodrama. But just as he had used Laudisi to add viewpoint and metaphysical depth to *Right You Are . . .*, here he does the same with the notion of a theatre in a theatre. There can be two kinds of actors, 'real characters' and 'real actors', and one actor is a Stage Manager and another is a Director, who can understand or reject the story, interpret it or stop it. Moreover the world of the theatre and the world of 'real life' and 'real people' are all seen as part of the multi-dimensionality and universality of drama. 'Don't you feel the ground sink beneath your feet as you reflect that this "you" which you feel today, all this present reality of yours, is destined to seem a mere illusion to you tomorrow?' says the Father to the Stage Manager. The 'characters' can assault both the artifice of art, because they are 'real', and the falsity of life, because they are aware of being part of a drama. The real and the artificial can thus be put under a massive variety of perspectives, not in order to deny the existence of reality but to show that we each have our own inward view of it, that we each construct our own fiction.

And yet when we enter that empty theatre and watch *Six Characters . . .* in a successful production, something extraordinary happens. We see the very creation of the illusion of reality. We know from the start that the play will never complete itself naturalistically, that everything will be foreshortened, each scene interrupted as another perspective is introduced. The characters are attempting to re-enact a reality that can never be wholly constructed, since they do not agree on it. Yet as each character attempts to construct him or herself, the magic of acting and the power of theatre achieves itself. The characters convince, each one with a separate story. 'For any character his drama is his very *raison d'être*,' Pirandello said, and in himself he has become real. 'I'm not acting my suffering . . .,' says the Mother, 'I'm alive and here now but I can never forget that terrible moment of agony, that repeats itself endlessly and vividly in my mind.' Each character inhabits a private world, and attempts to justify it, but there is no common understanding of what the overall drama is, for characters are also perspectives. 'We all have a world of things inside ourselves and each one of us has his own private world,' the Father tells us. 'How can we understand each other if the words I use have the sense and value that I expect them to have, but whoever is listening inevitably thinks they have a different sense and value?'

What Pirandello does in *Six Characters* . . . is something that theatre has done virtually since the beginning of drama: creating but also undermining the power of theatrical illusion. Theatre has always insisted that it stands in paradoxical relationship to reality, and that all the world is indeed a stage. But Pirandello handles the powers of theatre-in-theatre in a novel and modern way, because his undermining of illusion is in the interests of a recognizably twentieth-century sense of the falsity and incompleteness of identity, of the relativity of all things. Pirandello's philosophy, rather than simply the exploitation of *avant-garde* stage effects, is what makes his work so powerful and so relevant. As the Father says in a key speech, none of us is one person, and we may see this 'when by some tragic chance we are, as it were, caught up whilst in the middle of doing something and find ourselves suspended in mid-air.'

As Pirandello had put it himself, when a man lives, he does not see himself in the act of living. If he does he is astonished at his own appearance, or spits at his image: 'In a word there arises a crisis, and that crisis is my theatre.' Pirandello's method is to arrest the moment of living, to halt the action, to reintroduce the mirror, to remind us of the theatre. Essential to the play is its movement from action to arrest, from the fluid motion of being to the moment of art and self-consciousness when we are trapped into form. For the individual, this is tragedy. For the writer, this is what Pirandello would call 'humour', an awareness of contradiction, a vision of absurdity. Thus, said Pirandello, the 'universal meaning which at first I had vainly sought in the characters came out of its own accord . . . Without wanting to, without knowing it, their passion and torment expressed the passion and torment that for so many years have plagued me: the deceit involved in understanding one another, the multiple personality of everyone, and finally the inherently tragic conflict between life, which is always moving and changing, and form, which fixes it, immutable.'

5

It was part of Pirandello's purpose to remain endlessly elusive, a shifting identity, and this is as true of the nature of the plays he continued to produce up to his death in 1936, writing to the moment he died, as of his personal temperament. He wrote over forty plays, many still not translated into English, as well as seven novels and hundreds of short stories. Pirandello himself as well as his critics distinguished them into groups. There were the 'theatre in the theatre' plays, starting with *Six Characters . . .* and continuing with *Each In His Own Way* (1924) and *Tonight We Improvise* (1929), which break open the theatrical frame by, for example, having a member of the audience object to the performance of her own life, or showing us the critics in the theatre, or a revolt of the actors. There are the 'mirror' plays, about the doubleness and strangeness of identity. And, especially after the flirtation with Fascism, there are the later 'mythic' plays, like *The New Colony* (1925), where he reflects on social and religious issues. But perhaps the most important new development was Pirandello's deepening of the art of modern tragedy – most evident in *Henry IV*, which many critics consider the greatest play of all, and which Pirandello himself most respected.

Henry IV deals with two themes that were of crucial importance to Pirandello: madness and acting. The two themes are intricately interwoven. A wealthy young man goes to a masquerade as the eleventh-century German emperor Henry IV, hits his head in a fall from his horse, and wakes to believe himself the real Emperor. His rich family humour him. In a villa transformed into a medieval castle he lives with costumed courtiers who sustain his role as the despotic monarch. He lives 'out of the world, out of time, out of life'. Now, twenty years on, friends come to the villa with a doctor, to release him from his madness. 'Henry', now nearly fifty, and grotesquely made up to defy his age, tells his courtiers that he has in fact been sane for some years, but has chosen to maintain his role to play with the world and shake its foundations, the structure of beliefs people build up around themselves. He has constructed the world on his own terms. We cannot be sure of his sanity, or his madness; nor can his visitors, caught in an unremitting sequence of contradictions and confusions. With typical complexity and philosophical subtlety, Pirandello sustains the story of madness and illusion, masquerade and disguise, to a tragic outcome. 'Henry' is driven to murder, and so compelled to remain forever in the role of madman, losing his mastery of a situation he seemed to control. The role has now become the actor; the mask is fixed firmly on forever.

'Henry' (the unnamed hero) ends the play a prisoner of the disguise and absurdity he had tried to master. The theatre of his mind has become real. He is trapped forever in his madness and masquerade, eternally the king in the historical play he had chosen to perform, on the stage of which he must remain, eternally separated from life elsewhere. In this fixity, this eternal imprisonment in delusion, lies his tragedy. He may have explored to the limits of his fiction, but he cannot pass outside it. Like *** in *When One Is Somebody*, he has become the fixed form he has set out to evade: 'It is true that when one is Somebody, one has to condemn oneself to death at a certain point and stay shut up, like this, guarding oneself,' *** concludes. In one of his novels Pirandello gave a definition of a modern tragedy. 'The whole difference . . . between ancient and modern tragedy is . . . a hole in a paper sky,' he said, for it is the difference between the story of Orestes staged as if it were true and that story staged in a puppet theatre, where the paper sky rips open and the hero sees the theatre he is in. This theme runs everywhere through Pirandello's work, but *Henry IV* is its most profound and darkest expression, his most serious and his fullest play.

The theatre of Pirandello's mind was to become real too. Towards the end of his life, Pirandello complained that the critics were writing about many Pirandellos he could not recognize – 'lame, deformed, all head and no heart, erratic, gruff, insane, and obscure.' Yet his drama itself spoke of the endless multiplication of identities, the endless improvisations of life. Since then there have been many more Pirandellos, as his drama has shaped and reshaped modern theatre everywhere – unlocking the nature of its stage, the metaphysical depth of its fiction, the basic laws of its act of creation, the power of im-

provisation, performance and theatricality. It is no surprise that his
image to this day is elusive and illusory, for no modern writer has
done more to bring home the importance of illusion both in theatre
and in life. Yet what is most important is that his theatre has come to
seem far more than a theatre of play or artful trickery. As in the story
of *Henry IV*, it has come to be a theatre of modern life itself, a deep
and total vision that it takes the very depth of the stage, the full
intensity of the dramatic experience – and the troubled nature of its
illusion – to explore.

For Pirandello's supreme gift was to bring intellect to passion, and
the greatest of all the things he brought to theatre was the lucid, ironic
and frequently bitter intelligence he revealed in his endless pursuit of
the formless energy of life. No one believed in that energy more; for
to him it was the heart of the creative process itself. Yet he knew that
as the mind observes that process and becomes self-aware, it can only
become sceptical. 'Whosoever understands the game can no longer
fool himself,' he wrote, though this would mean losing the pleasure
of life. Here was the tragic fate of intelligence, and the reason for the
bitter humour that is the final legacy of Pirandello. 'Ordinarily in the
conception of a work of art, reflection is like a form of feeling, almost
a mirror in which the feeling is watching itself,' he wrote in *On
Humour*. 'Pursuing this idea, one might argue that, in the conception
of humour, reflection is, yes, a mirror, but of icy water in which the
flame of the feeling is not only watching itself, but plunges and ex-
tinguishes itself.' He may half have feared that icy water, but he
plunges us into it always, with that sense of contradicton that made
his work so modern.

Pirandello kept it to the end: 'For a long time I have been considered
a pessimist . . .' he said, 'but I have been misunderstood. My art is free
of that pessimism, which causes a lack of faith in my life. And I am
not even a nihilist since, in the spiritual activity which torments me
and animates my works, there is an incessant desire to create.' Pessimist
or not, he always continued to apply intelligence to the endless flux of
life, in which he hoped to find pleasure, only to discover absurdity.
'The taste for life! – that is never satisfied,' he wrote, 'because life,
even as we are in the very act of living it, is so ravenously hungering

after itself that it never lets itself be fully tasted. The taste for life comes to us from the past. From the memories that hold us bound, but bound to what? To this folly of ours, to this mass of vexations, to so many stupid illusions, to so many insipid occupations.' Pirandello, we know, never felt he had really tasted life, and for all the final fame his late years were bleak.

And what we find in the end is that dark humour, that ironic solitide, that exiled separateness that is the mark of the most unnerving and profound of our modern writers, from Kafka to the absurdists. Perhaps it was the taste for life as vital energy that drew Pirandello to Fascism, but his plays never came to have the mass-hysteria and savage vitalism that might have appealed to the party. This in turn led to his increasing disfavour within Italy, even as his fame grew elsewhere. So came what has been called the 'inner emigration' of his final years. 'I no longer have a home, a country of my own,' he wrote; 'My mind is completely alienated.' The self-mocking irony, the sense of contradiction, continued to his death. When his will was opened after his death in December 1936, when the state came to honour him, it was found he had left careful instructions for his funeral. 'When I am dead, do not clothe me,' he wrote. 'Wrap me naked in a sheet.' He forbade any public ceremony, religious or political: all he wanted was a hearse, a horse, a driver, nothing more. He wished nothing to remain to serve the pomp of church or state, though he asked that if he could not be completely disposed of his ashes be placed in a rock at his birthplace. Not until another war (in which that birthplace was damaged) was over were his wishes entirely fulfilled. But in 1949 – just as his bitter vision of existence was influencing the post-war generation of Existential dramatists – his ashes were returned at last to Chaos, the place from which he always knew he had come.

VIRGINIA
WOOLF

I

1922 – the year when T. S. Eliot published *The Waste Land*, James Joyce *Ulysses*, and Marcel Proust died – was undoubtedly a key year for the modern movement. It was also the year in which Virginia Woolf brought out her third novel *Jacob's Room*, her most experimental work so far, and the book where, she said, 'I have found out how to begin (at 40) to say something in my own voice.' The great events of the year certainly did not pass Virginia Woolf by. Indeed it was the Hogarth Press, run by herself and her husband Leonard, that published the British edition of *The Waste Land*, following on from the American edition of that year. She and Eliot also discussed *Ulysses*, and he attempted to persuade her that it destroyed the whole of the nineteenth century in fiction, and showed the futility of all the English styles. Mrs Woolf, an exact but not always kindly judge of her own contemporaries, was more sceptical. She recognized a considerable quality in the novel, but she also pronounced it a 'misfire'. Possibly a touch of puritan outrage unusual amongst the Bloomsbury circle to which she belonged had something to do with it. 'It is underbred, not only in the obvious sense, but in the literary sense,' she wrote in her diary. It was a typically magisterial Bloomsbury opinion – critically acute, but with an unmistakable touch of social condescension. It was an opinion she was to revise (but only somewhat) later, when, more and more, Joyce's work came, very reasonably, to be compared with her own. Joyce pushed further, but, she felt, in the same direction as previous fiction; she was looking somehow for a different direction in which to go.

Meanwhile her own work was proceeding with its typical business. There are few modern writers who have been more genuinely creative, more productive, or have provided us with such an extraordinarily rich written record of their lives, their feelings, and their times.

She had been reviewing regularly for very many years, and was beginning to tire of the burden. She typically dealt with this by starting on the major project of putting together a collection of her essays on past and modern literature. It would express and distil her literary position, and bring her critical standards to the common reader. And this was the book she duly published in 1925, along with her next novel, as *The Common Reader*. Aside from T. S. Eliot's *The Sacred Wood* – published, of course, by the Hogarth Press – this is probably the best work of modern criticism in Britain to come from the 1920s, an era when criticism grew more active as the modern movement stabilized. Then there was the question of that next novel, and what she should do now in fiction.

It was clear the next step would not be easy if she was to realize herself as what she wished to be, a truly modern writer. She had come to see that she was not really destined to be a popular novelist – and that her interest as an author lay not in strength, passion, or anything startling, but in what she called her 'queer individuality'. It was in this spirit that she now began a complex fictional project which was itself, over the next two years, to turn into one of the most important, and probably the most English, works of fictional modernism. It began life as a short story called 'Mrs Dalloway in Bond Street', which she completed in October 1922, and published in 1923 in the American magazine *The Dial*. However, when the story was done, it continued to preoccupy her. She now began to consider expanding it into a novel.

Her initial ideas were not quite what we read today in the novel, which became *Mrs Dalloway*. It would have six or seven chapters, deal with London social life, make the Prime Minister an important character, and it would all, as now, be 'converging on the party at the end'. The spirit of this version, of which drafts survive, was light – 'There should be fun,' she wrote in her notebook – but there was also gloom. As she explained in a preface found in some editions of the book, the central figure, Clarissa Dalloway, was to kill herself, or perhaps die at her party. This view was to change, but the preoccupation with death was an important part of the story, and it was in time to give rise to a new central character she added to the book, the shell-shocked war-victim Septimus Warren Smith, whose death is announced at the party with which the novel still ends.

Over the rest of 1922, Mrs Woolf continued to reconceive and replan the book, making detailed comments in her writing notebook about how to go on, and remarking 'At any rate, very careful composition.' In the new plan, it was not only the storyline that changed. A key notion was an emphasis on presentation through consciousness ('The question is whether the inside of the mind in both Mrs D[alloway] and S[eptimus] can be made luminous,' she noted). Like *Ulysses*, and probably thanks to its influence, the book was to deal with the flow of consciousness and awareness. And all its events, like those in Joyce's novel, were to take place on one single day – the day Clarissa Dalloway holds her party. The ideas were demanding, and the book – at first, presumably in deference to the concern with outer and inner time, called *The Hours* ('If that's it's name?') – developed only with great difficulty. 'I am blown like an old flag by Mrs Dalloway,' she noted, 'I must stop myself; think what I mean to say.' After it was done, she called it 'that agony . . . all agony but the end.' It was clearly a work of intense self-discovery, a probe into creation. It swung with the rhythm of her own upward and downward moods, and demanded that she face up to her views about reality in life and art, much expressed in her criticism. She was still anxiously in the process of finding confidence in her own literary voice and sensibility, and discovering, too, a voice for her times. 'At forty I am beginning to learn the mechanisms of my own brain,' she noted in her diary.

Virginia Woolf had been keeping a diary since 1915 and was to continue doing so up to her death in 1941. It is one of the great literary diaries, a remarkable record of her social life, her observations, her emotional feelings, her literary instincts, her reading, and above all of her process of composition. By her death there were 27 volumes, and the parts to do with her literary activities and the writing of her books were published in 1953 by her husband Leonard as *A Writer's Diary*. More recently, substantial selections of the larger diaries have been published in four finely-edited volumes, and so have her letters. In these diaries, letters, and in notebooks, Virginia Woolf kept an extraordinary and a careful analysis of her writing method. The history of modern fiction offers us several such records – of the writing of Thomas Mann's *Dr Faustus*, and Andre Gide's *The Counterfeiters* – and these greatly help us to understand the changed creative assumptions behind twentieth-century literary art. The account Mrs Woolf gives of *Mrs Dalloway* in her diaries and notebooks does the same, providing us with a vivid compositional history of one of the most important modern novels. That novel was very carefully and elaborately planned, though the writing – very considered – actually came in fits and starts, elation and doubt. There were times when she felt she was writing it too quickly, with too much glitter; at other times things came to a halt, provoking dismay and despair. And there was always the question of how far to take it, how much to put in it, how to connect together the tissues that made it, when it was done.

For two years the worrying process of composition continued. Was it all becoming too unfelt and artificial? 'One must write from deep feeling, said Dostoyevsky,' she noted, 'And do I? Or do I fabricate with words, loving them as I do?' Was she creating 'true' characters, and did she have what she called 'the "reality" gift'? 'People like Arnold Bennett say I can't create, or didn't in *Jacob's Room*, characters that survive,' she observed, 'I insubstantiate, wilfully to some extent, distrusting reality – its cheapness.' This matter of reality, and whether she enhanced or falsified it, was a lasting issue. She distrusted the materialism and specificity of fictional realism of the Arnold Bennett kind, and confronted it in an essay she wrote during the composition of the novel – the essay 'Mr Bennett and Mrs Brown', which was published in 1924. It is a repudiation of the Edwardian novel, and particularly the naturalism of Bennett, and it established a distinction between conventional fiction and 'aesthetic' fiction that was to last long. Reality was not a matter of fact, as many novelists made it; it was an aesthetic and metaphysical question. But the new way of doing things, the kind of novel that expressed it – that was the challenge she tried to face in *Mrs Dalloway*. As she observed, the book was becoming 'the devil of a struggle. The design is so queer and so masterful. I'm always having to wrench my substance to fit it.' After a year, in October 1923, she was noting, 'I took a year's groping to discover what I call my tunnelling process, by which I tell the past in instalments, as I have need of it . . .' And the cycle of creative urgency and creative crisis, of elation and depression, was to continue for another year, to October 1924.

2

Today we think of Virginia Woolf as a novelist of the 1920s and 1930s, the author of a central group of novels – *Mrs Dalloway* (1925), *To the Lighthouse* (1927), *Orlando* (1928), and *The Waves* (1931) – which played a central role in British fictional modernism. In their different ways, they all explore and assert the dominance of the aesthetic sphere and certain essential states of human sensitivity and intensity, and link the two through a sense that life itself, modern godless life, is constructed like a work of art, with a secret of reality hidden within it. These are her greatest books, but she was a long-established writer when she began on them. Her career, her literary sensibility and her attitude to modern fiction were very largely shaped long before the First World War broke out. Following in the path of her father, Leslie Stephen, a reviewer of enormous influence at the end of the nineteenth century, she had herself begun as a reviewer of books, and published her own first piece in 1904, the year her father died. From 1905 to the War she was a leading essayist for the *Times Literary Supplement*, drawing on her wide reading, strong scholarly inclinations, sharp sense of judgement, and indeed on her father's excellent library. She was also part of a literary and intellectual community that was perhaps the nearest thing to a continental intelligentsia the Britain of the first forty years of this century possessed – though it was highly British and rather imperial in character. This was the group of friends and Cambridge contemporaries that came to be called the 'Bloomsbury Group', in which she was close to the centre. For the friends gathered round the homes the various tribal Stephen children had inherited in Gordon and Fitzroy Squares, in, of course, that Georgian, central part of London around the British Museum from which the name comes.

Much – perhaps too much – has been written about Bloomsbury, but it did provide British life with an experimental intellectual and artistic centre it had not had for a long time, along with a considerable flamboyance of life-style, one reason why the memoirs, recollections, histories and biographies continue to pour out. Bloomsbury was an intellectual community, but also a social caste, an attitude to life and values, a complex web of friends, an intricacy of relatives, marriages and liaisons. Many of those involved were the children of the Victorian upper-middle-class intelligentsia, against whom they began to revolt in what, thanks to the influence of Freud, was coming to be called an 'Oedipal' way. But if it was a social grouping, it was also an active mood, a determinedly artistic attitude to life. When Roger Fry organized the Post-Impressionist exhibition at the Grafton Galleries in 1910, that was a Bloomsbury event. For Bloomsbury was also made up of important artistic moments and fundamental modern ideas – such as Fry's belief in 'significant form' in art. Clive Bell, married to Virginia's sister Vanessa, explained the Bloomsbury spirit as 'a taste for truth and beauty, intellectual honesty, fastidiousness, a sense of humour, curiosity, a dislike of vulgarity, brutality and over-emphasis . . .' It was also a modern revolt into a new idea of art that in turn linked with changed ideas about personal relations, sexual emancipation, and the nature of consciousness. Its convictions were to be found not just in art but in politics, feminism, economic theory and the writing of history and biography. Indeed its bible was really Lytton Strachey's book *Eminent Victorians*, published in 1919, a mocking history of Victorian moral seriousness and respectability. It was the great separation, the book with which the Victorian age has been said to have come to an end.

Bloomsbury can be fairly seen both as a revolt against the Establishment, and a new Establishment in itself, especially as the 1920s went on, and it took a central place in literary and artistic life – in publishing and magazine editing, in critical opinion, in social influence. Virginia Woolf was in some ways apart, an often lonely figure detached from the more flamboyant side of the Bloomsbury spirit. But she was also central to its attitudes, and was its major recorder. She was Bloomsbury's literary conscience, long before she was its novelist. Her views in the *Times Literary Supplement* and elsewhere established her as a cogent, sensitive and magisterial critic. Her essays judged the literary past and responded to the literary present with a spirit of living quarrel, exploring the achievement of many of the most important new figures – Conrad, James, Dostoevsky as he became available in the Constance Garnett translations – and many of the issues to do with the modern spirit in writing. As for Virginia Woolf's strong opinions on modern fiction, and its need to offer a new rendering of life, these were formed well before she completed her own first novel, *The Voyage Out*, in 1913 (it was not to appear until two years later). As she put it in 1918, 'It is not that life is more complex or difficult now than at any other period, but that for each generation the point of interest shifts, the old forms put the interest in the wrong places, and in searching out the severed and submerged part of what to us constitutes form we seem to be throwing fragments together at random and disdaining the very thing we are trying our best to rescue from the chaos.'

But Virginia Woolf's sense of the new task for the novel was most forcefully expressed in an essay called 'Modern Fiction'. It came out in 1919 (the same year as her second novel *Night and Day*) and was an appeal for a far more inward kind of fiction, a sort of novel freed of the old conventions and chronologies, a work of modern aesthetic freedom. In a famous passage that seems to offer to do for the novel what Marx had tried to do for the proletariat, she explained:

> If a writer were a free man and not a slave, if he could write what he chose, not what he must, if he could base his work upon his own feeling and not upon convention, there would be no plot, no comedy, no tragedy, no love interest or catastrophe in the accepted style, and perhaps not a single button sewn on as the Bond Street tailors would have it. Life is not a series of gig-lamps symmetrically arranged; but a luminous halo, a semi-transparent envelope surrounding us from the beginning of consciousness to the end. Is it not the task of the novelist to convey this varying, this unknown and uncircumscribed spirit, whatever aberration or complexity it may display, with as little mixture of the alien and external as possible?

The conventions of the novel are, in short, not fixed, but changeable, and what drives them forward is a sense of reality forged out of an intensified awareness of the texture of life as consciousness. This incorporates the experience of those who live within the novel, and are its characters or subjects, and those who create the novel as an aesthetic experience, the writers themselves. Modern fiction is modern by virtue of its changed sense of life, and that is not simply a changed awareness of society or human relations. It is dependent on a sense of life as it is experienced aesthetically, and this was becoming increasingly the subject of the novels she now set out to write. The feeling of the 'semi-transparent envelope' of life, surrounding and creating consciousness, is what Virginia Woolf set out to achieve in *Mrs Dalloway*. Indeed it could almost be said that that is what Clarissa Dalloway's party is all about.

As many writers know, it is one thing to have a critical idea of the nature of fiction, and something else to be able to compose it. It was a difficulty Virginia Woolf acknowledged in her diary: 'how my brain is jaded with the conflict of two types of thought – the critical and the creative.' This inner conflict had a good deal to do with the 'agony' of *Mrs Dalloway*. It had something to do with the fact that she became a novelist *after* being a critic, and had had to find her way. Indeed *The Voyage Out* and *Night and Day*, though they won respectful attention at the time, now look like tentative starts in the formation of a distinctive and more modern way of writing. *Jacob's Room* had been an important step toward becoming a surer novelist, a writer with her own strong sense of 'queer individuality'. But if she was now a much surer novelist, she was still not entirely a confident one. This was partly because she *was* determined to risk something new, partly because she felt somewhat out of the mainstream both of the traditional *and* the new experimental novel, and partly because she was a woman – and women, as she said later in her *A Room of One's Own* in 1929, were not supposed to compete with Shakespeare or to write novels. But perhaps, she proposed in another essay, 'Women and Fiction' (1929), women writers could be less absorbed than men in the facts: 'They will look beyond the personal and political relationships to the wider question which the poet tries to solve – of our destiny and the meaning of life.' This meant making a new poetry of prose, the one thing Joyce, she felt, had somehow not done. Could the new sort of thing be managed? And, if so, was she really the person to manage it?

3

For Virginia Woolf 1924 was the important year. It was the year she was to finish *Mrs Dalloway*. It was the year in which her own literary reputation was showing signs of moving towards its peak. It was the year she meant to do a great deal of writing, and she hoped to make £300 from it to spend on a bath and hot-water range for the house (she never did make much money from authorship). It was a year of major personal events, 'the most eventful in the whole of our (recorded) lives,' she noted. At the beginning of 1924 the Woolfs bought a ten-year lease on a Georgian town house, 52 Tavistock Square, in the heart of magical WC1, the district of Bloomsbury. It was where she had grown up and lived until her marriage in 1912 to Leonard Woolf. Even then they had lived close by, at Clifford's Inn, off the Strand, up to a moment of crisis in 1913, when Virginia had attempted suicide. Afterwards they moved out to the more suburban circumstances of Hogarth House in Richmond, where they founded the Hogarth Press.

Now they sold the house, moving themselves and the press back to the area of Georgian houses and squares around the British Museum which was not simply a postal district but a state of mind and, for Virginia, an essential condition of culture. The return to Bloomsbury and central London delighted Virginia, as her diary records. She wrote that 'the whole of London – London thou art a jewel of jewels, a jasper of jocunditie, music, talk, friendship, city views, publishing, something central & inexplicable, all this is within my reach, as it hasn't been since August 1913.' Indeed the diary of this time is filled with a sense of walking out into London and 'getting carried into beauty without raising a finger,' and she noted down her promise that she would write about the city. However, she said, 'my mind is full of *The Hours.*' The book was 'reeling off my mind fast, and free now,' and becoming more human, less lyrical. The return to central London helped write the book. 'I like London for writing it, partly because, as I say, life upholds one,' she noted.

Another house was important. During the summer Virginia went down, as she did over many summers, to Monks House at Rodmell, near Lewes in Sussex, the house where she died in 1941. She and Leonard had bought it for £700 five years earlier, and it was a retreat where she loved to work. Bloomsbury life did not cease even down in Sussex, for many of their friends had houses and cottages in the area. Indeed it was a continuation of Bloomsbury by other means, but for Virginia it always represented a sharp change of mood. There was a massive writing plan for the summer, 'a very animated summer . . . lived almost too much in public.' There was the novel and the essays, stimulated by the lecture for the Heretics Society in Cambridge which was to become the piece called 'Mr Bennett and Mrs Brown'. There was the death of Conrad, whom she deeply admired, and on whom she wrote a valedictory essay. There was also dejection with the book, which had reached the death of Septimus: 'A feeling of depression is on me, as if we were old and near the end of things.' That depression indeed enters the later pages, which display the sense of solitude and death, of the irrelevance of society, that she was feeling in her own life.

Yet the diary is also filled with the characteristic buoyancy, the delight in life, the wonderful perception and self-criticism in her nature ('Were it not for my flash of imagination, & this turn for books, I should be a very ordinary woman'). And soon 'blessed Mrs Dalloway' moved to the final excitement of the party and the summing up, and she was 'swimming high' and writing 'this might be the best of my endings, & come off, perhaps.' Then, on 17 October, back in Tavistock Square, she records that she had been interrupted in writing down 'that astounding fact', that a week ago yesterday she had written the last words of the last page: 'For there she was.' Afterward there followed the usual period of revision, but, rightly, she felt she had written the most satisfactory of her novels. Still, worries continued. Would the reviewers feel she had not properly linked the two essential themes as well as the two essential characters of the book – Clarissa Dalloway and her world, and the shattered world of Septimus Warren Smith, whom Mrs Dalloway never meets directly, but who becomes a very present ghost at her party? And was it unreal, mere accomplishment? 'I think not . . . it seems to leave me plunged deep in the richest strata of my mind. I can write and write and write now: the happiest feeling in the world.'

London and Bloomsbury, the life of society and the inner life of feeling, the rhythms of creative elation and concentration and the distilled experience of despair – all of these things had much to do with the spirit of *Mrs Dalloway*. It was a London book, about a great imperial city as it survived after the war. It perhaps owed something to Conrad, whom she admired, and to *The Secret Agent*, since it is a tale of two cities that interfuse – Clarissa's social London, and the second London which has 'swallowed up many millions of young men called Smith.' It was also a book about the flowing of consciousness and awareness, the life of the inner city of existence, which whether she was quite ready to admit it or not had something to do with her reading of Joyce. And Bloomsbury, so influenced by the Cambridge philosopher, G. E. Moore, played its part. Moore had said, 'By far the most valuable things which we know or can imagine are certain states of consciousness, which may roughly be described as the pleasures of human intercourse and the enjoyment of beautiful objects.' That sense of consciousness is strong in the book, but so is the sense of solitude, of deathly loneliness, of separation and the breaking of the human bond. The modern novel, departing from older representations of reality, was what she was striving for, and it was not meant to be complete in the way that older novels were. It was part of a modern age of changed relations and altered connections, 'a season of failures and fragments', she wrote in the essay 'Mr Bennett and Mrs Brown'. 'Tolerate the spasmodic, the obscure, the fragmentary, the failure,' she added, however, near the end of that essay. 'Your help is invoked in a good cause.'

4

Mrs Dalloway was not a failure, and when it came out in March 1925 many of the reviewers hailed it as a masterpiece. But it was certainly spasmodic, obscure and fragmentary, in ways that we now recognize as part of the inheritance of the modern novel. In the 'Modern Fiction' essay, Virginia Woolf had said that the modern novelist would probably not choose to create plot, comedy, tragedy or catastrophe in the conventional way. Elsewhere, in 'Mr Bennett and Mrs Brown', she had insisted that the modern novel was a novel of character, and that our idea of character had changed – somewhere around 1910, she suggested. All this is evidently reflected in the book. It is a book about life's semi-transparent envelope, and of 'the atoms as they fall'. In fact it is a novel of moments – the bright, luminous moments that belong to one day in 1923, the day that Clarissa Dalloway holds her party – and it has the symbolist's desire to reveal their deeper meaning. The comparison with *Ulysses*, and Joyce's idea of the 'epiphany', is inescapable. There is a deliberate slowing down or halting of time, intended to break the developing and progressive chronology of plot and character that is the general rule in the classic novel. The story proceeds through methods of loose association and connection, giving it a verbal plot as well as a plot of action. Like Joyce's novel, or Proust's, it is the story of its own act of creation. Like *Ulysses* – and for that matter like another novel that came out in the same year as her own, John Dos Passos's *Manhattan Transfer* – it distils time and experience through the dense, congested experience of a city.

In Joyce it is the second city of the British Empire. Virginia Woolf's subject is the first imperial city, which she sees in a very different way from Conrad, though here too there is light and darkness. It is a city proud of its past and its history, but also a very modern city, still touched by the aftermath of war and overflown by aeroplanes with banners that advertise toffee. It is a city that defeats and destroys some, and elevates others, a city in which despair can walk but which is also the 'jewel of jewels' that had excited Virginia Woolf when she returned to Tavistock Square. It is a city of great parks, military parades, fine doorways that open to reveal a life of grace ('A splendid achievement in its own way, after all, London; the season; civilization,' thinks Peter Walsh as he walks through it, following a girl who has caught his attention in the crowd), of royalty, power, and pride. It is also the city of dull flats and basement railings that swallows up Septimus Smith. The gap between Clarissa and Septimus is a complex social space that is never crossed directly, and the two central characters of the book never meet face to face. But the city, the streets, the sounds of Big Ben, the areas of common territory, link them, as does the stylistic habit of the book, its free, poetic flow and its sense of connection and transition.

But the day of the novel is certainly not occupied by very great events. Clarissa Dalloway goes out to buy flowers, she walks through London, she returns home, she receives a guest, Peter Walsh, whom thirty years before she might have become engaged to, she sees her daughter grow away from her, she gives a party. Beyond the domestic world we see glimpses of a much vaster society in which social and political power is exercised, radiating perhaps from the mysterious figure behind closed blinds in the motorcar in Bond Street, whose presence is announced by the 'pistol shot' of a backfire. The mysterious figure, the gloved hand, the flowers Mrs Dalloway carries – the images pile up and extend in meaning. In the sky above a plane writes its commercial messages, and on a park bench sits Septimus Warren Smith, who begins to see that the world is senseless. On the other hand, Mrs Dalloway herself is there to give it ceremony. When she returns home, she becomes a heroine back from her travels, a venerated figure. Her maid takes her parasol off her, 'handled it like a sacred weapon which a goddess, having acquitted herself honourably in the field of battle, sheds, and placed it in the umbrella stand.'

At the same time the story spreads away from its own immediate events. The clock is important, especially London's great clock, Big Ben, in its place of power, whose leaden sounds mark out the seventeen hours of the story – nearly the same time-span as *Ulysses*. Its beats mark out a central pattern for the book – something like the rhythm and beat of the sea in her later novel *The Waves*. The clock helps link consciousness to consciousness in a world of apparently

common time, which nonetheless drives them apart and then together. There is also the world of interior time, as the present flows
into the past. The fragments of the book are not entirely the 'fragments shored against my ruins' of *The Waste Land*. They may be
the chaotic fragments of image, remembrance and prophetic conviction that haunt the mind of Septimus Smith and drive him to
suicide. But they are frequently illuminations, revelations, part of
the 'luminous halo' of life – such as the crucial moment when Clarissa remembers being kissed by Sally Seton, and has a feeling of 'a
match burning in a crocus; an inner meaning almost expressed.' For
Clarissa herself the fragments are both a disorder and order, a breaking apart and a pulling together, part of the rhythmic nature of
being. For Virginia Woolf they are part of the 'tunnelling method'
that makes the novel.

Clarissa Dalloway is not in any conventional sense a romantic
heroine. She is in her fifty-second year, has been ill, seriously weakened
by the influenza epidemic. She feels a sense of emotional loss and of
the narrowing of her existence. But she is an exemplary hostess, herself
a part of the social domain of Britain, the wife of an important
Conservative Member of Parliament who has much to do with public
affairs, affairs which do not in any direct way interest her. But the
social life does, with its power to give meaning to life; and 'she, too,
was going to kindle and illuminate; to give her party.' And in different
ways the novel is the story of her capacity to 'kindle and illuminate',
and to respond to the things that kindle and illuminate the world. Her
one gift is 'knowing people almost by instinct . . . If you put her in a
room with someone, up went her back like a cat's; or she purred.' It
is at best a fragile gift, from which she often feels the need to retreat,
as indeed she does at her party. Peter Walsh, who thirty years before
had wanted to marry her, and now reappears, had in the past recognized these qualities: 'the perfect hostess he had called her (she had
cried over it in her bedroom), she had the makings of a perfect hostess,
he said.' Indeed one story of the book is that of his rediscovery,
through walking through London, of her unifying wholeness. He
finds postwar London again, by day and by night, takes impressions
of its urban beauty – the straight streets, the lighted windows, 'a sense

of pleasure-making hidden.' At the party he feels a sense of ecstasy and excitement, and asks where it comes from:

> It is Clarissa, he said.
> For there she was.

One critic has sharply recognized in Virginia Woolf's work a fascination with the 'metaphysical hostess', the woman gifted not just in party-giving but in distilling domestic and social relations, concentrating the felt meaning of life, a wholeness intuited in reality, into her own centre. The figure is indeed important in her books. We find it again in the next one, *To the Lighthouse* (1927), in the central figure of Mrs Ramsay, the mother and maker of the family, in whom all energies concentrate. *To the Lighthouse* is the story of the family in two phases, broken by the war and Mrs Ramsay's death, so that we see a world with her and a world without her. The book has several themes central to Virginia Woolf's work – the relation of male to female, of reason to intuition, of the difference between the isolation of pure thought and the social and humane value of living, as Mrs Ramsay does, 'in beauty', and of living life and painting it. But Mrs Ramsay is the unifying sensibility of the book:

> Mrs Ramsay, who had been sitting loosely, folding her son in her arm, braced herself, and, half turning, seemed to raise herself with an effort, and at once to pour erect into the air a rain of energy, a column of spray, looking at the same time animated and alive as if all her energies were being fused into force, burning and illuminating (quietly though she sat taking up her stocking again), and into this delicious fecundity, this fountain and spray of life, the fatal sterility of the male plunged itself, like a beak of brass, barren and bare.

This fecund female energy and its transcendental implication is more muted in *Mrs Dalloway*, but we can recognize it as part of the essential consciousness of the book. It has much to do with her conception of a feminine modernism – something that feminist critics have subsequently come to celebrate. It is also intimate with her style, the method of taking prose in the direction of poetry which gives her writing its distinctive lyric qualities. The lyricism is usually most intense when she responds to what in *Orlando* she calls 'the red, thick stream of life', and it generates – as in the passage above – some of her most luminous and complex imagery. Clarissa Dalloway functions in the novel to gather this sort of force to herself, and her party is its natural outcome.

Yet Clarissa's party is indeed interrupted by death, and her sense of wholeness is never complete. Throughout the book she is sadly conscious of the narrowed choices of her life, and a sexless chill in her nature. The luminous halo holds the past inside the present, and she recalls still her moment of choice between Peter Walsh and Richard Dalloway, and between the love of men and the love of women, and feels an absence. She sleeps alone, badly, in an attic room at the top of the tower of her house, where the sheets pulled tight on the bed remind her of sterility and mortality: 'Narrower and narrower would her bed be.' Everywhere there is a sense of some wholeness lost, some relationship – perhaps the one with Sally Seton, with whom she has half fallen in love – unfulfilled. The alternatives of her life have largely closed, and left her the wife of Dalloway, tied to the world of power and government. The memory of Sally, and the return of Peter Walsh from India, when he visits her and plays with his pen-knife, opens her wounds – just as her own flowers, as she carries them through Regent's Park, open wounds in the mind of Septimus Smith. And the book is not just Clarissa's story, though she is the radiating, at times the chilly, centre. The rhythms of consciousness move to other minds, including Peter Walsh's and Septimus Smith's. They also flow outwards into the city, and gather up the crowds, the people in the street, the nursemaids in the parks who watch the spectacles of pomp and power or the advertising plane flying over with its obscure message.

Virginia Woolf's method of narrating through consciousness owes something to James Joyce, but it is not the same. In her work the rhythms of consciousness are essentially those of the author's own sense of aesthetic creation – as she structures not just the narrative of the story but the texture of it, and its basic images and symbols: the flowers, Peter's pen-knife, the tolling of clocks, the ominous bed-clothes in the tower of the attic room. All this is one way in which *Mrs Dalloway* feels to us a modern novel. But another is the strong sense of a world changed by modernity itself. In many ways Virginia Woolf was always to be a traditional novelist. She respected the social order in which she lived, attached high value to its social life, engaged with its public institutions, and had her share of snobbery. But she saw it not as her male characters do, as they devote themselves to power and politics, to signing treaties and ruling India, but as a metaphysical society of the spirit. It was, as she said herself, a world seen from a feminine point of view, and like Clarissa it has an aesthetic coherence, a kind of beauty. But it is also a postwar world, not as solid as it was. The aeroplane over the city reminds us of recent war as well as of modern commerce. The car of the public personage erupts into the story as 'a pistol shot in the street outside'. The car is a reassurance to the crowds, the voice of authority. It is also what brings Septimus Smith, with his vision of a horror that has come to the surface and is about to burst into flames, into the story. The World War that started with another pistol shot haunts the novel in various ways, but above all through Septimus and his images of the world as a battlefield.

By introducing Septimus into the book, Virginia Woolf was able to create a story of two worlds that overlap and interlock, not by traditional narrative devices but by webs of indirect connection. Would the reviewers see how the themes interlocked, she wondered. They interlock, of course, through the great method of narrative by consciousness that was to become so important to the modern novel, and of which Virginia Woolf was a very distinctive explorer. They also interlock as part of the urban mesh of the novel, which is about the coincidence of lives in one complex community. But they interlock in another way, as Septimus becomes the spirit of another London wracked and damaged by the war. Like many figures in postwar literature he belongs to the 'tragic generation', part of a new fragility and instability which the novel seeks to recognize. He is one of Mrs Woolf's stranger figures, though we can find his counterpart

in a good deal of the fiction of the 1920s. He is a figure of a consciousness fragmented in a very different way from Clarissa's, belonging to
a world of force, violence and defeat. His other world resonates
through the final scenes: 'Up had flashed the ground; through him,
blundering, bruising, went the rusty spikes. There he lay with a thud,
thud, thud in his brain, and then a suffocation of blackness. So she
saw it. But why had he done it? And the Bradshaws talked of it at her
party!'

Virginia Woolf is a transcendental writer, a writer reaching to
metaphysical wholeness. The party, where everyone has six sons at
Eton, continues. The clock strikes again, and Clarissa Dalloway must
go back: 'She must assemble.' Thinking of death, she returns to her
party, to recreate in all its ambiguity the sense of aesthetic completeness
in which Virginia Woolf believed. At the end of *To the Lighthouse* the
painter Lily Briscoe looks at a world that has been deprived of much
of its feeling, but she completes her modern painting – just as Mrs
Woolf completes, with a strong sense of the power of art, her novel.
Mrs Dalloway concludes with a similar affirmation of presence, and it
is clearly shared by her author, who too believed in the radiant force
of the moment: 'it is or will become a revelation of some order; is a
token of some real thing behind appearances; and I make it real by
putting it into words.'

                                        5

With *Mrs Dalloway* and the novels that followed, Virginia Woolf
became perhaps the most essential representative of fictional modernism in Britain, winning both the veneration and the distrust that goes
with such a role. She was the writer most likely to be compared with
Proust, Mann, Gide or Faulkner, and the voice of an experimental
ideal with whom many of her contemporaries felt they had to come
to terms. Not all who were sympathetic felt that her kind of experiment represented the only or even the best path, and she became

used to a kind of criticism that she was, indeed, capable of turning against herself. 'I insubstantize, wilfully to some extent, distrusting reality – its cheapness,' she had noted in her diary, though of course she always insisted that there was a larger reality open to the power of creative intuition. Her friend E. M. Forster, who shared some but not all of her assumptions about the modern novel, put the critical point best: 'She is always stretching out from her enchanted tree and snatching bits from the flux of daily life as they float past, and out of these bits she builds novels.' It was part of the point of his *A Passage to India* – a book of almost the same date as *Mrs Dalloway*, and one with which it can be fairly compared – that we cannot live in a perpetual state of vision, and that visionary states can reveal not final joy but the muddle of the spirit, and even the despair of nihilism ('wait until you get one, dear reader').

Forster's charge that Virginia Woolf's books not only ended but always started in poetry, and so reached their lyrical state too readily, has an important truth. In turn she questioned his endeavour to retain a mixture of materialism and symbolism as the method of the modern novel: '. . . when the uncompromisingly solid should become the luminously transparent . . . he fails, because the conjunction of the two realities casts doubt on both.' The two positions – one half-realist and the other confidently symbolist – have become a central quarrel about the fate and future of the modern novel. As Iris Murdoch once sharply observed about Woolf's work, 'some people think there's a bit too much luminosity based on not enough stuff,' and, when, in a famous essay called 'Against Dryness', she suggested that the contemporary novel may require something of the 'crystalline' but also had to contain something of the 'journalistic', she was challenging the kind of novel represented by Mrs Woolf.

In 1941, tragically, Virginia Woolf, agonized by her bouts of madness, deeply distressed by the war and the bombing of London, the jewel of jewels, drowned herself in depression close to Monk's House. With the coming of another threatening war, an era was coming to an end. By this time her work was recognized as one essential strand in the modern movement, and perhaps the most influential example of it in the novel in the British line. During the

1940s and 1950s, in the aftermath of another war which demanded a new chronicle of historical change, when there was a return to social realism in the novel, the reputation of her work declined. There was a strong reaction not just to her kind of lyric modernism, but to Bloomsbury and all its works, as another literary generation, largely from different social origins, began to take its place in fiction. To them Virginia Woolf was not only the representative of what came to be called, somewhat dismissively, the 'experimental novel', which in a public time had come to seem a mannered and private affair, but also of the social caste that had been too dominant in the British literary scene and claimed the rights of aesthetic understanding to itself. Virginia Woolf, who was a scourge as well as a member of Bloomsbury, would herself have recognized some of the criticisms, and she acknowledged in her later years, as the sense of political crisis increased, that much British fiction had been built upon a tower of social confidence which had increasingly begun to lean.

Since that time, though, the centrality of Virginia Woolf's work has been increasingly acknowledged. The prodigious scale and achievement of *all* her writing – not just the nine novels, the feminist essays, the critical books, and the biography of Roger Fry, but also the periodical articles, the diaries, and the letters, a good part of these published posthumously, and some of them still appearing – have made her work, once accused of narrowness, seem more and more central to her own time, her intellectual world, and modern artistic ideas. A second questioning of realism, a new experimentalism, and the rise of feminism have all contributed important new understandings of her work and the nature of her significance for the present. By comparison with some of the other great modern writers of her age, Virginia Woolf remains a somewhat enclosed writer. Her sense of society, of history, and of the human condition is set within its chosen limits. She did not lack a sense of history and society – far from it – but she quarrelled with the central role social and historical forces had been given in the task of creating a modern writing. Certainly, as her diaries, her life-history, and her unhappy death itself display, she possessed as a personal pain that sense of crisis and extremity that has so understandably been a part of great modern writing, though she believed, like Clarissa Dalloway, in a metaphysical defiance: 'Death was defiance. Death was an attempt to communicate, people feeling the impossibility of reaching the centre which, mystically, evaded them; closeness drew apart; rapture faded; one was alone. There was an embrace in death.'

Virginia Woolf's was an achievement both of centrality and idiosyncracy, but then perhaps that is a definition of a major writer. Her novels are one essential aspect of modernism, in some ways an unusual one. They are more domestic than most of the great modern novels, and more enclosed in their own sense of aesthetic wholeness. They speak to an enchantment that is not there in much of modern fiction ('Didn't she know, she asked, that they were surrounded by an enchanted garden?' thinks old Mrs Hilbery at Clarissa's party), and they sustain a poetry of prose that many other modern authors felt had been fractured – though her pen, as her diary, and some of the satirical scenes in *Mrs Dalloway* show, could also become a poison one, sometimes in the interests of snobbery but usually in the interests of sharp moral truth. As more and more work by her comes into print, we can see the enormous variety of her tones and voices, the width and sharpness of her attention, the spread of her powers, and the major part she played in conveying the modern spirit in the arts. Nonetheless even she might have found an irony in the kind of emblem she has become. Today, a major American literary review offers its readers 'the chance to sport your literary preferences' by offering the choice of two tee-shirts. One is emblazoned with a drawing of Shakespeare. The other displays the fine-featured face, an image of intellectual sensitivity, of Virginia Woolf. The advertisement adds 'To allow for shrinkage, order one size larger than usual.' It seems appropriate, for Virginia Woolf was a writer who knew perfectly well the ironies of fame, and she always allowed for shrinkage.

FRANZ
KAFKA

I

'Someone must have been telling lies about Joseph K., for without
having done anything wrong he was arrested one fine morning.' This
is the terrible opening sentence of *The Trial*, the second of the three
novels written by Franz Kafka. Kafka, the young German-speaking
Jew from Prague who was to be acknowledged as one of the twentieth
century's greatest writers, wrote the book over the years of 1914 and
1915. He began it in the August during which the Great War started,
when the great age of German culture and the old labyrinthine world
of the Austro-Hungarian Empire in which he had grown up began its
slow collapse around him. This was also a time when his personal and
sexual life had fallen into disorder, and when the early signs of the
tuberculosis which would bring him to an early death ten years later
were just becoming apparent. Like so many modern novels, *The Trial*
was a book that came out of the breaking down of an era – and out
of the personal sickness that so often and so illuminatingly seemed to
accompany it.

And, like so many modern novels, Kafka's book then had a troubling, ironic history. In fact that history is so darkly ironic that we can
appropriately call it Kafka-esque. Not one of the three novels Kafka
wrote appeared in his lifetime. He never totally completed *The Trial*,
or put it into a fixed order. He had written it in a period of deep
personal upheaval, and in any case he wished to remain silent before
posterity just as he had remained silent in a number of crises in his
life, with his father and the girl he had wanted to marry. After the
war he handed the manuscript over to his old friend Max Brod; the
two of them had been students together at the German University in
Prague, and had followed similar careers in government service and
on the Prague literary scene. In 1924, at the age of 41, Kafka died of

the tuberculosis that had for so long made him fragile, lonely, and unwilling to marry, and constantly sent him to spas and sanatoria. Just before his death he issued his last instructions to Brod: 'Everything I leave behind me . . . is to be burned unread and to the last page.' Even those books which he had thought important and which had been published he wished to disappear forever. Fortunately for us, Brod well knew the self-cancelling and self-suppressing side of Kafka's nature. Almost everything Kafka had published had had to be teased from him. 'In spite of these categorical instructions I refuse to commit the incendiary act demanded of me,' Brod explains in his epilogue to the book. He set the not-quite-complete manuscript in order (some people still disagree with the order he selected) and *The Trial* appeared in Germany in 1925.

But the trials of the book were only just beginning. In fact it is not simply its dark story but its dark history that makes *The Trial* seem to belong so centrally to our bleak experience of the modern world. Like a terrible prophecy, Kafka's wish see his book suppressed and burned came true, and his writing was cancelled by just the kind of state terror about which he had written. With the rise of Nazism, the work of this German-speaking Jew was first confined to Jewish bookshops, and then suppressed and burned. Other works by Kafka which Brod wanted to publish could appear now only in Prague, the city of Kafka's birth and death. Prague itself fell before the Germans at the beginning of the Second World War, and afterwards was entered by the Russians, to become one of the Communist states. To this day, by a terrible irony that seems to come directly from Kafka's own imagination, his work is still suppressed there in his own city, as it is throughout most of Eastern Europe. Kafka is a forbidden and officially unmentioned author – presumably because his imaginary creations, which he described as personal fantasies, so closely resemble the actuality of a real daily existence that the many Czechs who re-member his work call 'Kafka-esque'. Meanwhile Kafka's international fame grew, but only slowly. *The Trial* became available in English only in 1937, in the brilliant translation by Willa and Edwin Muir. As the world increasingly came to resemble the imaginary one he con-structed, he became a writer for a new time of darkness. His surreal

methods and his exiled imagination became an influence on a generation of writers who saw before them a new world of war and the
ominous apparatus of the modern totalitarian state.

The war brought an age of new and unbelievable horrors. After
1945 came a full knowledge of the Holocaust, in which six million
Jews in Central Europe were murdered in the gas chambers and the
concentration camps. Many came from the large Jewish community
in Prague, in which Franz Kafka had grown up. Three of his sisters,
two of the women he had so anxiously loved, and other members of
the family from which he became half-exiled were among the victims.
After the Russian occupation and the coming of the Marxist state,
Prague, one of Central Europe's loveliest cities, city of golden spires,
of alchemists and goldsmiths, of cultural plurality and craftsmanship,
became a city of silence and suppressions, where writers were cautious
and Kafka went unacknowledged. Though many Marxist critics have
written understandingly of his work, his voice was thought unsafe.
Nonetheless, even in Eastern Europe, Kafka's silence has lasted, while
in the rest of the world he has been a writer who has caught and
captured the modern imagination as perhaps no other twentieth-
century author has.

Kafka's image is indeed one both of the humanity and the fragility of
the modern writer in the face of power and of the spirit of anxiety
that has belonged to our times. 'Logic is doubtless unshakable, but it
cannot withstand a man who wants to go on living,' he says at the end
of *The Trial*. Logic here represents power, history, and the inevitable;
and in the book it is logic and not the man, Joseph K., which survives.
It may well be that what concerned Kafka, as he wrote these words,
was whether he himself wanted to go on living in the world about
him: he was often to say that his tubercular illness was itself an expression of his character and his sense of defeat. But Kafka was to go
on living through his words, and indeed has become vastly larger
than any single work that came from his pen. His very appearance, as
it stares at us from the sleeves of his own books, and the many more
that have been written about him, has turned into a symbol. It is
emaciated, anxious, sensitive, pallid, the face of a man whose expression
says that he has never been at home anywhere, that he has been accused

of life. It is an image that links him directly with a postwar world
that W. H. Auden called, in a notable poem, 'The Age of Anxiety' –
the world after World War Two, the Holocaust and the atomic bomb,
after totalitarianism and the power of the masses. The Kafka who
lived in his own age of anxiety speaks clearly to our own sense of
victimization and superfluity, of labyrinthine oppressions and inward
exiles. Kafka has lasted, and become more than Kafka.

And, despite or rather because of its modernity, that first sentence
of *The Trial* became one of the most famous openings in all literature,
and it still resonates through contemporary experience. Clearly the
reasons are not the usual ones which make the first lines of great
novels memorable: elegance, wit, surreal strangeness. Its words evoke
not elegance but terror, the wit ('one fine morning') is terrible too,
and the strangeness of an absurd event is made to seem perfectly
natural. In fact, like everything thoughout Kafka's work, the sentence,
the situation, has the power of seeming both real and strange at once.
It is simply the plain statement of a state of affairs – but that state of
affairs is both timeless and very contemporary, just as it is both
metaphysical and social, psychological and political. As Max Brod
said, it was Kafka's gift to turn the surreal into the matter-of-fact.
But it is a sentence that represents the beginning of a sentence, for
Joseph K. here comes under the view of an accusation. He, as all are,
is sentenced to the condition of life and death. To be alive is to be on
trial.

Nonetheless, as George Steiner has said, these few phrases represent
probably the most graphic moment of clairvoyance, of prophetic
imagining, in twentieth-century literature. Like everything else in
Kafka's work, they at once raise life to the level of high anxiety.
There is the abbreviation of Joseph K.'s name, a habit of writing that
is common in Kafka's work, but which at once reduces his identity
and seems to turn him into a case or a file. In Kafka's next novel, *The
Castle*, the name of the bewildered and victimized hero would be
reduced even further, to a simple K. Joseph K. is arrested one fine
morning 'without having done anything wrong'. This sudden arbi-
trariness, which turns justice into injustice, is very much in the Kafka-
esque spirit. Soon we will begin to wonder just what wrong it is that

Joseph has not done – and why already he seems half-willing to accept the accusation, as if we are all accused of something. After all, he exists, in a modern state, and in a modern state. That modern state is partly an inward condition of the Kafka hero, who shares his author's neurotic and self-accusing nature. It is also a modern political condition – for that morning knock on K.'s door is the knock that summons him and us into the terrible world of contemporary history.

'He over whom Kafka's wheels have passed has lost forever any peace with the world,' the German critic T. W. Adorno once wrote, in a compelling phrase. It was curiously fated that Kafka, who is in some ways the most private, the most self-enclosed, indeed the most bourgeois of modern writers, should become one of the most powerful and most terrible. 'Had one to name the author who comes closest to bearing the same kind of relation to our age as Dante, Shakespeare and Goethe bore to theirs, Kafka is the first one would think of,' Auden said of him, acknowledging this most anxious of geniuses as a central expression of the modern spirit. Kafka, it should be clearly said, had himself little idea of the scale or nature of the historical prophecy he was constructing, and was a man little concerned with politics. Much that happened during the First World War, for instance, passed him by at a distance. He was an emotionally and intellectually self-engrossed writer. The disorientation he revealed was an inner state of existence. The nihilism he seemed to express in his writing was something which he himself distrusted. The world he wrote of was not ours, but the world of the dislocated Jewish heritage in an older and declining order of European affairs. And, like Dostoevsky, or indeed like other writers of his generation – the Austrian Robert Musil, for example, who produced *The Man Without Qualities*, the Triestean writer Italo Svevo, who wrote *The Confessions of Zeno*, or the Thomas Mann of *Death in Venice* – he wrote of a sense of superfluity, failed identity, sickness and irrelevance that deeply afflicted many of the sensitive intellectuals of a rising bourgeois and industrial age.

Yet this strange, retiring, sickly Jewish insurance clerk of Prague was to shake and shatter the modern imagination far more than any other. None summons the fragility and terror we feel in our age and our hearts more completely. As George Steiner says, Kafka was a prophet, and in the most literal sense:

> the key fact about Kafka is that he was possessed of a fearful premonition, that he saw, to the point of exact detail, the horror gathering. *The Trial* exhibits the classic model of the terror state. It prefigures that furtive sadism, the hysteria which totalitarianism insinuates into private and sexual life, the faceless boredom of the killers. Since Kafka wrote, the night knock has come on innumerable doors, and the name of those dragged off to die 'like a dog!' is legion. Kafka prophesied the actual forms of the disaster of Western humanism which Nietzsche and Kierkegaard had seen like an uncertain blackness on the horizon.

It is a profoundly telling fact, Steiner remarks, that in more than a hundred languages we can describe the harried and victimized condition of modern man with the adjective *kafka-esque*.

The Trial begins with Joseph K.'s arrest, and it ends with his execution. As he dies, the window of a house goes up nearby, and an insubstantial figure stands there and stretches out both arms. 'Who was it? A friend? A good man? Someone who sympathized? Someone who wanted to help? Was it one person only? Or were they all there? Was help at hand? Were there some arguments in his favour that had been overlooked? Of course there must be.' The figure of watching humanity, who might bring compassion to the condemned, is the last thing Joseph K. sees, apart from the faces of those who kill him. The last words he says are 'Like a dog!', and it was, Kafka adds, 'as if he meant the shame of it to outlive him.' What outlived Kafka was all of this: the great condemnation and victimization, the inward shame, and the vague hope for the good man, someone who sympathized. If the opening of *The Trial* terrifies us, that ending too resonates throughout our present world, revealing Kafka as one of the most profoundly troubling, as well as the most modern, of our twentieth-century writers.

2

The Trial begins in Joseph K.'s bedroom 'one fine morning' when he finds the world has changed. It is his thirtieth birthday, but things do not happen as usual. His breakfast does not come as it should ('That had never happened before') and two warders enter to tell him he is under arrest, though they do not know what for. From the opposite house people watch him; perhaps they are the ones who have been telling lies about him. The inspector in the next room who interviews him cannot explain who has accused him, or of what offence. His arrest will not prevent him from carrying on his ordinary life as a bank official. Joseph K. suggests that in that case being arrested is not so bad, and he hardly need be told about it, but the inspector explains 'It was my duty.' Three of his colleagues from the bank are present for some reason, and they accompany him to the office in a taxi, while Joseph K. looks behind to try to understand what has happened to him. All that has changed is that he is now being judged and observed from outside. Evidently to be alive is to be accused of an unknown crime.

'If someone else is observing me, naturally I have to observe myself too; if none observes me, I have to observe myself all the closer,' another K., Franz Kafka, wrote in the extraordinary diary he kept for many years and which is our best clue to his nature as a man and a writer. 'We often ask: who has been telling lies about us? Who could have told such things?' This self-observing and self-accusing imagination, which we find also in Joseph K., is the very spirit of Kafka. For every word Kafka wrote – the three novels he never intended for publication, the various stories and sketches, a certain number of which he did choose to publish, the extraordinary diaries, and the letters to Brod and above all those to Felice Bauer, the girl from Berlin to whom he was twice engaged but never married – bears the distinctive stamp of the same kind of imagination. It is haggard, haunted, ominous, neurasthenic. It is also curiously self-exposed and un-protected. As he noted once: 'Balzac carried a cane on which was carved the legend: I smash every obstacle; my legend runs: Every

obstacle smashes me.' Kafka writes in the spirit of self-exile, as no
other major writer has. His very identity as man and writer is rooted
in a pervasive inner guilt and exile, without which, it would appear,
he could scarcely feel he existed.

To understand Kafka's work, we need to understand that strange
yet representative sensibility, and what shaped it. Kafka was born in
Prague on 3 July 1883, the weak and delicate child and the only
surviving son of a German-speaking Jewish family. His father was a
powerful, hearty man from the countryside who had turned himself
by an effort of will and ambition into a successful merchant. His
mother came from a different and much more aesthetic Jewish
background, to which Franz felt closer. The quarrel of father and son
over almost everything in life was the crucial fact of Franz's existence.
'You asked me recently why I am afraid of you,' begins Kafka's
famous, and in some ways infamous, 'Letter to His Father'. This letter,
never sent to its destination, constitutes a crucial record of his early
life and his nature, perhaps the best emotional autobiography we have
of this confessional but reticent writer. It is the story of a succession of
revolts — against the family and the idea of the family, the life of
business, the Jewish inheritance of the ghetto — and the growth of an
anguished personality. 'I had lost my self-confidence where you were
concerned, and in its place had developed a boundless sense of guilt.'

This revolt of son against father has much to do with the whole
spirit of Kafka's writings. In that relationship, which became terrible
to him, Kafka found the basis of the disturbing, fatal relationship
between man and God, man and Law, Jew and Gentile. Throughout
his life he was to presume that he was judged by a paternal authority,
which rebuked everything that he did, every act he performed. Even
his illness was a crime against his father's health. His father educated
him, he says, in mistrust, 'which oddly enough was no particular
burden to you (the fact was that you were strong enough to bear it,
and besides, it was in reality perhaps only a token of the aristocrat),
this mistrust, which for me as a little boy was nowhere confirmed in
my own eyes, since I everywhere saw only people excellent beyond
all hopes of emulation, in me turned into mistrust of myself and into
perpetual anxiety in relation to everything else.' He particularly recalls

one hideous moment, when as a child he asked one night for water, and his father had carried him out onto the balcony and left him. 'Even years afterwards I suffered from the tormenting fantasy that the huge man, my father, the ultimate authority, would come almost for no reason at all and take me out of bed in the night and carry me out on to the *pavlatche*, and that therefore I was such a mere nothing for him.'

The conflict of the hearty and business-like father and the timid and weakly son was, as Kafka knew, no isolated phenomenon. It belonged to the experience of a whole transitional generation of Jews who had moved from the reasonably devout countryside into the secular world of the cities. And it became focused in Kafka's ambitions as a writer, themselves a revolt against the father who despised such things. It was a way of withdrawing from all the father expected his son to be – a loyal family member, a businessman, a husband, a faithful Jew. His writings were, Kafka said, 'an intentionally long-drawn-out leave-taking from you'. Not for nothing did Kafka come from the same Austro-Hungarian world that produced Sigmund Freud – Freud in the more urbane Vienna, Kafka in the lesser capital of Prague. And yet nothing was exactly what Kafka came to see himself as. He was a vacancy, a cipher, the defeated son of a patriarch. Like Freud, what he went on to explore was the repressive power of all such patriarchal authorities – but also that neurasthenic self-suppression that seemed required of the individual in the world of civilized and bourgeois society.

The battle went on throughout Kafka's schooldays at the German-speaking school in Prague, and then during his career at the German university in the city, where he first read chemistry and took an interest in literature and philosophy. It was at university that he met Max Brod, and it was here in 1906 that he took his Doctorate in Law. This was, in his father's view, a preparation for a life of employment in the government service of a state where Jewish employment had always been a struggle. Kafka had, to say the least, no admiration for the world of legal regulations. Nonetheless, like Brod, he saw the advantages of an official government post, where work finished at two in the afternoon, giving him time to meet Brod and the literary society of the city at the Café Arco, and plan his career as a writer. Thus he became a clerk in the Workers' Accident Insurance Institute, responsible for interviewing the victims of factory accidents. He became, in short, himself a part of the labyrinthine bureaucracy of the late days of the Austro-Hungarian empire, with its great offices and its cumbersome apparatus. That official world was something always reflected in his work, not least in the daily duties of Joseph K.

Thus, if Kafka's writings always presented himself as a victim, he was a knowledgeable victim who had power over others. He knew the world of law, and, like Dickens and Melville, Gogol, Tolstoy and Dostoevsky, the nineteenth-century writers to whom his work provides a link, experienced the life of bureaucracy and officialdom from the inside. Both adminstrator and subject of the system, he knew exactly the world of paperwork and hierarchy, rule and regulation, indifference and incompetence, which his work always summons up. He also came to know well the terrible working and living conditions of the urban proletariat, not only through his work for the Institute but through the experience of his own father's factory, where he sometimes worked in the afternoons. All this he did to buy income and time to be what he wished to be, a writer. At the same time, that writing became in turn the release from the daily duties that oppressed him. Indeed it became the expression of a mutual antipathy between himself and the world outside. Yet Kafka also sought to see *himself* from outside, creating an internal separation, an ironic view of himself. He was becoming not quite 'I', but 'K.'

The self-exile inside the writing was also intensified by his existence as a German-speaking writer in Prague, a city he does not often directly name, but which permeates his work. Prague, sometimes called 'The Dublin of the East', set in the very centre of Europe, is one of the loveliest and most ancient of mid-European cities, the 'city of golden spires'. It was an intellectual capital, but also a province. Its cultural history was divided, between a German heritage and the political influence of Austria-Hungary, between a Western European spirit and Czech cultural nationalism. It was a medieval city and a major Jewish centre, still flavoured by the spirit of the old alchemists and goldsmiths, the folklore of the countryside and the ghetto. The cultures multiplied and divided. Prague had four major ethnic sources: the German, the Czech, the Jewish, and the Austrian. The large Jewish minority of 25,000 was itself divided between Czech- and German-speakers. The latter was in the minority of the minority, and Kafka was one of them.

It is not surprising that the literature of minorities preoccupied the early notes Kafka made in his diaries. Nor is it surprising that writers like Rilke and Franz Werfel made for larger centres elsewhere, above all Berlin and Vienna, which between them dominated Prague's intellectual life. 'Always this one principal anguish,' Kafka noted during the war, 'What if I had gone away in 1912, in full possession of all my forces, with a clear head, not eaten by the strain of keeping down living forces!' Kafka went irregularly to Berlin, which he liked, and Vienna, which he liked less, but esentially he remained a writer of Prague. 'Prague does not let go . . .' he noted. 'This little mother has claws.' It became an unreal city through whose labyrinthine streets he walked, a city dominated by the high castle above, the river, the great hill, the cathedral, the state buildings, the cattlemarket, besides which he went to school. An early work, 'Description of a Struggle', contains a remarkable account of such a walk. 'Are you trying to make me believe I'm unreal, standing here absurdly on the green pavement?' he asks, 'You, sky, surely it's a long time since you've been real, and as for you, Ringplatz, you never have been real . . . I'm the only one who's afraid.'

On Prague's Laurenziberg hill, he records, he defined his artistic wishes: 'I found that the most important and most delightful was the wish to attain a view of life (and – this was necessarily bound up with it – to convince others of it in writing), in which life, while still retaining its full-bodied rise and fall, would simultaneously be recognized no less clearly as a nothing, a dream, a dim hovering. A beautiful wish, perhaps, if I had weighted it rightly.' The beautiful wish Kafka did attain; his writing is both full-bodied and dream-like, a nothing. It became a vivid witness to the fullness of life outside him, and the inward exile and separation he felt from it. As he noted, just around the time of the writing of *The Trial*: 'What will be my fate as a writer is very simple. My talent for portraying my dreamlike inner life has thrust all other matters into the background. My life has dwindled dreadfully, but nothing else will ever satisfy me. But the strength I can muster for that portrayal is not to be counted on.' That dreamlike inner life, that strength that cannot be counted on, these are the things that turned the young and tubercular Kafka, in provincial Prague, into a major writer.

3

Exile, we have seen, is a persistent condition of modern writing, much of which has been a revolt against the homely, the domestic, and the provincial. But no modern writer has carried his fragility as far as Kafka, or made it so inward and so central to his writing. From his early years Kafka kept a diary in which he recorded many things – the tales he heard, the glimpses of life he saw, the stories he started. Above all it shows the exact sensibility of his anxiety and his inner exile, his persistent self-denigration: '. . . if I lacked an upper lip here, there an ear, here a rib, there a finger, if I had hairless spots on my head and pockmarks on my face, this would still be no adequate counterpart to my inner perfection,' he notes. These are the diaries of a nightmare dreamer, for whom the terrible experiences of the gothic, the perverse, and the self-accusing come like threatening myths in the night. In this world, even waking in one's bed, as Joseph K. does at the start of *The Trial* and Gregor Samsa in the opening sentence of 'Metamorphosis', is terrible, dangerous, momentous. 'Sunday, July 19, slept, awoke, slept, awoke, terrible life,' runs an early entry.

These are also the diaries of a hungry reader, above all in the work of those thinkers about the modern anxiety with which Kafka was so intimate. 'Now read in Dostoevsky the passage that reminds me so of my "being unhappy",' he notes in one characteristic entry. Even the quotation marks somehow appear typical and revealing, a sign that unhappiness is not just a personal fact but a literary condition. Dostoevsky, perhaps the first of the modern writers, was an obvious source of his own imaginings, and Kafka and his own characterless heroes are clear descendants of his underground man. In other similar writers, like Gogol, Tolstoy and Strindberg, the great writers of Europe he admired, he found those images of the superfluous man, the man condemned to inner exile, that modern social life and modern self-awareness created. In his favourite modern philosophers, particularly Nietzsche and Kierkegaard, he discovered the universality of his sensations. So, after reading some passages from the Danish existentialist Kierkegaard, he comments: 'As I suspected, his case, despite essential differences, is very similar to mine, at least he is on the same side of the world. He bears me out like a friend.'

Unmistakably, though, these are the diaries of a writer, one who can strangely capture us within the world of his pained and crippled existence. He is a writer who constantly defines pessimism, depression, self-accusation and guilt as the very conditions of creation. Writing comes best when he is most disappointed, most guilty, most in despair. He describes himself as a night-time writer, one whose work is born from the time we cannot sleep because of our feelings of dread. He has 'a great yearning to write all my anxiety entirely out of me, write it into the depths of the paper just as it comes out of the depths of me, or write it down in such a way that I could draw what I had written into me completely.' The stories abound, and he writes them down; often they contain figures very like himself, figures who deserve the name of K. They share in the same world of illusion and bafflement in which the writer is enclosed: 'Everything is an illusion: family, office, friends, the street, the woman, all illusion, drawing nearer and further away; but the nearest truth is merely that I push my head against the wall of a cell without doors or windows.'

Where does the writing come from? 'Writing is a sweet and marvellous reward – but for what?' he writes to Max Brod. 'Last night it came home to me with the clarity of an object lesson for children, that it is the reward for serving the devil.' It has been rightly said of Kafka that everything he wrote he wrote with the fervour of the religious man, but what he sought to achieve was a view of no-thingness. 'I represent the negative elements of my age,' he writes, observing that he is not even guided by the sinking elements of Christianity, as Kierkegaard is, or attempting to catch at the flying prayer-shawl of the Jews. Yet he wishes, he declares, to create his own Kabbala, while remembering that 'What is laid on us is to accomplish the negative, the positive is already given.' According to Brod and other critics, Kafka was essentially a religious writer, for whom the primary exile is from the divine and transcendental world itself. This emphasis has sometimes been over-exaggerated, at the expense of recognizing his power as a fantasist of the modern world. But like many of the great modern Jewish writers, from Babel and Singer to Bellow and Amos Oz, he writes at no vast distance from a religious view of things, while expressing a secular vision. His writing everywhere carries a metaphysical charge, even though the transcendental world seems dismayingly far away, like a remote tribunal, a lost or refused father, a distant imperial power.

But this leaves the world unreal, detached from itself, suddenly made unhomely. It metamorphoses from a safe domestic space into a 'naked den' – as it does in the story so appropriately called 'The Metamorphosis'. Kafka's short stories are some of the finest of the century, and each contains in some form or another this sensation of defamiliarization. In 'The Metamorphosis' a man wakes to find himself a giant cockroach, which has to be 'got rid of'. In 'In the Penal Settlement', an officer demonstrates a terrible machine that writes a prisoner's sentence agonizingly into his flesh; he then becomes its victim. At a meeting of the academy an ape gives an account of his life, and a 'hunger artist', famous for his circus fasting, confesses that he hates and revolts against food, so the fasts are reality, and the falsehood is the food the circus gives him to keep him alive between performances. In the novels, a man goes to an imaginary, half-dreamt-of America that Kafka never was to visit (*America*), and another attempts to understand the strange bureaucracy of a castle that has come to govern his life (*The Castle*). In *The Trial* Joseph K. becomes subject to a system of law with absolute rules that he cannot understand and yet which he finally acknowledges.

Kafka prepared himself as a writer for many years, and pieces appeared in magazines; he also constantly decided his writings were worthless. Not until 1913 did a volume appear, *Betrachtung* (*Medita-*

tion), largely gathered from the diaries, and running to ninety-nine pages of large type. It was around this time that his creative energies seemed to reach a new release, and this was probably for emotional reasons. For in 1912, at Max Brod's, he met Felice Bauer, the young girl from Berlin who became the recipient of some of his most complex affections and most remarkable letters. During 1913, when this correspondence was at its strongest, Kafka wrote 'The Metamorphosis', and a good deal of the novel *America*. Even the entries in the diaries take on a new creative sharpness and vigour. And the outcome of this relationship undoubtedly has to do with the creation of *The Trial*.

The correspondence with Felice is indeed an extraordinary affair, filled with self-accusation, an almost daily record of evasions, physical anxieties, a strange confession of impotence and of the fact that his deepest feelings toward human beings are those of fear and indifference. From the start we can see that this is a relationship that will destroy itself, as Kafka faces his baffled anxiety in the face of the familiar things of life – love, attachment, marriage, fathering, the sharing of his rooms. When he proposed marriage to Felice, the list of reasons he gives for and against matrimony is extraordinary and contradictory: 'Inability to bear living alone' is the one point in favour; 'I must be alone a great deal. All that I have accomplished is the result of being alone,' is one of many points against. The engagement renewed the crisis with his father and all fathers, and the entire idea of marriage, family and children became a persistent threat to his writing – which is the task of revealing oneself to excess, only to be achieved by remaining totally alone.

A strong erotic charge runs through all of Kafka's writings, along with a troubling sexual guilt. In *The Trial* Joseph K. hopes that a woman will intercede for him, but his careless sexual activities seem part of his crime and instinct for self-destruction. Kafka himself had casual encounters with whores, and there is even a legend of an illegitimate son. He seemed to feel hunger for sexual contact with any woman who showed interest in him, and this included Felice's friend and intermediary Grete Bloch, to whom he writes as persistently as to Felice, confiding his sexual unease about her in ways that suggest that

Grete is more attractive to him. It was this that was to lead to the great crisis in the relationship, when in 1914 he went to Berlin to see Felice and became engaged to her for a few weeks. Then, in humiliating circumstances for Kafka, the engagement was broken off in a family 'tribunal' at his Berlin hotel, after Grete revealed the content of some of his letters to her. At this 'tribunal' Kafka remained silent. Even so the relationship was to persist, and into a second much later engagement.

This was one crucial event of the summer of 1914. The other, of course, was the coming of war. 'August 2. Germany has declared war on Russia. – Swimming in the afternoon,' Kafka notes in the diary, and a little later: 'I discover in myself nothing but pettiness, indecision, envy and hatred against those who are fighting and whom I passionately wish everything evil.' There are patriotic parades: 'I stand there with my malignant look.' At the same time he defined his fate as a writer, 'the talent for portraying my dreamlike inner life', even as his life started to dwindle. And it was in that August when the engagement collapsed and war was declared that he started writing *The Trial*. There is no doubt that the two major events in Kafka's life over the year – one personal, the beginning and end of his engagement, his attempt to enter the world, and the other historical, the coming of war – had enormous influence on the making of that book, and were somehow interlinked in his imagination. 'Again barely two pages,' he notes in September 1914. 'At first I thought my sorrow over the Austrian defeats and my anxiety for the future . . . would prevent me from doing any writing. But that wasn't it, it was only an apathy that forever comes back and forever has to be put down again. There is time enough for sorrow when I am not writing. The thoughts provoked in me by the war resemble my old worries over F. [Felice Bauer] . . .'

These are the two shadows hanging over the book, with its pervasive sense of separation from and failure in the courts of the world. Elias Canetti has indeed suggested, in an interesting and flamboyant interpretation of *The Trial*, that the episode with Felice is the major theme. 'The engagement [to Felice] becomes the arrest in the first chapter; the "tribunal" appears as the execution in the last,' he proposes.

He goes on to apply various details of the unhappy engagement to various episodes in the book, and some of the connections evidently fit: 'Had they set me down in a corner bound in real chains, placed policemen in front of me and let me look on simply like that, it could not have been worse. And that was my engagement,' is how Kafka described the famous 'tribunal.' Kafka himself suggests that the agonies of the year helped bring the book into being. But of course none of these things explain its extraordinary power, and the way these personal defeats, depressions, and feelings of sexual guilt, became a work of enormous metaphoric and mythic imagining.

4

Strangeness in *The Trial* is so matter-of-fact that we often do not remember how strange the events of the novel actually are. Joseph K. is notified of his arrest, but he completes a day's work at the bank and then returns to his apartment. Normality appears to be resumed, but Joseph follows his fellow lodger, Fraulein Burstner ('F.B.'), into her room, the one where the Inspector has interviewed him and has thus been 'polluted,' and attempts to make love to her. Afterwards he 'fell asleep almost at once, but before doing so he thought for a little about his behaviour, he was pleased with it, yet surprised that he was not still more pleased . . .' It is after this he is informed that an inquiry will take place into his case, to be held on Sundays in order not to interrupt his professional work. He has great difficulty finding the courtroom, in a great house in an ordinary street. He remembers what one of the warders has said, that 'an attraction existed between the Law and guilt, from which it should really follow that the Interrogation Chamber must lie in the particular flight of stairs which K. happened to choose.'

Children and sick people lie in the building, where he asks a young washerwoman for 'a joiner called Lanz'. She guides him to a crowded courtroom and shuts him in. Before the crowded room K. makes his defence, saying that this is only a trial if he recognizes it as such. K. enjoys his outburst, and explains he is quite detached from the affair. Indeed he attempts to become the champion of all who are accused. Evidently, he announces, there is 'a great organization at work', employing not only corrupt workers and Examining Magistrates, but a judicial hierarchy of the highest rank. Its task is to ensure 'that innocent persons are accused of guilt, and senseless proceedings are put in motion against them, mostly without effect, it is true, as in my own case.' In fact most of those there seem to be officials of the court. Despite the fact that he is not called again, K. returns the following Sunday, to find the court is not sitting. The washerwoman, the wife of a court official, offers herself to him. Now K. considers he may be able to lure her away from the court, but she is carried off by a bandy-legged student to the Examining Magistrate's office. He is shown round the offices, and begins to faint, discovering that most men accept the fact that there is an accusation against them. Now he starts to feel that he too is being incorporated in the universe of those 'accused of guilt'.

From this moment onward K.'s struggle to remain independent of the world of 'us' (the warders at the beginning ask K. why he cannot accept his position and become one of them) weakens, and everything in his life seems to be part of the court and the trial. He relationship with Fraulein Burstner seems affected, and so is his life at the bank, where, one evening, he hears groans behind the door of what he had thought a lumber-room. The two warders who had arrested him are being whipped by a third man. When he checks the next night the scene is still the same, and he orders the lumber-room cleared. The situation makes it clear that K. does not expect the clerks to find the warders and their torturer; it is a vision suffered by him. K. himself is thus the source and cause of all the events, as if he is living in a dream which is from time to time separate from reality. Nonetheless the dream-reality grows more and more inclusive, and the gap between the familiar and the strange closes. It is part of the extraordinary quality of *The Trial* and Kafka's other writings that we are led into a world where we cannot directly distinguish between what is objective reality and what is consciousness, the stuff of the mind of the hero, or his author, 'the tremendous world I have in my head'.

The second half of *The Trial* largely consists of K.'s encounters
with figures who seem to know well the world of the courts, and can
explain its affairs to him. By now K. *pleads* for his trial in the complex
modern world of crime and punishment. K. is taken to see an old,
ailing Attorney who strangely seems to know something of his case,
and is told that the charges in the case are inaccessible to the accused
and his counsel. K. disgraces himself by beginning to flirt with the
Attorney's importunate nurse, Leni, and is told that accused men are
often sexually attractive: 'It's a remarkable phenomenon, almost a
natural Law.' It is not the sense of guilt, nor the punishment they
receive, since not all are guilty or will be punished. It is 'the mere
charge preferred against them that in some way enhances their attractive-
ness.' K. joins Leni, and is told that he should admit his fault. 'I seem
to recruit women helpers,' he thinks. In this scene the sexual anxiety
in the novel is evidently great, as K. finds himself in a complex world
of the erotic, the legal and the religious. A portrait of the Judge hangs
over him as he kisses Leni, and thus 'exchanges' her for his less exotic
girl-friend Elsa. 'You belong to me now,' she says, as if emphasizing
the sexual nature of his guilt.

K. also seeks out a painter, Titorelli, who paints the Judges of the
court. Again there are complex erotic overtones, for K. has to walk
up a staircase in a dirty building which is lined with teenage girls,
who are both childish and sophisticated, and chase him into the room.
Titorelli tells him they belong to the court too. The anxieties of Justice
and Law are everywhere, even in the paintings Titorelli paints.
Titorelli accepts K.'s claim to innocence, and undertakes to get him
off, asking him what sort of acquittal he would like – definite acquittal,
ostensible acquital, or indefinite postponement. But definite acquital
has never been heard of. Ostensible acquittal means that one is
ostensibly free only, and likely to be constantly re-arrested, and
postponement means preventing the case from getting past its first
stage. Both are simply ways of deferring sentence. When K. says they
also prevent real acquittal, Titorelli declares that K. has found the
kernel of the matter. And, leaving the studio, K. finds himself again in
the offices of the Law Court – for everything is an aspect of the
Court.

And this is true not only in the world of Art but also in that of Religion, as K. finds in the culminating scenes of the book. He is required to go to the Cathedral, apparently on business. Before he goes Leni calls him on the telephone and says, 'They are driving you hard.' In the great cathedral, he wanders with a tourist guidebook in his hand. As he is about to leave, the priest calls out his name. He tells K., who slowly approaches, that he is a prison chaplain, and knows about K.'s case. It is going badly: 'You cast about too much for outside help,' he says, 'especially from women.' After K. has asked the priest to come down from the altar, he is told a parable – the key moment of the novel. Indeed Kafka chose to print the tale as a separate story called 'Before the Law' in 1916. It is undoubtedly the mythic core of the book, and the closest it comes to a revelation, both for Joseph K. and the reader. It is a story of the impenetrable nature of the law that governs us, and the impenetrability of meaning itself. It belongs to the tradition of Jewish myth, and in its sense of life's victimization it has been compared with the Book of Job.

The story the priest tells is of a man from the country who waits outside the door of the Law. The doorkeeper will not admit him, yet. He waits a lifetime, and at the end asks the doorkeeper why, if all men seek Law, no one else has sought admittance. The doorkeeper explains that this door has been intended for him alone, and that he is now going to shut it. K. protests that the doorkeeper has deluded the man. In a brilliant parody of religious exegesis, the priest interprets the story in a variety of ways. It shows that: 'The right perception of any matter and a misunderstanding of the same matter do not exclude each other.' It indicates that the man may go anywhere he chooses, and that only the Law is closed to him. It implies that the doorkeeper shut the door out of his devotion to duty, or else to bring the man to regret in his last moments, and perhaps that the doorkeeper will not in fact be able to shut the door after all. Nor need the waiting man accept his statements as true: 'It is not necessary to accept everything as true, one must only accept it as necessary.' The parable is a parable of life's quest to discover meaning and significance, though it also implies the ambiguity of all significance. It is, of course, the parable of K.'s own story, and it forbids any release from guilt or any possibility of acquittal. As the priest says, he too is a servant of the Court, for religion and law are intertwined. The Court he represents receives you when you come, and only relinquishes you when you go. It is both impenetrable and always there, like existence. And its meanings are not fixed but multiply endlessly, like Kafka's story.

5

Joseph K.'s long wait before the law now comes to its inevitable end. On the evening before his thirty-first birthday two men come to his door. He waits as if expecting guests. No one watches from the windows. Fraulein Burstner appears and seems to lead the way. He reminds her of a lesson he has tried to keep in his mind, to keep his intelligence calm and discriminating to the end: 'Are people to say of me after I am gone that at the beginning of my case I wanted it to finish, and at the end of it I wanted it to begin again?' K. is taken through streets filled with policemen to a quarry, where the two men, who seem like tenth-rate actors, remove some of his clothes, which K. folds, as if to use them again, 'although perhaps not immediately'. They pass a knife across his body, and K. sees he is supposed to seize it and plunge it into his breast. 'He could not completely rise to the occasion, he could not relieve the officials of all their tasks; the responsibility for this last failure of his lay with him who had not left him the remnant of strength necessary for the deed.' He sees the house and the figure at the window, with outstretched arms. He wonders where the Judge is, whom he has never seen. He spreads out all his fingers, as Leni, with her webbed hands, had done. 'Like a dog!' he says as the men stab him to the heart. 'It was as if he meant the shame of it to outlive him.'

The Trial is itself an inexorable parable, in which Love, Art and Religion are arrayed before the power of Law and Death. Like the dark parable of the Law which the priest seeks to unravel to Joseph K., the book is subject to many interpretations, some more darkly pessimistic than others. For in Joseph K.'s quest there is a kind of macabre comedy, a desire for humanism, reason and intelligence, and an overwhelming sense of its absurdity before the powers that rule life. Talking to the priest, Joseph finds himself too tired to follow all the conclusions arising from the story, 'and the trains of thought into which it was leading him were unfamiliar, dealing with impalpabilities better suited to a theme for discussion among Court officials than for him. The simple story had lost its clear outline . . .' *The Trial*, in a great tradition of metaphysical writing, creates both the simple story and the endless possibilities of hermetic interpretation. As we read Kafka's diary over the months he wrote the book, it is not hard to see how the story relates to the inner crises of his own mind, preoccupied as it is with guilts, dark dreams, a re-reading of the Bible, with its 'unjust Judges', terrible imaginings ('Between throat and chin would seem the most rewarding place to stab'), and his awareness of his own nullity. At the same time, in its hunger for knowledge and self-aware-ness, his mind reaches out the more into the greater world of the mythical imagination. It is out of this that *The Trial* comes.

It has been noted that Kafka is one of the least problematic of all the modern writers. His work is profoundly ironic, but it does not have, say, the devious and cunning irony of Conrad or Mann. It does not spawn the complex and self-aware forms of Joyce or Proust. It does not present the dialectics of argument, like *The Magic Mountain*, or capture, like Proust, a complex activity of consciousness. Nothing seems contentious, except the very fact of existence itself. Kafka deals in states of affairs at once profoundly imaginary and strangely surreal while yet being very real. For this reason his work seems to defy interpretation — or else, like the parable in the Cathedral, to generate many interpretations. For Max Brod, Kafka was essentially a religious writer, who 'applied the highest religious standards to all work (al-though he never actually said so)'. For the postwar French exist-entialists like Camus and Sartre, who revived his work, he was a philosophical writer, in the absurdist spirit (Camus wrote brilliantly on him in *The Myth of Sisyphus*). For Marxist critics he has been a writer concerned with the alienations of the modern industrial system; for the anti-Marxist critics, he has been the great writer of humanism in revolt against the totalitarian state. *The Trial* has attracted Freudian interpretation, and, more cunningly, it has been read as a novel of the modern anti-hero, characterless, superfluous, and always presuming himself innocent, in his timeless conflict with the Law that can nevermore be understood.

What this makes clear is that Kafka did indeed encompass much of the dark history that came into the world after his death. Yet his stories are not in the first instance political tales. They are complex modern fantasies, half-allegories that come from the inner spirit and from a deep sense of the mysterious rules governing existence. They come from an inner spirit that knows well those lies, the morning knock, the staring spectators, the great labyrinth of arbitrary law, the indifferent officials, the insufficient papers, the hierarchies above the hierarchies, the tribunals, the endless process of trial, the wait before the door that never opens. These are the metaphysical anxieties of a troubled mind, the visions of a temperament that sees a world where benign divinity has been replaced by random arbitrations and absent authorities. That these should also be the actualities of modern history, that the humiliations, the dream-like passivity before strange powers, the strange bondage between the punishers and the punished, should also be the hideous inner psychology of the political world of our age, is a terrible truth that he could only have seen through foreboding.

Yet Kafka is the most modern of the modern writers, and in many respects it is this slight figure who saw himself as little more than K. who casts the longest shadow. It is a dark and alien vision, the inheritance of Dostoevsky realized and cast into a deeper gloom and extremity. We might challenge its universality – and yet there is scarcely a major writer in the wartime and postwar world who has not somehow been touched by him. The rise of surrealism in the 1930s and 1940s draws on his sense of modern history as terrible metaphysical fantasy. As Camus and other admirers in postwar Paris saw, his methods resembled theirs. It was said of Camus that he wrote like a condemned man, and so did Kafka. Samuel Beckett's reduced heroes, with their abbreviated or absent names, owe much to Kafka, and so does his sense of the hermetic isolation of the writer, condemned to the world of the word, and writing from an unnamed agony, only in order to see his work collected and distributed by others. The great rise of the Jewish-American novel in the United States of the 1950s, written by authors who saw themselves as the 'survivors' of the ghetto world which had so hideously perished in the Holocaust, came under his clear influence, and not just their sense of exile and of agonizing history but their awareness of the way in which the real world secretes the metaphysical one, owes much to him. The writers of Eastern Europe, particularly those who, like Milan Kundera, are exiles from his own city of Prague, have sustained the imaginative connection with the writer whose absence is a presence, and represents the humanity of art in an age of politics.

Of all the modern writers, Kafka has received the largest literary homage, sometimes in unexpected forms. In Philip Roth's novel *The Breast* (1972), for example, the central character, David Kepesh, is turned into a female breast – a surreal transformation that evidently owes its origin partly to Gogol's story 'The Nose', but above all to Kafka's 'The Metamorphosis', in which Gregor Samsa turns overnight into an enormous insect. At least, Kepesh consoles himself, he has out-Kafka-ed Kafka, asking who is the greater artist, he who imagines a marvellous transformation, or he who transforms himself? In *The Professor of Desire* (1977), Kepesh returns. He is a Jewish professor of literature, at odds with his father and his Jewish heritage. He is also teaching a course on Kafka, and finds in the strange erotic quality of Kafka's world something of his own troubled preoccupation with sexual desire. He goes to Prague, and visits Kafka's grave, to find, surprisingly, that he lies between his father and his mother. Though Kafka is forbidden reading, he meets many people who remember him, and someone offers to take him to meet Kafka's barber. In an extraordinary dream in the arms of his mistress, Kepesh imagines a conversation with an old woman who in her young days had provided Kafka with her services – 'Kafka's whore'. Kepesh performs many strange homages, but one in particular. At the Jewish cemetery he places a pebble on Kafka's grave, and notes that of the many there only his seems well looked after. 'Only the childless bachelor seems to have living progeny,' he notes. 'Where better for irony to abound than *à la tombe de Franze Kafky?*'

POSTWORD

If there ever was any doubt that the literary arts between the 1860s and the 1930s underwent a major revolution comparable to the other great literary revolutions, and that this revolution merits the name of Modernism, there is one thing that seems to settle it. That is the current popularity of the term 'Postmodernism' to describe the somewhat quieter revolution of our own times. Just what Postmodernism is may not be entirely clear. The major writing of our era has been extensive, eclectic and hard to bring under a single umbrella. But the name clearly suggests that there was indeed a Modern movement, and also that it is over. Our own arts must follow on from Modernism, though whether as its progeny or its adversary the term Postmodernism does not make clear. The answer, undoubtedly, is that our experimental and innovative writing shows something of both. It continues the avant-garde tradition into an age when the avant garde itself seems less urgent and necessary; it continues the spirit of Make It New in a time when novelty is not in short supply. The great adversaries, the powers of Victorianism, of sure faith, of fundamentalism, have gone, or are just possibly around the corner and waiting to return. But the age of the great transition, the massive fracture, is over.

Nonetheless, sometime just after the Wake, another World War did leave the arts with another gap to clamber over, another large transition to make. In the postwar atmosphere, Existentialism flourished and a new sense of crisis came. A 'new novel' emerged in France, with the work of Beckett, Butor, Robbe-Grillet, and the spirit of fiction transformed, especially in Germany, Italy, and the United States. In quieter terms, change even came to the novel in Britain. The theatre of the Absurd developed, flourishing with, again, Beckett,

Ionesco, Albee, Pinter and Frisch; this made a larger mark in Britain. Poetry too has had its succession from Modernism, especially in the work of the new American poets. A new generation was apparent, a new theatrical and literary practice came, and the Modern movement seemed to recede into the past. Few of its greatest writers still lived, its political associations seemed compromised, and its intellectual origins and its social or anti-social vision appeared to belong to a past age. It seemed possible to look back on it all and see it as something over, something complete.

Yet if few of its writers survived, and the formative conditions had passed, in many ways its arts seemed never more alive. The dark existential vision of Dostoevsky, the destructive element of Conrad, Eliot's perspective of sterility, Kafka's awareness of the annihilation of the self – all these belonged perfectly to the era of the atom and the Holocaust, the Age of Anxiety and the Age of Existentialism. Modernism, and especially that element in Modernism that was aware of the destructive element, conscious of the abyss, declared its continuity with the disturbing and profound experiences of the twentieth century, and its arts deepened in their authority. New writers either wrote in its shadow, or else attempted to depart for other climes, looking for other – often far more traditional – traditions, only to find their authority compromised. It was hard to be either the progeny of the Tradition of the New, or its adversary. At the same time the avant garde had become traditional itself; the sense of troubled modernity was no artistic secret but a universal commonplace. Modernism had been and gone, and as one commentator, Harry Levin, put it, in his aptly titled essay 'What Was Modernism?', the shocking had lost its ability to shock, and we had moved from the age of the outrageous Picasso to the age of bourgeois apartment blocks called 'The Picasso'.

Thus 'Postmodernism' might be thought of as the experimentalism of an age beyond outrage, an age which, nonetheless, has produced its own major arts which will, I believe, acquire with distance the clarity of a major achievement. The danger of the term is that it suggests that we all know, understand, and have fixed and assimilated the arts that went before. But, as I have emphasized here, though there was self-evidently a Modern movement, it meant many things. It was never single nor coherent, for the ideas came from many sources, moved in many directions, and produced many versions of new art. The writers themselves almost never called themselves 'Modernists', and they were often in dispute with one another. Ibsen would not, I think, have understood Kafka, though Dostoevsky might. 'I regret that I do not know M. Joyce's work,' said Proust: 'I have never read M. Proust,' replied Joyce. Modernism was many things, and passed through many stages in many places, as I have tried to emphasize in this book.

Nonetheless it is clear that most of these writers possessed a strong and deep sense of a condition that can be called 'modernity.' 'One characteristic of the works we call modern is that they positively insist on a general frame of reference beyond themselves,' write Charles Feidelson and Richard Ellmann in their anthology *The Modern Tradition* (1965); 'They claim modernity; they profess modernism.' That modern awareness takes many forms, but one obvious aspect was the Nietzschean desire to balance the sensibility of transition itself. Much of this writing holds in suspension the forces that have driven the past and those that create the new present. Out of this they generate ambiguous images: of the new city as place of possibility and place of sterility and crisis; of the new machine, at once a novel vortex of energy and a dehumanizing and destructive force; of an age of multiplicity, which offers both freedom and a terrible emptiness; of an age of exile, which offers both a free space for the creation of the unknown arts and also a terrible homelessness and a deep self-alienation.

The themes of the writing we call Modernist are usually ambiguous and troubled themes. They point to the loss of an older order of meaning and art, to the age of the unheroic hero, the age beyond classic tragedy, the age beyond realism and communitarian feeling. The major forms of Modernist art are largely the most sceptical of literary forms: irony, as in Conrad and Mann, tragi-comedy, as in Ibsen and Pirandello, parody, as in Eliot or Joyce, aesthetic fragmentation, as in Proust or Woolf, or existential absurdity, as in Dostoevsky and Kafka. They are the forms which challenge, which undermine, and which then reconstruct, the entire inherited convention of the arts. There is a negation and a despair in the Modern movement, which dismays many readers who find its scepticism and irony hard to comprehend. There is still something contentious about the most notable works of Modernism. They set out to shock, outrage, and transform, and their artists did not expect to received easily. Some still retain the outrage. Kafka to this day cannot be read in his native Czechoslovakia, though we should remember that Joyce's *Ulysses*, Lawrence's *Lady Chatterley's Lover* and Nabokov's *Lolita* were forbidden books in both Britain and the United States in recent times.

These writers took the avant-garde gamble that one day their books might be better understood, and take their place in the world they set out to transform. To a great degree that has happened. *The Waste Land*, Eliot's poem of fragments, once thought to be understandable only by the select few, is now a set text in schools; Joyce, who thought that since he took seventeen years to write *Finnegans Wake*, we should take seventeen years to read it, has become the best known of twentieth-century authors. Not everyone takes to the Modernists, and even a fine poet like Philip Larkin thought them best left to Americans. Yet, just as our cities have been transformed by Modern architecture, our houses by Modern design, our arts by the Modernist techniques of film, so our views of the world have been transformed by these writers. We know what a Kafka-esque situation is, and have probably often been in one. We acknowledge the Proustian obscurities of memory when we seek to find our relation to the past. Ibsen's concentrated naturalistic stage is totally familiar to us, just as the slammed door at the end of *A Doll's House* still sounds through our sexual politics, but Pirandello's spirit of the play-in-the-making is also a convention of our theatre.

The Modern movement may then be over, but it is still ours. It is almost exactly fifty years ago, in 1939, that Joyce published what still seems to remain the climactic book, *Finnegans Wake*. As, over the following two years, Joyce and Woolf, Yeats and Freud died, the climate of modern writing changed. For a time the signs were ominous: George Orwell wrote, just at this time, in his essay 'Inside the Whale', that writers now faced 'the age of totalitarian dictatorships – an age in which freedom of thought will be at first a deadly sin and then a meaningless abstraction.' The darker vision, the gloomier aspects, of Modernism seemed to point to the crisis, and insofar as it has departed from us we may feel ourselves moving away from the Modernist spirit. But Modernism was far more than an art of despair and crisis; it spoke for the innovative powers of art, their force as an essential philosophy, a principle of the discovering imagination. That was the spirit of Making It New – the spirit that maintained the modern arts as a moral, intellectual but above all creative power in our century. They became as inescapable as the fact of modernity itself: which makes us all Postmodernists.

BIBLIOGRAPHY

INTRODUCTION: MAKE IT NEW

This book owes much to an earlier one, *Modernism* (1976), in the 'Pelican Guides to European Literature', which I edited with James McFarlane. There the reader will find a detailed study of the whole modern movement in literature – its history, intellectual and social background, its international setting, its movements, and its developments in poetry, fiction and drama. It gives a bibliography of several hundred titles in all those areas, and there are truly thousands of books on the Modern movement. My list here covers titles specially relevant to this introduction and to the book as a whole.

Ezra Pound published his essays called *Make It New* in 1934. Holbrook Jackson's *The 1890s* (1913, recently reissued) is an early study of the origins of British Modernism, and the story is followed up in Frank Kermode's *Romantic Image* (1957) and C. K. Stead's *The New Poetic* (1964). The first major study of international literary Modernism was Edmund Wilson's *Axel's Castle* (1931), while Herbert Read's *Art Now* (1935, rev. ed. 1960) dealt with modern painting. See also Robert Hughes, *The Shock of the New* (1980). Stephen Spender's *The Struggle of the Modern* (1963) gives a provocative and interesting account of the development of modern writing, Hugh Kenner has written on *The Pound Era* (1971) and Julian Symons has just produced a lively book on the British modernists called *Makers of the New* (1987).

For the development of the modern novel, see Eric Auerbach's brilliant study of changing attitudes to realism, *Mimesis* (Princeton, 1953), David Daiches's *The Novel and the Modern World* (rev. ed. 1960), Alan Friedman's *The Turn of the Novel* (1966), and my own *Possibilities* (1973). For modern poetry, see C. M. Bowra, *The Heritage of Symbolism* (1943), Cleanth Brooks, *Modern Poetry and the Tradition* (1948),

David Daiches, *Poetry and the Modern World* (1940) and F. R. Leavis's influential *New Bearings in English Poetry* (1950). Important books on drama are Eric Bentley's *In Search of Theatre* (1954), Robert Brustein's *The Theatre of Revolt* (1964), Richard Gilman's *The Making of Modern Drama* (1974), George Steiner's *The Death of Tragedy* (1961), and Raymond William's *Drama from Ibsen to Brecht* (1968).

On the themes of Modernism see Wylie Sypher, *Loss of the Self in Modern Art and Literature* (1962), Monroe K. Spears, *Dionysus and the City* (1970), Paul Fussell's *The Great War and Modern Memory* (1975), Erich Heller's *The Disinherited Mind* (1959) Walter Kaufmann (ed.) *Existentialism from Dostoevsky to Sartre* (1956), and George Steiner's *Extraterritorial* (1972). Richard Ellmann and Charles Feidelson (eds) *The Modern Tradition: Backgrounds of Modern Literature* (1965) is a fine background anthology.

FYODOR DOSTOEVSKY (1821–1881)

Two interesting biographies are E. H. Carr's *Dostoevsky, 1821–1881* (1931, reprinted 1962) and David Magarshack's fuller and more modern *Dostoevsky* (1961). Dostoevsky put himself on record in *The Diary of a Writer* (trans. Boris Brasol, two vols, 1949). The chief studies are Donald Fanger's *Dostoevsky and Romantic Realism* (1967), Robert Lord, *Dostoevsky* (1970), Edward Wasiolek, *Dostoevsky: The Major Fiction* (1964) and George Steiner's brilliant *Tolstoy or Dostoevsky* (1959). Rene Wellek edited an anthology of criticism, *Dostoevsky: A Collection of Critical Essays* (1962). Robert L. Jackson's *The Underground Man in Russian Literature* (The Hague, 1958) shows how important the Dostoevskian hero has been, and Gilbert Phelps in *The Russian Novel in English Fiction* (1956) shows his impact on British writers.

There are various English editions of *Crime and Punishment*, including David Magarshack's Penguin Books translation which I quote from. A very useful edition edited by George Gibian for Norton Critical Editions (1975) has plentiful background material and modern criticism. Edward Wasiolek edited *The Notebooks for 'Crime and Punishment'* (1967), and A. D. Nuttall's *Dostoevsky's 'Crime and Punishment': Murder as a Philosophical Experiment* (Falmer, Sussex, 1978) is good on the philosophical problems of the book. See also Ronald Hingley's *The Undiscovered Dostoevsky* (1962) and John Jones' *Dostoevsky* (1983).

HENRIK IBSEN (1828–1906)

Ibsen's place in modern drama is discussed in most of the books on modern drama already mentioned, but also useful are Martin Esslin's *Reflections: Essays on Modern Theatre* (1971), Francis Fergusson's excellent *The Idea of Theater* (1949) and Raymond Williams, *Modern Tragedy* (1966). There is a brilliant life by Michael Meyer, *Ibsen: A Biography* (1967). There are various editions and translations of his plays, but the key edition is the Oxford Ibsen edited by James McFarlane. Two excellent anthologies of criticism are James McFarlane, *Henrik Ibsen: A Critical Anthology* (1970), which follows the development of his international reputation, and Rolf Fjelde (ed.), *Henrik Ibsen: A Collection of Critical Essays* (1965).

Other main studies are G. Wilson Knight's *Ibsen* (1962) and F. L. Lucas, *Ibsen and Strindberg* (1962). George B. Bryan's *An Ibsen Companion* (1984) is an excellent aid. The most famous, typically flamboyant account is of course George Bernard Shaw's *The Quintessence of Ibsenism*, which was first published in 1891 and is widely reprinted. See also Michael Meyer's *Henrik Ibsen: The Making of a Dramatist 1828–1864* (1967), Edward Beyer's *Ibsen: The Man and his Work* (1978) and David Thomas's *Henrik Ibsen* (1983).

JOSEPH CONRAD (1857–1924)

For Conrad's position in the modern British novel see F. R. Leavis, *The Great Tradition* (1947), William V. O'Connor (ed.), *Forms of Modern Fiction* (1948), and Dorothy Van Ghent, *The English Novel: Form and Function* (1953). The main life is Jocelyn Baines, *Conrad: A Critical Biography* (1960); see also Frederick J. Karl, *Joseph Conrad: Three Lives* (1979) and Norman Sherry's *Conrad's Eastern World* (1966) and *Conrad's Western World* (1971).

A valuable collection of critical essays is Marvin Mudrick (ed.), *Conrad: A Collection of Critical Essays* (1966). Other useful books are: A. J. Guerard, *Conrad the Novelist* (1958), D. J. Hewett, *Conrad: A Reassessment* (rev. ed. 1969), F. R. Karl, *A Reader's Guide to Conrad*

(1960), and R. W. Stallman (ed.), *The Art of Conrad: A Critical Symposium* (1960). There are valuable chapters in Irving Howe, *Politics and the Novel* (New York, 1957; London, 1961) and J. Hillis Miller, *Poets of Reality: Six Twentieth-Century Writers* (1965). On *The Secret Agent* the best book, with plentiful background, is Ian Watt (ed.) *Conrad, 'The Secret Agent': A Casebook* (1973), which includes the preface written for the book by Thomas Mann. See also Jacques Berthoud's *Joseph Conrad: The Major Phase* (1978) and Zdislaw Najder's *Joseph Conrad – A Chronicle* (1984).

THOMAS MANN (1875–1955)

For Mann's central place in the modern novel, see J. G. Brennan, *Three Philosophical Novelists: Joyce, Gide, Mann* (1964), Roy Pascal, *The German Novel* (Manchester, 1965) and H. M. Waidson, *The Modern German Novel* (1959). Mann published *A Sketch of My Life* in 1960, his polemic *Reflections of a Non-political Man* was translated in 1985, and his book *The Story of a Novel* (1961) is a fascinating reflection on his writing process, dealing primarily with his late novel *Doctor Faustus*.

His most famous critic is Georg Lukacs, whose book *Essays on Thomas Mann* appeared in English in 1964. A valuable collection of critical essays is Henry Hatfield (ed.), *Thomas Mann: A Collection of Critical Essays* (1964). Erich Heller's *The Ironic German* (1958) is a key study. Other important books are J. G. Brennan, *Thomas Mann's World* (1962), Henry Hatfield, *Thomas Mann* (rev. ed. 1962), R. H. Thomas, *Thomas Mann: The Mediation of Art* (1956) and Andrew White, *Thomas Mann* (1965). H. J. Weigand's *Thomas Mann's Novel 'Der Zauberberg'* (1933) is an extended early study of *The Magic Mountain*. See also Hermann Kesten (ed.), *Thomas Mann Diaries 1918–1931* (1985), Nigel Hamilton's *The Brothers Mann* (1978), and Richard Winston's *Thomas Mann: The Making of an Artist 1875–1911* (1982).

MARCEL PROUST (1871–1922)

Proust's place in modern fiction is explored in many of the books on the modern novel mentioned, but also useful are René Girard, *Deceit, Desire and the Novel* (Baltimore, 1965), A. A. Mendilow, *Time and the*

Novel (1952) Martin Turnell, *The Novel in France* (1951), Harry Levin, *The Gates of Horn* (1966), and Henri Peyre, *The Contemporary French Novel* (1955). There were early excellent essays on Proust by Joseph Wood Krutch in *Five Masters* (1930, reprinted 1959) and Edmund Wilson, *Axel's Castle* (1931). Samuel Beckett's brilliant short book on *Proust* was first published in 1931 and reprinted in London in 1970.

A la recherche du temps perdu was reprinted in the corrected Pléiade edition in two volumes in Paris in 1954. The new English translation by C. K. Scott Montcrieff as revised by Terence Kilmartin was published in 1981, and in Penguin in three volumes in 1983. The great biography of Proust is George Painter's *Marcel Proust* (2 vols 1959–1965; 1 vol. 1983). Some key critical essays about Proust are collected in René Girard (ed.), *Proust: A Collection of Critical Essays* (1962). Other useful studies are: Adele King, *Proust* (1968), Milton Hindus, *A Reader's Guide to Marcel Proust* (1962), and the same author's *The Proustian Vision* (1964), Germaine Brée, *Marcel Proust and the Deliverance from Time* (1968), and Wallace Fowlie, *A Reading of Proust* (1967).

JAMES JOYCE (1882–1941)

James Joyce's *Ulysses*, which first appeared as a small press publication from 'Shakespeare and Company' in 1922, has at last come out in a carefully annotated edition, *Ulysses: The Corrected Text* (1986). For Joyce's position in modern fiction, see Edmund Wilson, *Axel's Castle* (1931), Mark Schorer (ed.), *Modern British Fiction* (1961), M. J. Friedman, *Stream of Consciousness: A Study in Literary Method* (New Haven, 1955), Leon Edel, *The Psychological Novel* (Philadelphia, rev. ed., 1964), Vivien Mercier, *The Irish Comic Tradition* (1962), Anthony Burgess, *The Novel Now* (1967), and Christopher Butler, *After The Wake: Essays on the Contemporary Avant-Garde* (1980).

There is a brilliant biography, Richard Ellmann's *James Joyce* (rev. ed. 1982). The main critical works are: Harry Levin, *Joyce: A Critical Introduction* (Norfolk, Conn., rev. ed., 1960), Hugh Kenner, *Dublin's Joyce* (1955), W. Y. Tindall, *A Reader's Guide to James Joyce* (1959), Walton Litz, *James Joyce* (1966), Arnold Goldman, *James Joyce* (1966), and Anthony Burgess, *Here Comes Everybody* (1965). T. S. Eliot's famous essay ' "Ulysses", Order and Myth', is reprinted in S. Givens,

Joyce: Two Decades of Criticism (1948). The key book on *Ulysses* is Frank Budgen's *James Joyce and the Making of 'Ulysses'* (rev. ed. 1972). Among the many more books on the great book are Stuart Gilbert, *James Joyce's 'Ulysses'* (rev. ed. 1952), Harry Blamires, *The Bloomsday Book: A Guide Through Joyce's 'Ulysses'* (1966), Clive Hart and David Hayman (eds), *James Joyce's 'Ulysses': Critical Essays* (1974), and David Hayman, *'Ulysses': The Mechanics Of Meaning* (1970). See also Herbert Gorman's *James Joyce* (1941), Stuart Gilbert (ed.) *Letters of James Joyce* (1957) and Richard Ellmann (ed.) *James Joyce, Selected Letters* (1976).

T. S. ELIOT (1888–1965)

The studies of modern poetry already mentioned show Eliot's central place in modern verse, but also useful are Yvor Winters's *On Modern Poets* (1959) and W. H. Auden's *The Dyer's Hand* (1963). There is a brilliant life by Peter Ackroyd, *T. S. Eliot* (1984). Eliot's 1935 volume of collected poems is now replaced by *The Complete Poems and Plays of T. S. Eliot* (1969); a useful companion volume is Frank Kermode (ed.) *Selected Prose of T. S. Eliot* (1975). Eliot's general reputation can be explored in Arthur W. Litz (ed.), *Eliot in His Time* (Princeton, 1973) and Allen Tate (ed.), *T. S. Eliot: The Man and His Work* (1967). Some of the many good studies are: Bernard Bergonzi, *T. S. Eliot* (1971), Helen Gardner, *The Art of T. S. Eliot* (rev. ed., 1968), Hugh Kenner, *The Invisible Poet* (1960), F. O. Matthiessen, *The Achievement of T. S. Eliot* (rev. ed., 1958) and Stephen Spender, *Eliot* (1975). Two good handbooks are George Williamson, *A Reader's Guide to T. S. Eliot* (1957) and B. C. Southam's *A Student's Guide to the Selected Poems of T. S. Eliot* (1968).

The Waste Land is one of the most studied poems ever. For the original draft see Valerie Eliot (ed.), *'The Waste Land': Facsimile and Transcript* (1971). Two useful anthologies are Jay Martin (ed.), *A Collection of Critical Essays on 'The Waste Land'* (1968) and C. B. Cox and Arnold Hinchcliffe (eds), *T. S. Eliot's 'The Waste Land': A Casebook* (rev. ed., 1975); also A. J. Wilks, *A Critical Commentary on 'The Waste Land'* (1971).

LUIGI PIRANDELLO (1867–1936)

To the books on modern drama listed for the Introduction, I would add here Lionel Abel's fine *Metatheater* (1963), Eric Bentley's *The Playwright as Thinker* (1967), Karl Guthke's *Modern Tragicomedy* (1966) and J. L. Styan's *The Dark Comedy* (1968), which all show the contribution of Pirandello to modern theatre, a story extended in Martin Esslin's *The Theatre of the Absurd* (rev. ed., 1983).

We await a major life of Pirandello in English, but the translation of Gaspar Giudice's *Luigi Pirandello* (1985) is invaluable. For the reader of Italian, Leonardo Sciascia captures his great predecessor in *Pirandello e la Sicilia* (Rome, 1961). Many editions of Pirandello's best-known plays are available, though a good many are still untranslated. Eric Bentley's *Naked Masks: Five Plays* (1952) is excellent. Criticism on Pirandello is collected in G. Cambon (ed.), *Pirandello: A Collection of Critical Essays* (1967). Other main books are: Susan Bassett-McGuire, *Luigi Pirandello* (1983), Oscar Budel, *Pirandello* (1966), Renate Matthaei, *Luigi Pirandello* (1963) and Walter Starkie's very evocative *Luigi Pirandello, 1867–1936* (Berkeley, 1965). More detailed studies are Roger W. Oliver, *Dreams of Passion: The Theatre of Luigi Pirandello* (1969) and Anne Paolucci, *Pirandello's Theater* (1974). To see how Pirandello's view of theatre applies to modern theories of social life, see Erving Goffman's brilliant *The Presentation of Self in Everyday Life* (1959).

VIRGINIA WOOLF (1882–1941)

Virginia Woolf's role in modern fiction is explored in several of the studies of the modern novel already mentioned, but see also E. K. Brown's *Rhythm in the Novel* (Toronto, 1950), Reuben Brower, *Fields of Light* (1951), and Erich Auerbach's *Mimesis* (Princeton, 1953). The chief biographies are Clive Bell's *Virginia Woolf* (2 vols, 1972, 1973) and Quentin Bell's *Virginia Woolf* (2 vols, 1976) which can be interestingly supplemented with J. K. Johnstone's *The Bloomsbury Group* (1954), Quentin Bell's *Bloomsbury* (1968), and Leonard Woolf's three volumes of memoirs, *Sowing* (1960), *Growing* (1962), and *Beginning Again* (1963). Leonard Woolf edited Virginia's *A Writer's Diary* (1953) and Anne Oliver Bell edited four volumes of *The Diary of Virginia Woolf* (1979).

E. M. Forster, *Virginia Woolf: The Rede Lecture* (Cambridge, 1942), is an important comment. Other main studies of her work are Bernard Blackstone, *Virginia Woolf: A Commentary* (1949), David Daiches, *Virginia Woolf* (Norfolk, Conn., 1942), J. E. M. Latham, *Critics on Virginia Woolf* (Miami, 1970), Jane Novak, *The Razor Edge of Balance: A Study of Virginia Woolf* (Miami, 1975), A. D. Moody, *Virginia Woolf* (1963), and Hermione Lee, *The Novels of Virginia Woolf* (1977).

FRANZ KAFKA (1883–1924)

Kafka's place or placelessness in modern fiction is considered in Ronald Gray, *The German Tradition in Literature* (Cambridge, 1965), Erich Heller, *The Disinherited Mind* (1961), Georg Lukacs, *The Meaning of Contemporary Realism* (1962), and George Steiner, *Extraterritorial* (1972). The chief biographies are Max Brod, *Franz Kafka: A Biography* (1960) and Ronald Hayman's *K: A Biography of Kafka* (1981). Brod's edition of *The Diaries of Franz Kafka* (2 vols, 1948) is also a major source for understanding him. So is the Penguin edition of Kafka's *Letters to Felice* (1978) which also contains the remarkable essay on him by Elias Canetti, 'Kafka's Other Trial'.

Criticism is collected in Ronald Gray (ed.), *Kafka: A Collection of Critical Essays* (1962) and Angel Flores (ed.), *The Kafka Problem* (1963). Gray also wrote two useful studies, *Kafka's Castle* (1956) and *Franz Kafka* (1973). Other important critical books are Franz Kuna, *Franz Kafka: Literature as Corrective Punishment* (Bloomington, 1974), Erich Heller, *Kafka* (1974), Paul Eisner, *Franz Kafka and Prague* (1950), Anthony Thorlby, *Kafka: A Study* (1972), and Clement Greenberg, *The Terror of Art: Kafka and Modern Literature* (1968). See also Ernst Pawel's *The Nightmare of Reason: A Life of Franz Kafka* (1984).